P9-DHB-378

# Cobden and Bright

## A VICTORIAN POLITICAL PARTNERSHIP

Is it not a grand history, that of the last forty years? Are not the changes such as all of us may be proud of, that they have been effected with so little, in fact with no disturbance? You cannot point, probably, to a revolution of violence in any country of late times where there has been so much done of permanent good, in the same period, as has been done for the people of this country by the wise changes in our law. And yet, I dare say, history will not say very much of these changes. The fact is, history busies itself with other matters. It will tell our children, I dare say, of conquests in India, of annexation, it may be in the Punjab, of Chinese wars—wars which were as discreditable to us as they have been unprofitable . . . of all these changes which have saved the nation from anarchy, and an English monarchy from ruin, history will probably say but little. Blood shines more upon her pages, and the grand and noiseless triumphs of peace and of wise and just legislation too often find but scanty memorial from her hands.

John Bright, 1877

Bright and Cobden in 1860

(*from The Mansell Collection*)

# Cobden and Bright

## A VICTORIAN POLITICAL PARTNERSHIP

DONALD READ

*Senior Lecturer in History, University of Kent*

NEW YORK: ST. MARTIN'S PRESS: 1968

942.081
R282

© DONALD READ 1967
*First published 1967*

*First published in Great Britain by*
*Edward Arnold (Publishers) Ltd.*

*First published in*
*the United States of America in 1968*

for

Martin

*Library of Congress Catalog Card Number:* 68–15436

SBN: 7131 5306 7

*Printed in Great Britain by*
*The Camelot Press Ltd., London and Southampton*

COLLEGE LIBRARY
HAMPDEN-SYDNEY, VA.

# *Contents*

81085

# Plates

# Acknowledgements

For help in the preparation of this book I am indebted to the Governors of Dunford House, who have deposited the Cobden Papers with the West Sussex Record Office in the knowledgeable care of the County Archivist and his staff; to Dr. K. Fielden, who gave me permission to consult his important thesis on Cobden and America; to the library staffs of the University of Leeds, University College, London, the Institute of Historical Research, the British Museum, the Manchester Reference Library, and the Leeds Reference Library, for guidance at various times over books and manuscripts; to Mr. F. C. Mather for reading the book in proof and making helpful comments; to Mr. G. C. F. Forster and my wife for careful proof-reading; and to Miss M. Spencer-Payne for assistance with typing. Last but not least, I gladly acknowledge the help given me by the library staff of the University of Kent, who have demonstrated how quickly and how completely a new university library can achieve the highest standards of service.

D. R.

# Introduction

FAMOUS partnerships in history range in time and character at least from that of Antony and Cleopatra to that of Bulganin and Khrushchev. In English history the Victorian partnership between Richard Cobden and John Bright is outstanding. Yet, although given its place in the textbooks, the Cobden–Bright connection has never been closely studied. Separate detailed biographies were published of Cobden by John Morley in 1881 and of Bright by G. M. Trevelyan in 1913; but neither volume analysed their relationship in any critical spirit. Both books accepted that the two men were in complete political agreement except in two instances (over Parliamentary reform in the 1850s and '60s, and briefly over the American Civil War) where Bright was thought to have been more progressive than Cobden. Their characters and styles are known to have differed markedly—Bright loud-spoken, Cobden much softer—but otherwise substantial identity of view has been assumed. The present study, which is a study only, not a complete double biography, sets out to modify this received version of the Cobden–Bright relationship. It tries to show that political agreement between them was not so nearly complete as has been assumed, and that, moreover, when they differed it was Cobden, and not Bright, who was the more progressive of the two.

Morley's biography of Cobden, which was outstandingly successful in many respects, can perhaps be excused for not making this last point. It was published in Bright's lifetime, vetted by him, and dedicated to him. Moreover, Morley did quote extensively from Cobden's letters and diaries, so that (intendedly or otherwise) we may collect evidence from his pages to support a different view of the partnership from that which he himself suggested. The letters printed in J. A. Hobson's study of *Richard Cobden, the International Man* (1918) are valuable in the same way, as are many of the thousands of unpublished letters to and from Cobden and Bright in the British

Museum, Manchester Reference Library, West Sussex Record Office, and elsewhere.

From the side of Bright, the biographies by Robertson and Barnett Smith, both published while he was still alive and active in politics, and both committed to proving that 'Bright was right', naturally did not consider the possibility that their hero might be less rather than more progressive than his partner. Unfortunately, Trevelyan's standard life, written a generation later, is no better in this respect. Trevelyan used letters and diaries of Bright's not available earlier, but he still overrated Bright's Radicalism while seriously underestimating that of Cobden. Trevelyan was perhaps himself too close to Bright in family background to be sufficiently detached.[1] J. L. Hammond, another Liberal historian of Trevelyan's generation might have produced a more balanced assessment, doing fuller justice to Cobden. In a penetrating essay, published in 1932, he truly remarked that the association of Cobden's name with that of Bright had worked to the disadvantage of Cobden's reputation. There was as much difference between Cobden and Bright, claimed Hammond strikingly, as between Gladstone and Palmerston. 'In comparison with Gladstone, Palmerston was an insular Englishman with the high spirit of a schoolboy; in comparison with Cobden, Bright was an insular Englishman with the stern conscience of a Quaker.'[2]

Bright himself in his old age, and perhaps throughout his career, believed that there was a more nearly complete identity of opinions and aspirations between himself and Cobden than was really the case. In 1861 Cobden made a revealing admission in a letter written to a mutual friend at a time when he and Bright were not in full agreement over the American Civil War. 'Our friend Bright', confessed Cobden, 'is so abused by other people that I never find it in my heart to tell him even when I differ from him.' This admission was very significant, even though it cannot be accepted without qualification. We shall see how in the years between repeal of the Corn Laws and the outbreak of the Crimean War Cobden did often make clear to Bright his disagreement with him over important issues. These years between 1846 and 1854 constituted a period of relative coolness in the friendship. Then the unpopularity brought upon them both, and especially upon Bright, by their opposition to the Crimean War drew the pair close together again. In addition, after 1857 Cobden was disgusted by the rejection of Bright by the Manchester electorate at a time when he was still recovering from a breakdown caused by his anti-war exertions. From the mid-'50s, therefore, because Cobden thought that Bright was being unjustly attacked for his opinions, he hesitated to admit to Bright that he too sometimes disagreed with him. In its last ten years Cobden was being careful not to strain the famous partnership. Yet Bright never seems to have realised this. Because Cobden deliberately played down the differences between them, Bright came to assume in his old age that such differences had hardly existed, and historians have tended to assume the same. At the unveiling of Cobden's statue at Bradford in 1877 Bright dwelt upon his twenty-five years of friendship with Cobden, 'unbroken and undisturbed by a single jar of any kind'. Admittedly, at the time of Bright's illness in the mid-'50s Cobden too had referred more than once to the 'transparent intimacy of mind' between Bright and himself. He told a meeting in 1857 that he did not believe that there was one aspiration in the mind of either unknown to the other. But such intimacy need not mean total agreement, and we shall see how Cobden was well aware in these later years of the limits of Bright's Radicalism compared with his own. As personal friends Cobden and Bright enjoyed a long intimacy. As political partners they sought much in common. But because Cobden was able to see wider and longer than Bright he was attracted by arguments and aspirations with which his friend had little sympathy. Cobden, not Bright, was the complete democratic Radical: Bright was a Radical only within clear limits. Such is the basic argument running through the present study.[3]

# I

## Cobden

### I. BACKGROUND

RICHARD COBDEN was born in an old farmhouse, known as Dunford, near Midhurst, Sussex, on June 3, 1804. This was, and remains, an area of attractive, rolling, well-wooded countryside. It stands far in distance and in spirit from the hard world of the industrial North, with which the name of Cobden is usually associated. Throughout his life Cobden loved his native district. He told John Bright in 1851 that, although he had seen much of the world's best scenery, he had found nothing in nature so beautiful as the wooded parts of Sussex. 'Their soft waving outline is Hogarth's line of beauty on the grandest scale. And then for smiles—what can compare with dimples on the face of the Sussex Downs.'[1]

Cobden was the second son and fourth child in a family of eleven, five boys and six girls. His ancestors were yeomen, traceable in West Sussex back into medieval times. His grandfather and namesake, born in 1739, had found moderate prosperity in the late eighteenth century as a maltster and farmer, who served for several years as bailiff of the borough of Midhurst. But when he died in 1809 he left only a modest inheritance to be shared between his five children. Dunford was sold, and William Cobden, the only son, father of the statesman, moved to a small farm on the outskirts of Midhurst. William Cobden was engaging in disposition but ineffective in business. Gradually he lost his capital, and in 1814 his farm had to be sold, so that he spent the last nineteen years of his life in more or less genteel poverty. Young Richard Cobden was to find his father a serious financial and psychological burden during his first years in business in the 1820s. Richard Cobden then became in effect head of the family, 'a second father' as one of his younger sisters described him in 1833.[2] He accepted this burden with an amiability which he no doubt inherited from his father and which later contributed much to his success in politics. But Cobden also possessed well-directed energy and intelligence to add to amiability, qualities which probably came to him from his mother. She had been born in the same year as her husband, with the pleasant Hardyesque maiden name of Millicent Amber. She died, much mourned by her children, in 1825. In her last years she had kept a village shop in an attempt to assist the declining fortunes of the family.

Cobden's schooldays were unhappy. After a spell at a Midhurst dame school, he was sent at the expense of his mother's brother-in-law, a London merchant, to Bowes Hall school in Yorkshire. Here he lived from 1814 to 1819, seeing neither parents nor friends. He was ill-fed, ill-taught and ill-used in a school which could have served as a model for Dickens' Dotheboys Hall. In later life Cobden could never bear to speak of his schoolboy misery. Fortunately, these unhappy years neither embittered him nor weakened his zest for education, both for himself and for others. The traits of amiability inherited from his father and of perseverance derived from his mother were perhaps even stimulated by the test of ill-usage. His suffering comes out indirectly in his surviving quarterly letters to his family. In one letter he assured his aunt and uncle that he was very comfortable; in another he asked his father if he knew of any other parents with boys needing a good school. 'I assure you most of the scholars at this place are taught very expeditiously and every care taken of them in every respect.' This enquiry, however, like the copperplate hand and stilted language in which it was conveyed, was too unnatural to carry conviction. Young Cobden was clearly writing to dictation.[3]

Cobden's schoolboy misery came to an end in 1819 when an usher at the school wrote privately to his father to tell him of his son's ill-health and unhappiness. Young Richard now went as a clerk in his uncle's warehouse in London. But Cobden's education did not finish at this point; rather it really began, as he undertook, at the same time as making his way in business, to educate himself both from books and from experience. His knowledge of the traditional two dead languages and cultures, such as he might have gained from a good formal education, remained limited to the end of his life; but in his young manhood he read widely in English and French literature and still more earnestly in social politics and political economy. At his death in 1865 the main works in his library seem to have been volumes of economics, politics and history. In the 1820s political economy was rapidly becoming known and accepted as the great living language, laying down rules of right conduct within the new national and international economic system which was being created by the Industrial Revolution. Laws were discovered by the new 'science' governing capital and labour, profits and wages, the relations between states and between employers and employees, the use of land, the development of manufactures, the functions of government, and the role of the individual. The father of the science was Adam Smith, whose classic work upon *The Wealth of Nations* had appeared as early as 1776, but whose influence was greater in Cobden's day than in his own. Cobden always revered the work of Adam Smith. In the last year of his life he was still saying that if he were young again he would 'take Adam Smith in hand' and promote a league for free trade in land just as, on the authority of Smith, he had promoted a league for free trade in corn.

The fundamental rule of the political economists was that trade needed to be as free as possible and Government interference as small as possible. This message was vigorously propounded, there being (in the phrase of a modern economist) a 'sense of crusade' in the writings of Smith and his successors. They were the intellectual spearhead of a national and international free trade movement of which Cobden became the political leader. The catchphrase of 'laissez-faire' soon became associated with the new political economy. As oversimplified by the man-in-the-street, it seemed to justify an economic free-for-all, with Government enjoying no larger role than to remove impediments and to keep out of the way. Ordinary workmen found their trade unions for raising wages, their agitations for legislative reduction of factory hours, and their claim for generous poor relief in unemployment or old age all strenuously resisted in the name of *laissez-faire*, and naturally they hated the new cry. By contrast, selfish employers revelled in a crude call for economic freedom. As one writer remarked in 1833, they had learned a few words of French, 'and each parrot from his perch, as he keeps swinging himself to and fro in his glittering cage, ejaculates, "laissez nous faire!" '

Richard Cobden was never one of these parrots. He had read the political economists carefully, and he knew that they had never advocated unlimited application of *laissez-faire*. McCulloch, for example, in his *Principles of Political Economy*, published in 1825, argued that individuals must fend for themselves as far as possible; but he went on to say that any economist or politician who proposed carrying a policy of *laissez-faire* 'to its full extent in all cases and at all hazards, would be fitter for bedlam than for the closet or the Cabinet'. When large numbers of workmen were unemployed, McCulloch accepted that they must be given help, because practical provision for the destitute was as much a part of political economy as theories of rent or of profit. Cobden understood all this. He was deeply concerned in politics to raise the standards of the masses. Political economy, he reminded John Bright in 1855, 'has a heart as well as a head. Such men as Chadwick, who shake the dry bones of the science like a scarecrow at ignorant people, do infinite injury to the benign truths of Adam Smith.' Cobden was nevertheless convinced that under a system of international free trade, as advocated by the political economists and for which he worked throughout his career, the need to temper *laissez-faire* with interference in the name of humanity would be limited. Trade would become so prosperous, the demand for labour would grow so much greater and steadier, that rates of employment and wages would reach and remain at new peaks.[4]

Young Cobden sought to educate himself not only in the science of economics, but also in what claimed to be the science of understanding personality. This was phrenology, then much in vogue. Even by the end of Cobden's lifetime phrenology had become discredited, but his interest in it during his younger days did him no disservice in that it reflected his eager enquiring mind. In any case he seems not to have taken its claims too seriously, for when sending copies of his first political pamphlet to his uncle in 1835 we find him humorously warning his relative not to waste them upon Tories, who, claimed Cobden, could be spotted at sight by the diminutive size of their heads. Extreme Radicals, Cobden suggested, could be recognised 'by the preponderance of their destructive organs', while sound Liberals could be detected 'by the superior magnitude of their frontal development'. Cobden even wrote a bad comedy called *The Phrenologist*, which was offered to, and rejected by, the manager of Covent Garden. Leading characters were Dr. Cranium, a phrenologist, and the amorous Sir Amory Intrigue. 'Heavens and earth!' exclaimed the doctor on feeling Sir Amory's head 'what do I discover? Fie! Fie! You have been a dreadful lover of the ladies! Oh, fie, Sir Amory, here is a dreadful bump indeed!' And so on, in a manner which sought to poke continuous fun at the new science.[5]

This play was penned in the mid-1820s when Cobden was a commercial traveller. Cobden always loved travel, and learnt much from it, at home and abroad, and his experience on the road at this time played a vital part in shaping his future political career. He was first sent out by his uncle with samples of muslins and calico prints in 1825. He told his father that his chief apprehension was that his health, which was never robust, might not stand the strain. If it did, he was characteristically optimistic that he would do well. His health did hold, and he successfully collected orders from all over the British Isles.[6]

Cobden's enthusiastic search for knowledge of facts and of people was now given full scope. He was still reading many books, but he knew that education did not come from books alone. As he toured the country he looked and talked and listened, and so began to build up an unequalled store of practical knowledge of the prospects and problems of British industry and agriculture, which was later to be one of his great assets in political controversy. On his very first journey we find him, for example, surprised and excited by the growth of Birmingham. His background up to this date had been predominantly agricultural and metropolitan. Now on his travels he began to learn closely and quickly about provincial industrial England. At first, London still provided his yardstick. He noted that Birmingham was shrouded in a canopy of smoke still more dense than that of the capital; and he found that the bustle of the Birmingham streets reminded him strongly of London. 'I was never more struck with any sight than the numerous fires I have passed in my journey through Staffordshire. They glare in the night from the very edge of the turnpike road to the remotest boundaries of the horizon, and give an effect the most novel and awful I ever observed.' These words are reminiscent of the description of the approach of Little Nell and her grandfather to the industrial Midlands given by Cobden's young contemporary, Charles Dickens, in *The Old Curiosity Shop* (1840–1). But revealingly, whereas Dickens was depressed and alarmed by what he called 'this dreadful spot', Cobden, though not unaware of its dirt and squalor, was excited and stimulated by its power. The counties of Lancashire, Yorkshire, Cheshire and Staffordshire, he was to claim in his second political pamphlet, published in

1836, possessed enough wealth, created by the skill and industry of their provincial inhabitants, to overcome the whole Russian Empire.[7]

By 1836 Cobden was well established as a master calico printer. After three years' experience of travelling, his enterprising buoyant nature had led him naturally into business on his own account. In 1828 he and two friends set up in Manchester, on capital more than half borrowed, selling goods for calico printers on commission. At first, as he admitted years later, he was so ignorant of Manchester business that he was forced to look up names of calico printers in the local directory.[8] But he learnt fast, and was soon well on the way to being a 'Manchester Manufacturer', under which pseudonym he was to publish his first pamphlet in 1835. In 1831 his firm decided to undertake calico printing on its own account. The export excise on calicoes had just been abolished, and prospects were good for a rapid expansion of trade. The three partners therefore took over an old calico printing factory at Sabden, near Whalley, at the northern edge of the cotton district, twenty-eight miles from Manchester. Cobden was now full of knowledge of the cotton trade and district; the fascinated outsider of a few years before had become an energetic insider. Manchester, he told his brother, Frederick, excitedly at the beginning of 1832, was 'the place for money making business'. With animation and growing sympathy he described the activity of its streets, the strangeness of its dialect, the roughness and riches of its cotton lords. Money was to be made in Manchester, and Cobden was determined to make it. He only regretted that his brother did not share some of his own 'Bonapartist feeling'. 'I would not give 2½*d.* to anybody to guarantee me a fortune if I live.' In 1836 Cobden's firm made a net profit of £23,000, although admittedly this was an exceptional peak.[9]

Manchester reflected industrial growth at its greatest intensity; but during Cobden's lifetime industry was developing rapidly throughout much of the Midlands, the North of England, and around Glasgow. Cotton manufacture, wool manufacture, coal mining, iron and steel making, engineering, the chemical industry, shipbuilding, were all in varying degrees undergoing a transformation. Between 1801 and 1861, from three years before Cobden's birth to four years before his death, the population of the United Kingdom more than doubled, from about ten and a half millions to well over twenty-three millions. Here was both a huge new labour force for industry and a huge new consumer demand for its products. In times of trade prosperity such population growth was stimulating, but in times of trade depression it was frightening. One of Cobden's favourite points in support of free trade was to claim that the population was increasing at a thousand per day, and to argue that complete free trade was needed in order to expand foreign markets for our manufactures.*

Cotton was the industry which grew first and fastest, and also which depended most upon foreign markets. By the end of the Napoleonic Wars in 1815 cotton manufacture contributed 7 or 8 per cent of the national income, far outstripping the much older woollen industry. By 1830, the period when Cobden entered the cotton trade, cotton textiles accounted for half by value of all British exports. Admittedly, right up to the time of Cobden's death in 1865 many more people worked outside the great factory industries of Britain than worked within them. At the 1851 census five and a half million workers were placed in non-mechanised occupational categories, compared with a million and three-quarters in mechanised occupations, including half a million cotton workers. But these half-million produced one half of British exports. Relatively few produced relatively much, and Cobden and Bright were to prove that the problems and aspirations of the Lancashire cotton trade were of foremost national importance.[10]

Under the stimulus of the Industrial Revolution Manchester had become the second largest city in England. Its population was mushrooming at an unprecedented rate, from about twenty thousand in the mid-eighteenth century to nearly ninety thousand in 1801, and to about three hundred thousand by 1841. Manchester was the metropolis of the Lancashire cotton district, the hub of the earliest industrialised area in the world. Cotton spinning and weaving had been followed on a domestic basis in Lancashire since at least the early seventeenth century, but the existence of this early cotton trade subtracts hardly anything < from the magnitude of subsequent developments. About 1760 the old cotton trade was supporting perhaps forty thousand people: by the time Richard Cobden entered it, taking account of ancillary occupations such as transport, building, engineering and chemicals, it was supporting

---

* During Cobden's lifetime population increase averaged 210–230,000 per annum, never 365,000. It did reach this rate during the last quarter of the nineteenth century.

perhaps a million and a half. The chronology of the Industrial Revolution in cotton falls into two parts, dividing about 1790. The first phase, beginning around 1770, saw the new cotton spinning machinery erected in water-powered mills beside fast-flowing Pennine streams. Then, after less than twenty years, coal-fed steam engines began to be introduced, and this brought the cotton factories down from the hills and into the towns, nearer to markets and to labour supply. By the end of the century Manchester housed some fifty spinning mills, pouring forth smoke from their chimneys. The town was becoming big, bustling and dirty, its centre increasingly dominated by warehouses, its polluted rivers and canals lined with factories, its workpeople packed in overcrowded houses and cellars. A visitor in 1808 found the town 'abominably filthy, the steam engines pestiferous, the dyehouses noisesome and offensive, and the water of the river as black as ink or the Stygian Lake'. Engels' grim description of Manchester a generation later in his *Condition of the Working Class in England* is well known. Yet Manchester's sense of power and achievement made it a place of fascination: British and foreign tourists visited the town regularly. A German visitor in the 1840s claimed (rightly) that there had never been anywhere like Manchester, in its appearance, in its activity and prosperity, and (alluding to Cobden and the Anti-Corn Law League) in its political organisation. Benjamin Disraeli, who visited Manchester about the same time, found it as great a human exploit as Athens. Only a philosopher, he exclaimed in his novel *Coningsby* (1844), could fully understand the 'grandeur of Manchester'. Thomas Carlyle, who aspired to be such a philosopher, described the noise of its mills starting up at half-past five on a Monday morning as 'sublime as Niagara or more so'.[11]

But even those who were excited by the achievement of Manchester and of the Industrial Revolution admitted its dangers. There was a human as well as a technological side to the story, and in the sphere of social adjustment Englishmen of Cobden's generation had proved themselves much less successful than in the sphere of technical invention. Society in the cotton district of Lancashire was sharply divided between cotton masters on the one hand and cotton operatives on the other. There were few gradations of status; masters and men faced each other almost alone, and social tension was endemic. The cotton operatives comprised two main types, factory workers employed in the mills and handloom weavers working at home. About 1840, when Cobden was beginning his national political career, perhaps a quarter of a million cotton factory workers lived in Lancashire (a majority of them women and children), and perhaps a hundred thousand handloom weavers. The weaving branch of the industry was just beginning to pass into power-loom factories, and most English handloom weavers were abandoning their trade. Unfortunately, their places were being taken throughout the 1830s by Irish immigrants, who were flooding into the cotton towns. Over a hundred thousand Irish lived in Lancashire by 1841, thirty-four thousand of them in Manchester, in addition to about half as many again English-born children of Irish parents. The attachment of the Manchester Irish to the decaying handloom trade meant that most of them lived in chronic poverty, chiefly in the worst slums in the worst parts of Manchester, notably the 'Little Ireland' district. In times of slack trade their misery became intense because they were always the first to fall out of work. A petition from Manchester during the depression of 1837 claimed that members of weavers' families were trying to survive on only $1\frac{1}{2}d$. per head per day.[12]

The gap between these weavers and the cotton masters was the widest of all, but the gap within each mill between masters and factory workers was wide enough. It poisoned the social atmosphere of the cotton district. The lot of employers was not easy. Competition between smaller mill owners was fierce, and bankruptcy rates in times of slump were much higher than would be accepted as normal today. But whereas employers might fear bankruptcy, workmen had to fear hunger. A Manchester song of the period, quoted in Mrs. Gaskell's novel of Manchester life *Mary Barton* (1848), reflected this sense of difference.

> How little can the rich man know
> Of what the poor man feels,
> When Want, like some dark demon foe,
> Nearer and nearer steals!
>
> *He* never saw his darlings lie
> Shivering, the flags their bed;
> *He* never heard that maddening cry
> 'Daddy, a bit of bread!'[13]

Already by the date of Cobden's arrival in Manchester an active
political tradition had developed among the cotton operatives. The
workers had soon found their political martyrs. These were the dozen
people killed and more than four hundred injured in the Peterloo
Massacre. A great meeting in support of universal suffrage held on
St. Peter's Field, Manchester, on August 16, 1819, had been brutally
dispersed by a charge of the Manchester Yeomanry, acting under orders
of the local Tory magistrates. To their credit, few cotton masters had
supported the Peterloo magistrates. They were themselves vaguely
liberal in politics, anxious for a degree of Parliamentary reform which
would give Manchester its own Members of Parliament, and still more
eager for commercial reform to remove trade burdens like the raw
cotton duty, the calico excise, and the Corn Laws. The calico excise was
abolished in 1831, encouraging Cobden to set up as a calico printer;
Parliamentary reform came with the Reform Act a year later.
This gave Manchester two representatives in Parliament, elected
on a middle-class £10 householder franchise. Significantly, however,
the lead in popular agitation for the Reform Act came not from
Manchester but from Birmingham, where Thomas Attwood formed
the Birmingham Political Union. Industry and society in Birmingham
were much more graduated and cohesive than in Manchester, and the
B.P.U. was able to draw upon a wide range of local support. Manchester formed not one but two Reform Unions at this time. A mainly
middle-class union supported the Reform Bill, while a rival working-
class body demanded universal suffrage.[14]

Richard Cobden was well aware of the social reasons for this political
separation. He described in 1841 how the huge factories of the cotton
district, 'with three *thousand* hands under *one* capitalist', gave to
Manchester society 'the worst possible tone' by placing an 'impassable
gulf between master and operative'.[15] In fact, only a few factories
employed thousands of workpeople, most employed hundreds or less,
but their owners were marked off from their hands by the system of
factory production. Use of the word 'hands' as a synonym for workpeople was itself revealing. We shall see how earnestly Cobden sought
to draw masters and men together in support of free trade, believing
that it would bring both classes equal benefit.

Social divisions in Manchester were coming to be indicated and
intensified by topographical division. In the early days of the Industrial

Revolution merchants and manufacturers had lived close to their warehouses and factories, and consequently near also to the homes of their workpeople. But from about 1830 the Manchester middle classes began to withdraw in large numbers to exclusive suburbs on the outskirts of the town, leaving the operatives behind in the crowded central districts. Cobden told his brother in 1832 how several of his neighbours in Mosley Street were selling their homes for conversion into warehouses at twice the price which they had paid for them as dwelling houses. His architect had assured him that he could now get six thousand guineas for his house as a prospective warehouse. 'So as I gave but three thousand, and all the world is talking of the bargain here, and there being but one opinion or criterion of a man's ability— *the making of money*—I am already thought a clever fellow.' Cobden himself moved out to such a suburb, Broughton, after his marriage in 1840. It was described in Chadwick's famous *Report* in 1842 as inhabited 'almost exclusively by the upper classes'. The houses were new, spacious and well built, and the death rate there was less than half that in central Manchester. In 1844 Cobden was wanting to move again. 'I can't be in the town', he told his brother, 'or in the suburb in a *row*. I must be in a detached place, and whether at two or five miles from the Exchange is of little consequence.' This physical separation intensified the separation in spirit between masters and men. By the 1840s Engels was noting how Manchester employers travelling to their homes in the suburbs were protected from a sight of the miserable living conditions of their workpeople by screens of shops set along the main exit roads. 'Out of sight' began perhaps to mean 'out of mind' for many Manchester businessmen, but it never did so for Richard Cobden.* [16]

---

* Commenting on various Negro riots in Los Angeles in August 1965 *The Times* pointed out that they were not strictly race riots at all. They were urban riots. 'In the big cities of the north and west the barriers are inextricably bound up with unemployment, poverty, educational deprivation, and the breakdown of social and family structures. As every American who can afford it moves out into the suburbs the city centres tend to become aesthetic and cultural deserts inhabited largely by the poor, who are mostly Negro. The result is a ghetto mentality and a bitter resentment of authority, or just of "them", that can explode over quite trivial incidents' (*The Times*, Aug. 14, 1965). Los Angeles' urban problem of today parallels that of Manchester in Cobden's day.

We have seen how Cobden had been introduced to national progress and problems through travelling round Britain in the 1820s. In the 1830s he widened his range and began to journey abroad. He found that he greatly enjoyed foreign travel, apart from the sea passages which often prostrated him. The same eager enquiring mind which had discovered Birmingham and Manchester now learnt about Constantinople and New York, collecting valuable stores of knowledge and impressions well reflected in his still readable travel letters. In his prime Cobden was the most travelled major figure in British politics. He possessed first-hand knowledge not only of the Grand Tour countries of Western Europe, but also of the Near East, Russia and the United States. Cobden had probed much deeper than any diplomat or Foreign Secretary. He had met foreigners of all sorts, merchants as well as princes, peasants as well as politicians. As a result, his ideas and arguments about international affairs were as well grounded upon knowledge as his attitudes upon domestic questions. The two were not indeed separated in Cobden's mind, for (as we shall see) the creed of free trade treated national and international problems and interests as closely linked.

Cobden first went abroad in July 1833 on a brief visit to Paris in search of designs for his calico printing firm. In the following year he travelled again to France and on to Switzerland. He was much impressed by Swiss scenery, and still more by Swiss institutions. He told his brother that the Swiss were the most prosperous and happy people in the world. Cobden was convinced that this was the result of free trade. Switzerland, he claimed, was the only country which did not employ one single customs officer.[17]

But Cobden reserved his greatest admiration for the United States, at a time when many Englishmen were inclined to smile at American provincialism. He arrived there on his first visit in June 1835, and stayed for just over a month, visiting the eastern states. His itinerary was intensive and exhausting. He found American boasting tiresome and American women unattractive, pasty in complexion and 'deficient in bust and bustle'. But he thought the American system sound in essentials and impressive in potential. He admired the democracy of American government, and the equality of American society (apart from the blot of Negro slavery). He was impressed by American material prosperity, and also by the success and equitability of the

American system of education. He forecast that the United States would capture the economic and political leadership of the world unless Britain adopted far-sighted and liberal economic and political policies.[18]

This had already been the theme of Cobden's first political pamphlet, *England, Ireland and America*, published a few weeks before his American visit as the anonymous work of 'A Manchester Manufacturer'. The style was already characteristic, clear, factual, cumulative in its persuasive effect. Cobden pointed out how the United States already possessed many natural advantages which could not be taken from her. Yet British manufacturers were still hampered in fighting American competition by two artificial disadvantages which ought to be immediately removed. These were, firstly, protection and restriction of commerce, and secondly, an aristocratic and expensive foreign policy of unnecessary interference in foreign wars and rivalries. This interference burdened us with heavy taxation and debt at the same time as the policy of commercial protection and restriction limited our use of resources. For the title page of his pamphlet Cobden chose an apposite quotation from George Washington. 'The great rule of conduct for us in regard to foreign nations is, in extending our commercial relations, to have with them as little connection as possible.' The case of Ireland, demoralised and desperate, seemed to Cobden the most striking illustration of the folly of traditional British economic and foreign policies.[19]

In the summer of 1836 Cobden published his second pamphlet, entitled simply *Russia*, partly provoked by alarmist fears of a Russian invasion. Once again the author described himself only as 'A Manchester Manufacturer', an indication that although his first pamphlet had been well received and had reached a fifth and cheap sixpenny edition by this time, Cobden's own name was still of little moment. In his first work he had argued that it was the rival economy of the United States which was likely to damage us, not (as British statesmen nearly always assumed) Russian 'efforts of barbarian force'. Cobden's first work had mainly elaborated the reality of the American economic danger: his second sought to demonstrate the unreality of the assumed danger from Russian military power. True, Russia might overrun the Balkans, and even Turkey itself, if we did not bolster up the Turks. Cobden did not countenance such aggression. But he contended strongly that it should not be part of British policy to prepare to fight the Russians for the sake of the Turks. The so-called 'Eastern Question', which absorbed so much of the time of our Foreign Secretaries and of the resources of our Treasury, ought to be no question at all for Britain. Russian military movements a thousand miles away constituted no real danger, whereas American economic progress three thousand miles away was a genuine threat. Economic strength made a country truly great, not military conquest. Watt and Arkwright, not Nelson and Wellington, had put Britain in the first place. Russia would add nothing to her real power even if she overran the whole Turkish empire. Such was Cobden's argument. And with a characteristic homely touch he rounded off his case in a footnote describing what he himself had seen of American economic potential during his tour. He had found that the Americans could mine high-grade coal with great ease. A steamboat on which he had travelled had stopped at one pit-head, and loaded on fuel at only three-farthings a bushel. Such material abundance and cheapness, concluded Cobden, bore more directly upon the future destiny of Great Britain 'than the marriages of crowned heads in Portugal, the movements of savage forces in Russia, and similar proceedings, to which we attach so much importance'.[20]

We shall return later to the general arguments which Cobden here first used against the balance of power conception of international relations. For the present we need notice only how through these pamphlets Cobden, the calico printer, had begun to make a name for himself as a political writer. Few of his ideas were new. He did not claim to be an original thinker. But he was consciously setting himself up as an 'agitator' (in the literal, non-pejorative sense) of public opinion, an agitator, moreover, whose principles and inclinations each kept him apart from ordinary Whig-Tory party politics.* *Russia* began with the plain assertion that 'this is not a party pamphlet'. And, for once, such a claim was true. The greatest non-party statesman ever to figure in British politics was now launched upon his career.

Through his Russian pamphlet Cobden met Lord Durham, the prominent Whig-Radical, then Ambassador at St. Petersburg, who

---

* The terms 'agitator' and 'public opinion' both seem to have been coined in the early years of George III, in response to the growing popular aspirations of the time. The existence of the one term required the other.

had been much impressed by Cobden's arguments.[21] At a lower political level, but one more immediately useful to him, he now began to be accepted as a coming man in Manchester. Here he owed something to Archibald Prentice, editor of the *Manchester Times*, a veteran Radical, who had realised Cobden's political promise and who gave his writings and activities steady publicity. The *Manchester Times* welcomed *Russia*, for example, as 'one of the most valuable pamphlets that has been issued from the press'. An interesting though slightly malicious piece of evidence about the Cobden–Prentice relationship has survived from the diary of Absalom Watkin, another Manchester reformer. In September 1837 Watkin dined at Cobden's house in company with a Mr. Grime. Conversation turned to the failure of S. J. Loyd as a moderate reform candidate at the 1832 Manchester election. In part, this was caused by Loyd's poor showing under Radical questioning from Prentice at a public meeting.

> 'Mr. Cobden, adverting to the prejudice against Mr. Loyd which had been produced by the questioning of Mr. Prentice, observed, "Prentice should have been bought over. Not", he added, "that I mean to say that our friend is on sale, but he should have been won over—such things are to be done—*he should have been consulted.*" '

Watkin noted in his diary how he and Grime exchanged meaning glances at this remark, and how not long afterwards Cobden's servant came into the room to tell his master that a messenger from Prentice wished to speak to him. Cobden apologised to his guests and went to see the man. 'Now, Prentice eulogises Mr. Cobden in the *Times*', commented Watkin, 'and, I have no doubt, *has been consulted.* In this manner reputation is maintained, and the way to distinction is smoothed.'[22]

Only a few days before this dinner Cobden had himself been defeated as a reform candidate for Stockport in the 1837 General Election. When the town clerk of Stockport had asked Joseph Parkes about Cobden as a possible candidate, Parkes, one of the leading political wirepullers of the period, had replied that 'he would be an honour to them, not they to him'. The *Manchester Times* backed Cobden strongly throughout the campaign. Prentice admitted in one editorial that at first he had been doubtful about Cobden's speaking power. A good pamphleteer might not make a good platform politician.

But, as Prentice remarked, Cobden had soon proved himself able to explain his programme effectively upon noisy election stages. In this programme Cobden, in his own phrase, went 'the whole hog' upon most of the issues of the time. He gave first place to the need for happiness and peace in Ireland. He blamed Irish distress mainly upon the Protestant Established Church, which, by provoking internal dissension leading to violence, had prevented the spread of education to the Catholic masses, and had thereby fostered bigotry and superstition. He called, therefore, for disestablishment of the Irish Church. In the name of freedom and equality he also pressed for disestablishment of the Church of England. Dissenters were no longer an obscure few whose rights could be ignored. Moreover, the example of the United States had proved that Church and State flourished best apart. Though himself an Anglican, Cobden therefore felt that he could consistently propose disestablishment. He called also for progress towards greater political equality. He proposed extending the Parliamentary franchise to all householders, on the ground that they had been given local votes under the Municipal Corporations Act and had proved themselves sufficiently intelligent and trustworthy to be granted the higher franchise. Linked with this must come triennial Parliaments and vote by ballot, the one increasing the influence of the electorate, the other removing the possibility of unfair pressure upon individual electors. At the same time, continued Cobden, a national system of education must be established so as to improve the quality of public opinion. And to ensure economic prosperity trade must be free. This meant, in particular, repeal of the Corn Laws. It meant also abandoning the colonies, for under free trade we would have no need to maintain them as markets for our goods. Withdrawal from the colonies would assist in reducing the over-large standing army. Our traditional interfering foreign policy must also be repudiated. Colonies, army, and diplomatic service had all been inflated to provide jobs for the dependants of the aristocracy. The House of Lords, the great stronghold of the landed aristocracy, must also be reformed, allowing proper influence for the manufacturing interest and its demand for equality and economy. Finally, humanity must be promoted alongside equality by removing the 'barbarous severity' of the criminal code.

Despite this wide-ranging programme, and despite an active campaign, Cobden came bottom of the poll. The *Manchester Times* claimed that this was largely because his Tory rival, a local mill-owner, had exercised unfair influence over voters in a manner which election by ballot would prevent. Probably a more important reason was that Cobden started as a stranger in the borough. In the circumstances it was no disgrace to gain only fifty-three votes less than his well-known local opponent (418 to 471). In his speech after the election Cobden forecast that within two years economic depression would make Tory mill-owners, such as his opponent, appreciate through their pockets the case for repeal of the Corn Laws.[23]

Despite this Stockport diversion Cobden's centre of both business and political activity was still Manchester. Here in October 1837 he was selected to serve as one of the Court Leet jurors, whose task it was annually to choose a Borough-reeve. Manchester was still partly governed, or more accurately mis-governed, through this inappropriate manorial form of government. Cobden's attention was now attracted to the need for the incorporation of Manchester under the terms of the Municipal Corporations Act of 1835. The local Radicals had long been aware of the need for reform in local government; now Cobden roused them into quick action. During the first half of 1838 he devoted much of his time to promoting an agitation for a petition in favour of incorporation. He circulated five thousand copies of a lively pamphlet, entitled *Incorporate Your Borough!* It was again anonymous, Cobden simply signing himself 'a Radical Reformer' and addressing his 'Fellow Townsmen and Brother Reformers'. This pamphlet was designed especially to win the support of the working men by showing them that incorporation would produce better and more democratic government. Cobden recalled the memory of the Peterloo Massacre, which, he claimed, would never have occurred if Manchester had been incorporated. The Lancashire and Cheshire county magistrates responsible for the outrage would then have enjoyed no more jurisdiction over Manchester than over Constantinople. Most Manchester workmen, however, refused to see any advantage for themselves in incorporation. The 1832 Reform Act which had enfranchised the middle classes, had been followed by the 1834 Poor Law, which threatened working men with the workhouse even if they were out of work through no fault of their own. Why should the poor seek to give the middle classes more power locally? A noisy and class-conscious agitation against the new Poor Law was just reaching a peak in Lancashire and Yorkshire, before merging during the summer of 1838 into the great Chartist agitation. The local anti-Poor Law and Chartist leaders went to the length of allying with the Manchester Tories in defence of the existing unreformed local government. 'Working Men Beware!', exclaimed one poster. 'The Whigs are at their dirty work again . . . no Middle-class Government . . . No Cotton-Lord Mayors . . . No Wine Cellars stored out of a New Borough Rate.'

Cobden and the incorporation party battled hard against this current, but without much success. Their support came mainly from manufacturers and shopkeepers. Rival petitions were got up, for and against incorporation, the opposition petition claiming over thirty thousand signatures, that of the incorporators upwards of eleven thousand. Close scrutiny reduced the number of valid signatures on both sides to not very different totals, eight thousand more or less. The Privy Council was convinced, however, that the incorporators represented a majority of 'respectable' local opinion, and that Manchester needed a modern system of government. A charter was therefore granted. Cobden and his friends had won an important victory, but it was not a total triumph. The Manchester Tories contested the validity of the charter of incorporation until 1842, boycotting the first borough elections in December 1838. The Whigs and middle-class Radicals therefore made a clean sweep at the polls.[24]

Cobden himself became one of the first group of aldermen. Already, however, he was becoming deeply involved in the anti-Corn Law agitation, so that he never found much time after incorporation to devote to local affairs. He regarded repeal of the Corn Laws as following logically and directly upon the incorporation of Manchester, as he explained in one of the most vigorous passages in his pamphlet. The lords of Clumber, Belvoir, and Woburn, wrote Cobden, could no longer storm and ransack the town at the head of their vassals. Yet they were just as effectively plundering its manufacturers and workmen through their 'infamous bread tax upon your industry'. Cobden called upon all classes in Manchester to claim a share in its government and protection. 'Give unity, force, and efficiency to the intelligent and wealthy community of Manchester, and qualify it by organization, as it already is entitled by numbers, to be the leader in the battle against monopoly and privilege. In a word, INCORPORATE YOUR BOROUGH.'[25]

In distributing its circulars and pamphlets the Anti-Corn Law League was to make great use of the penny post, introduced at the beginning of 1840. Alongside his work for the incorporation of Manchester, Cobden played an active part in the campaign for cheap postage. In May 1838 he gave evidence on behalf of the Manchester Chamber of Commerce before a Parliamentary select committee enquiring into the postal services. He argued that both the national revenue and all classes would benefit from cheap postage. Manchester businessmen, professional men, and ministers of religion all desired it. He described how among the working classes, although many were not so well educated as they deserved to be, there was usually one member of each family who could write. Given cheap postage, scattered members of working-class families would be able to keep in touch much more easily. As for the revenue, Cobden estimated that four-fifths of all correspondence between Manchester and London was being conducted outside the national postal network because of its high charges.

Cobden came to know and to admire Rowland Hill, the man chiefly responsible for securing the penny post. In May 1838 he sent Hill a characteristically lively invitation to lecture in Manchester. Cobden recommended that the lecture should 'appeal strongly to the *moral* sympathies, shewing its connection with an indulgence of our best affections, and the intimate relation it has to the increase of education'. A few months later in working up the anti-Corn Law campaign Cobden was again to emphasise the relationship between reform and morality. Less than a month before his death in 1865 he looked back with satisfaction upon the moral and educational benefits which had resulted from twenty-five years of penny postage. Rowland Hill would be remembered, wrote Cobden, when Napoleon III had been long forgotten. In 1843 he had told Hill that the work of the Anti-Corn Law League was 'the spawn of your penny postage'. After his work during the first half of 1838 for incorporation and cheap postage Cobden began during the second half of the year to lay the foundations of this great movement.[26]

## 2. INDUSTRY AND AGRICULTURE

At the opening of the nineteenth century the prosperity of the British economy still depended primarily upon the condition of British agriculture. By mid-century the Industrial Revolution had overturned this agricultural hegemony. About 1750 the share of agriculture in the gross national product approached one-half; by 1800 it was down to about one-third, and by 1850 it had dropped to one-fifth. Agricultural production had not fallen in absolute terms, indeed it had grown, but it had not matched the remarkable growth of industry. Moreover, the emergence of a huge new urban industrial population had transformed Britain from a grain exporting to a grain importing country. In the mid-eighteenth century Britain sold enough corn overseas to feed a million people per annum; by the 1840s, when Cobden was leading the campaign against the Corn Laws, she had become committed in years of normal harvest to feeding 10 to 15 per cent of her population on foreign grain.

Throughout these changing hundred years, control of the levels of grain import and export was attempted through the Corn Laws. These laws went back to the Middle Ages, but during the later eighteenth century they began to alter in their application. Up to the middle of that century they were important because they provided a bounty for corn exports; the fact that importation was also regulated was of less importance. Then gradually, as Britain began to import corn on a large scale, the restrictive aspect of the Corn Laws came to the fore. The new industrial employers and workers wanted the price of bread as low as possible, and began to press for relaxation of grain import restrictions in hopes of a larger and cheaper inflow of Polish and Prussian corn. Landlords and farmers, however, opposed this strongly, and because the landed interest controlled a large majority of seats in the unreformed House of Commons their views prevailed. Although the corn export bounty was abolished as an anachronism in 1814, a new and more rigorous Corn Law was passed in the following year. The existing sliding scale of corn import duties was replaced by absolute prohibition of import up to a fixed price (eighty shillings per quarter in the case of wheat) with free admission thereafter. The cry went round the industrial districts that the landed interest had passed selfish legislation to keep prices high and profits inflated. And so for the next thirty years the Corn Laws became a symbol of potential conflict within British society, conflict between the interests of old agriculture and new industry, between free trade and protection. The 1815 law provoked many hostile petitions from industrial towns. Nearly fifty thousand people signed a Birmingham petition, over fifty thousand another from Manchester. At this time many provincial Tories supported the attacks of Whigs and Radicals, even though the 1815 law was the work of a Tory ministry. The Tory *Nottingham Gazette*, for example, condemned a measure designed to 'encourage one class of the community in preference to another'. 'An Enemy to Restrictions' wrote to the normally Ministerial *Manchester Mercury* newspaper in 1816 complaining that Parliament had recently acted 'as if to add to our prohibitive laws could be a remedy for all our evils'.[1]

Hostility to the Corn Laws was not yet, however, on the scale of thirty years later. Richard Cobden was still at school. Cotton manufacturers in the 1820s were anxious chiefly to secure abolition of the direct taxes upon the cotton trade, notably the raw cotton import duty and the export excise upon printed cottons. The latter was removed in 1831, but the raw cotton duty was actually increased at this same time in order to compensate the revenue. Despite continuous pressure, it was not repealed until 1845.[2] By contrast, Manchester's criticism of the Corn Laws was vigorous only at times of trade depression. It needed Cobden and the Anti-Corn Law League to stimulate Manchester opinion into continuous and complete opposition to the Corn Laws. In his 1835 pamphlet even Cobden was still prepared to accept a fixed duty upon imported corn for revenue purposes. Soon afterwards he became convinced of the need for complete repeal, but his early attitude was revealing.[3] J. B. Smith, a cotton dealer, who tried during the prosperous mid-'30s to rouse the Manchester Chamber of Commerce in favour of total repeal earned for himself the nickname of 'mad Smith'. The Manchester Chamber would have been glad to accept a fixed duty in place of the 1828 Corn Law. This measure had reintroduced a sliding scale of duties related to import price in place of the absolute prohibition of 1815.

Then in 1837 the coincidence of a bad harvest with renewed trade depression gave new intensity to feeling in Lancashire on the Corn Law question. In July 1836 the United States President had ordered that payment for public lands should be made in gold, not in notes. To protect its reserves the Bank of England raised its rate from $4\frac{1}{2}$ to 5 per cent, and refused to discount American bills. Import houses cancelled orders for cotton, and American merchants withdrew orders in England. The *Manchester Times*, edited by Archibald Prentice, a veteran advocate of Corn Law repeal, reported in June 1837 that fifty thousand workers in the Manchester area were unemployed or on short time. The directors of the Manchester Chamber of Commerce complained that the price of wheat had risen by half and that eighty-eight cotton mills had stopped working.[4] In December J. B. Smith persuaded the board of the Chamber to approve a petition criticising the Corn Laws and asking for freer trade. Then at its annual meeting in February 1838 Richard Cobden made his first major move on the Corn Law question. Hoping to exploit this intensified feeling against corn legislation, he proposed that the Chamber should hold quarterly instead of annual general meetings. But Manchester opinion refused to be rushed, and Cobden's motion had to be withdrawn.[5]

The real chance for the reformers came towards the end of the year. On September 10 Dr. John Bowring, sometime secretary to Jeremy Bentham and an ardent advocate of free trade, lectured to an audience of about sixty people at the York Hotel, Manchester. Bowring described the power of the new German *Zollverein*. He claimed that Germany and other countries had reluctantly begun to manufacture cotton goods because the Corn Laws prevented them from exchanging their corn for Lancashire manufactures. After the meeting Archibald Prentice began to canvass the idea of forming an Anti-Corn Law Association in Manchester. Cobden was not present, as he was on a month's tour of Germany studying its growing economic strength. But on the Continent he too was coming to the conclusion that the reformers must make a new effort to collect opinion against the Corn Laws. In his first pamphlet in 1835 he had briefly mentioned the need for organisation by businessmen in support of free trade propaganda, but the bodies which he seems to have envisaged at this time were more philosophical than the future Anti-Corn Law League. 'We have our Banksean, our Linnaean, our Hunterian Societies; and why should not at least our greatest commercial and manufacturing towns possess their Smithean Societies?' Cobden told his brother in October 1838 that he could give the question 'a great lift' on his return home by publicising what he had discovered about economic progress in Europe and especially in Germany.

A fortnight after the Bowring meeting Prentice and six others met again at the York Hotel, Manchester. After a further fortnight the names of thirty-eight members of a provisional committee were

` Plate I

Cobden in his prime

announced. J. B. Smith was treasurer, and members included George Wilson, future chairman of the Anti-Corn Law League, and 'John Bright, Rochdale'. A week later a list of additional names included that of 'Richard Cobden, Mosley Street'.[6]

In this manner was the great anti-Corn Law movement started in Manchester in the autumn of 1838. The Anti-Corn Law League, the national body which was to embrace the Manchester Association as its chief component, was not formed until March 1839. There could be no suggestion yet that Manchester was leading a mass national movement. Nevertheless, from the first it set out to give such leadership. The association's subscription, as Prentice explained, was deliberately set as low as five shillings per annum in order to attract 'popular' support. Yet this figure was still far beyond the means of ordinary working men, and it confirmed that in this first phase the Manchester reformers were seeking mainly to create a mass movement of middle-class businessmen like themselves.

The Manchester Association soon began to act. On October 25 the first anti-Corn Law lecture under its sponsorship was given at the Manchester Corn Exchange. The speaker was A. W. Paulton from Bolton, who had been engaged as a full-time lecturer. He and Smith next embarked upon a speaking tour of industrial towns, reaching as far as Birmingham, an indication that the Manchester men were thinking nationally from the start. Their base, however, was not yet secure. The Manchester Chamber of Commerce was still reluctant to come out clearly for total repeal of the Corn Laws. A special general meeting was called on December 13, 1838 to support an anti-Corn Law petition, but its terms were vague and mild. J. B. Smith inveighed against any restrictions upon trade. Then in a short speech Richard Cobden successfully proposed an adjournment of the meeting for a week to allow time for a stronger petition to be prepared. With this move Cobden began his seven and a half years of continuous agitation against the Corn Laws. During the intervening week the first Manchester municipal elections were held, emphasising how, with this smaller local victory won, Cobden was now advancing to promote larger national and international progress.

At the adjourned meeting of the Manchester Chamber of Commerce the directors again submitted their original draft petition, though with a stronger conclusion asking that the existing laws be repealed.

This, however, left room for the imposition of some new Corn Law, and was unacceptable to Cobden and the total repealers. In his speech to the meeting Cobden skilfully used fear of the Chartists to win the support of the many hesitant middle-class members of the Chamber for total and immediate repeal. The working-class agitation for the six points of the Charter (universal manhood suffrage, vote by ballot, equal electoral districts, annual Parliaments, payment of Members of Parliament, and abolition of the property qualification for election) had begun in the summer, and under the spur of economic distress had quickly spread throughout the industrial districts. As winter set in the Chartists began to hold meetings by torchlight, and the language of some Chartist orators became as inflammatory as the torches around them. Most of this was bluff, but middle-class men of property in Manchester and elsewhere were given grounds for expecting a working-class rising. As recently as December 12, the *Manchester Guardian*, the favourite newspaper of the cotton merchants and manufacturers, had carried a long editorial which quoted outbursts from O'Connor and Stephens threatening to burn the cotton factories. Here, concluded the *Guardian*, was an attempt to 'strike terror' which must be quickly curbed.

Against this tense background Cobden presented his case for complete repeal of the Corn Laws to the Manchester Chamber of Commerce. He asked why 'incendiaries' were able to call torchlight meetings. Because thousands of workpeople lacked work and decent homes. And why was this? Because of the Corn Laws and other restrictions. Cobden then produced his own petition in place of that of the directors. In forcible language it drew the attention of the landlord-controlled House of Commons to the vast size and imperative needs of the new cotton manufacture, which had become 'essential to our well-being as a nation'. Foreign cotton manufacture was developing rapidly. Soon it would offer dangerous competition, because foreign rivals could buy food at half the price which, under the Corn Law, it was being sold in Britain. Bad as was present distress, the future for those dependent upon the cotton industry was thus blacker still, unless we adopted free trade. 'Already the millions have raised the cry for food. Reason, compassion and sound policy demand that the excited passions be allayed, otherwise evil consequences may ensue.' Every man, concluded Cobden, had an 'inalienable right . . . freely to exchange the results of his labour for the productions of other people.' Cobden's persuasive arguments carried the meeting with him, and his petition asking the Commons to repeal the Corn Laws and to adopt 'the true and peaceful principles of free trade' was adopted almost unanimously.

## 3. LEADER OF THE ANTI-CORN LAW LEAGUE

This was Cobden's first great success as a speaker against the Corn Laws, and it was a characteristic triumph of personality plus argument. Before we follow the story of the anti-Corn Law agitation from these beginnings in 1838 to its end with repeal of the Corn Laws in 1846 we need to study the personality and arguments which Cobden brought to it as leader.

Personality was to count even more with Cobden than with most politicians, for he never held office. He owed his success to the influence of his character and his intellect. Walter Bagehot, the most perceptive of Victorian political commentators, remarked in an obituary notice that, quite apart from Cobden's specific political achievements, he would be remembered for his 'unique character'. His engaging nature was well expressed in his face. Kindly eyes looked out from under a wide brow; an alert yet gentle expression played round a mobile mouth. A contemporary commented upon the attractiveness of Cobden's countenance which, 'when he became interested, would light up and almost fascinate one on account of the vivacity and strength of intellect which became clearly displayed.' Harriet Beecher Stowe confirmed that Cobden's 'frank fascinating smile' was 'a sufficient account of his popularity'.

For all his friendliness Cobden always knew what he wanted. Abuse left him unruffled. He told his wife at the height of the anti-Corn Law campaign that he was never angered by slights or neglect because he was able to 'take refuge in a certain self-esteem which tells me I am not despicable, whatever other people may think to the contrary'. Yet he could usually respect the arguments of all rational opponents. Because of this, although he took a decided line on political issues, Cobden was not treated (at least by those who knew him personally) as a narrow partisan. He was much helped here because, as Bagehot pointed out, he arraigned principles not persons, an attitude probably unique among political agitators. When he entered Parliament in 1841 he found himself regarded by the agriculturalist majority as a 'Gothic invader' from the industrial North. Yet four years later he could claim that he was on cordial terms with all parties in the Commons, 'and especially with two ultra-monopolists who three years ago would have skinned me alive'.[1]

Cobden's attitude towards Lord Palmerston is revealing in this context. Palmerston, Prime Minister 1855–8 and 1859–65, was the great opponent of Cobden's view of foreign affairs in the 1850s and '60s. They differed profoundly in origins, character and ideas. In 1864 Cobden complained that after fifty years of public life, 'during which almost centuries of change have been effected in our political and economical systems', Palmerston had not been associated with one movement towards prosperity and freedom. But Cobden felt less and less acrimony towards Palmerston personally. 'I believe he is perfectly sincere,' he remarked towards the end of both their lives, 'for the longer I live, the more I believe in men's sincerity'. Palmerston came to reciprocate these generous feelings. Cobden used to remark jokingly that whatever he said about Palmerston's policy, 'the old rascal will always insist upon calling me his honourable friend'. Both could hit hard in debate, but mutual respect grew.[2]

As leader of the Anti-Corn Law League Cobden showed unlimited enthusiasm, great patience and much good humour. Above all, he shared the great soldier's gift of being able to encourage and to stimulate others. His ability to arouse enthusiasm can still be felt as we read his letters and speeches today. His public speaking style was as straightforward and unpretentious in matter and manner as his private character. There were no histrionics in a Cobden speech. At the end of his very last public address he remarked how he had never wound up in peroration: 'when I have done I leave off, and sit down'. Cobden always gave a logical, factual statement of his case, spiced at intervals with humour, holding his listeners by his clarity and impressing them by his continuous good sense. Justin McCarthy, who knew Cobden well, described his speaking manner as essentially characteristic of the man himself: 'plain speaking, a constant appeal to the reason, the judgment, and the better qualities of men, without any proclaimed right to control by mere rhetorical display'.

This style came naturally to Cobden, but its naturalness did not mean that he was unaware of it. He took care, for example, not to overcrowd his material. His rule was never to use more statistics than he could carry in his head, in the hope that what he could easily remember his hearers might also remember. He was careful, too, not to be boring when addressing mass audiences. He tried, he said, to teach people almost without their knowing it. 'If they are simply lectured, they may sit out the lesson for once, but they will not come again; and as I have required them again and again, I have been obliged to amuse them, not by standing on my head or eating fire, but by kindred feats of jugglery.' Cobden was indeed rather ashamed at having to enliven his matter in this way. Yet he need not have felt concern. He was no demagogue; he never lapsed into amusing and stirring his audiences simply for effect. On the other hand, he was always ready to learn from his public. He admitted on one occasion that there was nothing like repeated speech-making for discovering the strong and weak parts of an argument: 'the audience by voice and eyes are infallible critics.' Of course, there were times during the long anti-Corn Law agitation when Cobden drove himself so hard that his speeches suffered. After speaking badly at a demonstration in 1845 he himself admitted to his wife that he had been talking too often on the one subject. Like many good speakers, he always felt slightly nervous before addressing a meeting. When he delivered his first major speech in Manchester in October 1835, supporting a proposal to establish a Manchester Athenaeum, he could not see a single face in the audience in front of him. Then as he got under way his confidence grew, so that this first speech, like most later ones, began to make its impact. In old age John Bright recollected another early Cobden speech, the first he ever heard by his future friend, given at Rochdale in 1837 in support of working-class education. Cobden's style, Bright remembered, was already the same as it was always to be, 'a conversational eloquence, a persuasiveness which it was almost impossible to resist'. Sir Robert Peel in his resignation speech after repeal of the Corn Laws in 1846 likewise praised Cobden's 'appeals to reason, expressed by an eloquence, the more to be admired because it was unaffected and unadorned'. Less well-known than these tributes is that from the great Corn Law opponent of both Peel and Cobden, Benjamin Disraeli. Disraeli's detailed description of Cobden's speaking style, given in his novel *Endymion*, is just and delicate:

'He was a pale and slender man, with a fine brow and an eye that occasionally flashed with the fire of a creative mind. His voice . . .

was rather thin, but singularly clear. There was nothing clearer except his meaning. Endymion never heard a case stated with such pellucid art; facts marshalled with such vivid simplicity, and inferences so natural and spontaneous and irresistible, that they seemed, as it were, borrowed from his audience. . . . When his case was fairly before them, the speaker dealt with his opponents—some in the press, some in Parliament—with much power of sarcasm, but this power was evidently rather repressed than allowed to run riot. What impressed Endymion as the chief quality of this remarkable speaker was his persuasiveness, and he had the air of being too prudent to offend even an opponent unnecessarily. His language, though natural and easy, was choice and refined. He was evidently a man who had read, and not a little; and there was no taint of vulgarity, scarcely a provincialism, in his pronunciation.'

It is instructive to compare this with Disraeli's verdict upon Thomas Attwood, leader of the Birmingham Political Union during the Reform Bill crisis, and the foremost provincial politician of the generation before Cobden. After a visit to Birmingham in 1832 Disraeli had reported that none of the local leaders was entirely satisfactory, although there was 'a simplicity about Attwood which is pleasing'. Disraeli found Attwood's organisation inferior, 'his voice good, his pronunciation most vicious and Warwickshire, altogether a third-rate man'. In short, Attwood's was the simplicity of mediocrity, whereas Cobden's was the simplicity of greatness.³

Cobden's effectiveness as a public speaker set him apart from earlier advocates of free trade. As one of them admitted in 1841, the free traders had not been orators since the early days of the Younger Pitt. They had hammered away with facts and figures, 'but we could not elevate the subject and excite the feelings of the people'. A knowledgeable observer exclaimed in 1838 that many Radical free traders in Parliament were not fit even to be abbots in a monastery. The nearest to a leader among them before Cobden entered Parliament in 1841 was the Hon. C. P. Villiers, brother of Lord Clarendon. From 1838 to 1846 Villiers annually introduced a motion in favour of repeal or at least of modification of the Corn Laws. As a member of a leading Whig family Villiers was at first much deferred to by Cobden and by other leaders of the League. But Villiers did not possess, and realised that he did not possess, the qualities to make him the leader of a mass movement. After repeal had been achieved Cobden wrote gratefully of the good temper with which Villiers had given place to himself.[4]

Cobden was as effective a private letter-writer as he was a public speaker. He wrote thousands of letters during his career, elaborating new arguments, suggesting new moves, encouraging the hesitant, praising the enterprising. Each one was characteristically clear in expression and infectious in enthusiasm. Cobden's skill as a correspondent was remembered years later by one of the League's legal agents. One evening in December 1844 the agent had waited to receive a letter of credentials from the League leader. Throughout the evening Cobden had received callers in his bedroom. Then he fluently dashed off the necessary letter, without needing to alter a single word even though he had been hard at work all evening. Cobden often composed a score of letters at one sitting, each in handwriting as clear as his thoughts. This was true even when he was travelling on his campaigns of agitation. As soon as he reached his inn after a long journey or noisy meeting he would sit down to write. Sorting through his anti-Corn Law correspondence some years after repeal, Cobden was himself surprised at the extent to which he had concentrated his time and thoughts upon the single object.[5]

Cobden devoted himself single-mindedly to the one target of 'total and immediate' repeal of the Corn Laws, and he insisted that the Anti-Corn Law League should do the same. Again and again in his speeches and writings he stressed the need to pursue this objective alone. To seek other reforms alongside Corn Law repeal, however desirable in themselves, would diminish the impact of the main demand upon the public. The Leaguers, Cobden told Villiers in 1841, must 'stick to their text. There is nothing but "no bread tax" that will avail us at the hustings.'[6]

Some historians have believed that Cobden regarded the Complete Suffrage movement of 1841–3 with hostility because it threatened this League singlemindedness. The Complete Suffrage party was led by Joseph Sturge of Birmingham, who had made his name in the 1830s as a leader of the successful movement for abolition of colonial slavery. Sturge set out in November 1841 to form a Complete Suffrage Union, demanding both Corn Law repeal and a wide extension of the suffrage.

He made his first moves at an anti-Corn Law conference in Manchester, raising the suffrage question after the main business had ended. Sturge had decided that repeal would come only after Parliament had been greatly reformed, probably to the point of universal suffrage. He was moved also by a desire to unite middle and working classes by giving them common political aims and organisation. This would reduce social tension and undermine the position of Feargus O'Connor, the demagogue Chartist leader, who revelled in attacks upon the middle classes. G. M. Trevelyan, the official biographer of John Bright, has argued that Bright was more sympathetic to Sturge than Cobden, and that this foreshadowed subsequent differences between them over the need for suffrage reform after 1846. Cobden's general attitude on the franchise question will be studied later. He was, in fact, more in favour of a genuinely democratic franchise than Bright himself. Nor was Cobden's view of the Complete Suffrage movement the negative one suggested by Trevelyan. Cobden told Sturge that 'as individuals' he welcomed middle-class Corn Law repealers also becoming Complete Suffragists. Conversely, Cobden hoped that working men who adopted Complete Suffrage might then decide to support the Anti-Corn Law League. This would broaden the social base of the League. And if this were too much to expect, Cobden still saw great good in drawing the masses round Sturge rather than O'Connor. 'At all hazards we must break the spell of Feargus and his hired retainers.' Simply to bring the working classes together under more effective leadership might advance the anti-Corn Law cause by making Government and landlords more amenable. 'I am not sorry to see Sturge taking up this question,' Cobden told Smith in December 1841. 'It will be something in our *rear* to frighten the aristocracy.' But all this could be done without the League becoming involved. The League might benefit from Sturge's move; by remaining detached it would not suffer if he failed. And by the early months of 1843 the Complete Suffrage effort had clearly failed, for O'Connor and the ultra-Chartists made it impossible for Sturge to work either with or without them.[7]

Cobden used the League to call exclusively for repeal of the Corn Laws. This seemed to him to be the all-important reform from which would follow a wide range of benefits to many sorts of people in many lands. Fundamentally, Cobden saw repeal as a moral and religious question. He was a quietly but deeply religious man. Gladstone thought that Morley's biography, though good in many respects, underestimated the importance of Cobden's religious feelings.* 'There is no other present refuge from doubt and despair,' Cobden was to write in 1858 after the death of his brother following a long and painful illness, 'but in the trust in God and the mistrust of our own powers.' Cobden was born and remained throughout his life an Anglican; yet he was characteristically tolerant in his Anglicanism at a time when many Anglicans were still trying to preserve exclusive secular privileges. He once admitted how strong was his sympathy for any religious sentiment, how he had sat in a Welsh chapel listening to a ranting sermon and unable to understand a word of it, 'watching with pleasing excitement the effects upon the countenance of the hearers; their glistening eyes, and compressed lips, and outstretched heads, were eloquence enough in themselves for me! But I sympathise with all moral men who are not passive moralists.' This last sentence was especially revealing. Cobden's was an active moral and religious code, related as much to the market place as to the church. Thus it seemed to him necessary and proper to judge the Corn Law question in religious and moral terms. In 1841 he challenged Gladstone, then a rising young Tory, to meet him in public debate on the corn question. Cobden promised to show Gladstone that the Corn Laws were 'calculated for the temporary enrichment of a small part of the community, at the expense of the millions who subsist by honest industry; that they are an interference with the disposition of divine Providence as proved by the revealed word of God and the obvious laws of nature, and that therefore they ought to be totally and immediately repealed'. Cobden told his brother at the beginning of the League agitation that he hoped for a spirit of moral elevation throughout the movement similar to that which had pervaded the successful anti-slavery agitation. 'It appears to me that a moral and even a religious spirit may be infused into that topic.'[8]

In August 1841 the Anti-Corn Law League organised a conference in Manchester of over six hundred ministers of religion in an attempt to prove the link between Christianity and repeal of the Corn Laws.

---

* Morley, an agnostic, did not repeat this mistake when writing Gladstone's own biography, admitting in his introduction that he was not competent to discuss Gladstone from a religious point of view.

'Henceforth', wrote Cobden, 'we will grapple with the religious feelings of the people. Their veneration for God shall be our leverage to upset their reverence for the aristocracy.' The clergymen who assembled in Manchester quickly agreed on the sinfulness of the Corn Laws, 'which violate the paramount law of God, and restrict the bounty of his Providence'. Thereafter Cobden carried with him a list of names of ministers who had attended the conference, so that on his speaking tours he would know where to look for support and hospitality.[9]

Religious feelings about the wickedness of interference with God's gift of food underlay Cobden's economic and social arguments against the Corn Laws. He was convinced that repeal would produce immense moral and material benefits both in the short and long terms and for people both at home and abroad. His economic and social arguments against the Corn Laws were many and not always mutually consistent. But his favourite argument emphasised how cumulative prosperity would follow Corn Law repeal in a manner which made it vital for the prosperity of both British industry and of British agriculture. We will look at Cobden's agricultural case later. In respect of industry he promised cumulative prosperity upon the following pattern:

(1) Repeal would benefit British manufacturers by opening wider markets for goods sent out in exchange for the much increased volume of foreign corn which would be imported after repeal.

(2) This in turn would benefit British workmen by creating a much greater and steadier demand for labour, and therefore higher and more regular wages, at the same time as it produced cheaper and more plentiful food.

(3) This greatly increased volume of international trade, by bringing peoples and Governments into closer relationship and interdependence, would encourage the opening of a new era of international fellowship and peace. Economic self-interest would discourage the outbreak of wars which disturbed this network of international trade.

As well as Corn Law repeal Cobden wanted repeal of the foreign timber and sugar duties (which were maintained to benefit West Indian and other colonial vested interests), and repeal of the Navigation Laws (which gave our merchant navy outdated and unneeded protection).

He believed that both the 'Condition of England Question', produced by the Industrial Revolution, and the 'Condition of Europe Question', which had been given a new intensity by the French Revolution of 1789, could be largely settled through general free trade. Free trade, exclaimed Cobden, was the international law of the Almighty:

'Every age, every generation, had some distinguishing struggle that marked its history. In one century we had the contest for religious freedom—another century marks the era of political freedom— another century comes, and the great battle of commercial freedom has to be fought; and Manchester, and those free cotton districts around it . . . were pledged to take the lead in this great contest. . . . It was not a mere contest for a few more pigs, a few more sheep, or a little more corn. If the mere physical, the material gain to which we were looking, was all that we had come to hope from the trial of our principles, why it would be a sordid and mercenary conflict after all. No: the triumph of free trade was the triumph of pacific principles between all the nations of the earth. . . . He saw in the distance—he might perhaps be dreaming—but he saw in the distance a world's revolution involved in the triumphs of free trade principles. The very motives which had led Governments and ambitious rulers to rear up great empires, and to aggrandise the world's territory—those motives would be gone, and gone for ever, when they had taught people that they could better profit by the prosperity and freedom of other nations, through the peaceful paths of industry, than they could triumph through the force of war or military conquest.'[10]

In economic terms, Cobden promised cumulative prosperity after the repeal of the Corn Laws. Before his time the main anti-Corn Law argument had followed cheap labour lines. It had claimed that the Corn Laws by raising the price of bread, forced up wages and thereby reduced profits and weakened British competitive power. Repeal was linked under this argument with reduction of wages. Employers therefore seemed likely to benefit from repeal, but not their work-people. Gladstone remembered how narrow and self-interested the pre-Cobdenite cheap labour case had seemed when argued in Parliament in the 1830s by Villiers and others. 'The answer was obvious. "Thank you. We quite understand you. Your object is to get down the wages of

33

your workpeople." ' It was Cobden, remarked Gladstone, 'who really set the argument on its legs'.[11]

Cheap labour logic assumed that wages rose and fell in relation to the price of bread. Part of the protectionist defence of the Corn Laws also assumed this, claiming that, even if the laws did increase the price of bread, wages always rose in proportion so that workpeople never suffered. Cobden entirely denied this idea of a link between prices and wages: 'wages do not fall or rise with the rise and fall in the price of food'. He contended that wages depended solely upon the state of the market, and that (under his cumulative prosperity argument) repeal would produce a high market demand for labour. Here was how in 1841 he appealed to Manchester workmen along these lines in characteristically straightforward language:

'Why should an increased trade in food lower wages? . . . Did any working man come there so ignorant as to suppose that his master had the power of reducing his wages as he chose? ("He has.") Then if he had, would any working man tell him why his master should be so good-natured as to be giving 18s. per week, when in Ireland they were giving only 4s. per week? (Great uproar.) He believed there was no one in that room who would not agree with him in saying that if the masters had the power of regulating wages, the working men would be put upon a much shorter allowance than they were. The price of labour was regulated, like the price of apples in the market, by the quantity there was, and the demand there was for it; and as the population of this country was increasing to the amount of a thousand a day, we must try to get an increased market for our own labour; and how was this to be done, if we refused permission to foreign countries to trade with us?'

In February 1842 Cobden exposed in the Commons the protectionist contention that wages rose with corn prices. During the last three years bread had been dearer than for twenty years, yet wages had fallen faster than in any previous three-year period. Peel was seeking to stabilise wheat prices at about fifty-six shillings per quarter by means of a new Corn Law sliding scale. Had Peel in mind, asked Cobden rhetorically, a sliding scale for wages? Of course not. And just as it was economic folly to try to control wages, so it was folly to try to control corn prices. 'By what right do you pretend to gauge the appetites and admeasure the wants of millions of people? Why, there is no despotism that ever dreamed of doing anything so monstrous as this; yet you sit here and presume to judge when people want food, dole out your supply when you condescend to think they want it, and stop it when you choose to consider they have had enough.'

Cobden told Sturge in November 1841 that it was wrong to argue, as the Chartists did, that the working classes might help the middle classes to repeal the Corn Laws if the middle classes would help the workers to gain the suffrage. This wrongly assumed that repeal of the Corn Laws was not primarily a working man's question. 'He is every day more and more a slave to the aristocracy every day it lasts, because every day adds a thousand more competitors for the short supply of work and food. A wolfish scramble for the means of life must go on so long as under such circumstances we are imprisoned with a daily diminishing share for each.'

In 1843 at a great Anti-Corn Law League demonstration at Drury Lane Theatre Cobden again emphasised that repeal was demanded by the League as much for the benefit of the operatives as for the profit of their employers. Employers already enjoyed enough to eat. Working men would consume the much increased quantity of foreign corn imported after repeal:

'They would be set to work to pay for that corn with the produce of their wages. They went to the shopkeeper; the shopkeeper was enriched by the custom of the labourer. The shopkeeper went to the wholesale dealer; each shopkeeper went to the neighbouring shopkeeper, and they again enriched each other. The wholesale dealer went to the manufacturer; the manufacturer could only supply the demands of the wholesale dealer by setting to work more operatives. Such was the beautiful order in which Divine Providence regulated this world. There was a circle of continuous links, which could be injured in any one part, but it would, like electricity, pervade the whole chain.'

Here was the essence of Cobden's economic and social case for repeal of the Corn Laws.[12]

Yet despite such persuasive arguments, couched in typically clear language, Cobden had to admit in August 1842 that most working men still stood aloof from the Anti-Corn Law League.[13] Many still believed that repeal would only reduce their wages. No matter how often Cobden denied this, his word was suspect. Class antagonism was strong, and Cobden was himself a middle-class manufacturer. Moreover, he was an opponent of factory reform, of legislation to limit the hours worked by adults in the factories. This seemed to prove to many operatives that Cobden was no less selfish than most of his fellow manufacturers. The League campaign was seen as either irrelevant to the needs of the working classes, or even as opposed to them. The politically active workmen, the Chartists, insisted that only universal suffrage could transform the position of the wage-earners. Only after the six points had been enacted might repeal of the Corn Laws be considered. The Chartist leaders differed among themselves whether repeal would then be advantageous; but they all agreed in refusing to accept Cobden's argument that repeal was the necessary first step for all reformers.

Cobden was himself in favour of a wide extension of the suffrage, but he had no patience with the Chartist demagogues who, he felt, were deluding the people over both means and priorities. He complained to Sturge in 1842 that the Chartists did not seem to understand their real position. They attacked capital, machinery, manufactures and trade, which were the 'only materials of democracy', while leaving alone the aristocracy and the state church, 'which are the materials of the oligarchical despotism under which they are suffering'. Feargus O'Connor, the Chartist leader and chief culprit in the eyes of Cobden, had evolved a fallacious scheme for assisting tens of thousands of workmen to set up smallholdings on the land. He seemed bent, wrote Cobden, upon destroying the new system of industry in order to restore the age of Gothic feudalism:

'We must deal boldly with these leaders, and expose them, and we must deal frankly with their deluded followers by telling them on all occasions that they are powerless without the aid of the middle class. The working class, as a class, have been flattered too much. They must be made acquainted with their weakness. At no time in our history was the *multitude* so powerless as at present in a physical point of view. In barbarous ages, when men fought with clubs or battle axes, a rude undisciplined mob had a good chance if they outnumbered their oppressors. But now, when the refinements of science have been applied to the art of war, mere numbers are as nothing in opposition to a disciplined force.'

Workmen should join their employers in demanding repeal of the Corn Laws, which was the most needed reform. After that, and under more reputable leaders than their present ones, the working classes might reasonably look for extension of the franchise.[14]

The opposition between Cobden's view of the Corn Law question and that of Feargus O'Connor was given its most striking demonstration when Cobden and Bright met O'Connor and his lieutenant, McGrath, in public debate at Northampton on August 5, 1844 before an audience of six thousand. O'Connor came confident of a verbal triumph. In a series of open letters addressed to Cobden in his *Northern Star* newspaper he had jeered at 'the glib philosophy and sophistry of mountebank cosmopolites, who would hang this vast world upon a free trade peg'. The meeting developed, however, into a victory not for O'Connor but for Cobden. A large part of the audience seems to have been uncommitted to either side, and much therefore depended upon the persuasiveness of the speakers. This gave Cobden the advantage, for he delivered a characteristically reasoned speech, calm but convincing, containing some typical homely points. 'There was a certain duty imposed on French shoes; but the smugglers brought them into this country at half the money; but wheat was a more bulky article, and could not be so dealt with, and the landlords had, therefore, the best of the bargain. Let them, then, have free trade in corn, for they had already done their worst with shoes.' O'Connor replied with an equally characteristic effusion. His contention was supposed to be that Corn Law repeal would place new burdens upon the working men unless preceded by enactment of the Chartist six points. But O'Connor's rambling harangues were effective only for stirring audiences already committed to him, not for influencing neutral listeners. Gammage, the Chartist historian of Chartism, who was present, recorded the disappointment of the O'Connorites at their leader's performance. 'All the time he was speaking his friends imagined that he was only introducing the question, and when after three-quarters of an hour's address he sat down, there was a look of blank disappointment.' McGrath followed O'Connor to little effect, and

37

then Bright wound up with a knockabout speech exposing O'Connor's incoherence and his inconsistent record on the Corn Law question. On the show of hands, the Leaguers claimed a clear majority in support of Cobden's free trade resolution. The Chartists denied this, but without doubt Cobden's persuasiveness and Bright's strong language had won the League at least a great moral victory. Revealingly, in the first number of the *Northern Star* to appear after the meeting O'Connor suddenly switched from warm abuse to warm praise of Cobden. 'He is decidedly a man of genius,' O'Connor now admitted, 'of reflection, of talent, and of tact—and while he is in part deficient in some of those qualities which are necessary to constitute a good mob orator, he lacks none of those properties which entitle him to pre-eminence in the front rank of orators.'[15]

The greatest appeal of the Anti-Corn Law League was always to the middle-class manufacturers. And yet we may still ask whether Cobden's anti-Corn Law arguments were ever understood by these men who subscribed thousands of pounds to support the League. 'Never did any unfortunate village by the moor ends require enlightening more pitiably than this Northern metropolis,' exclaimed John Bright writing from Manchester as late as May 1841. We have seen how the pre-Cobdenite case against the Corn Laws had been a selfish cheap labour one. The cheap labour motive remained strong among typical manufacturers during the early 1840s despite all Cobden's efforts to place the case against the Corn Laws in a wider and more elevated context. Most manufacturers either still adhered to the old cheap labour belief or were interested in Cobden's cumulative prosperity line only in so far as it promised them more trade and higher profits; they were much less interested either in higher wages or greater inter-national harmony. Cobden admitted and deplored the continuing attachment of many manufacturers to what he called 'their gross pocket question'. He tried to persuade them to give more thought to matters outside their factory walls. If only, he exclaimed at the outset of the League campaign, his countrymen possessed more of the '*mind*' of the merchants and manufacturers of Germany, with their present opportunities they could become English Medicis or Fuggers. Cobden's ambitions for his order were thus very high ones, even though he was not seeking to serve that order alone. But this vision was not shared by most manufacturers. Events after repeal of the Corn Laws were to show that, rather than form a new purer commercial aristocracy, they were anxious only to ape and to be accepted by the old landed aristocracy, the very group which had burdened them with the Corn Laws.[16]

Cobden paid a high price in personal terms for devoting so much of his time and energy to attempting the moral elevation of the manufacturers. He suffered both as a businessman and as a family man. In 1839 he dissolved the successful partnership which had made his name as a calico printer, and formed a new one with his elder brother, Frederick. They took over from the old partnership a print works at Crosse Hall, near Chorley, and a warehouse in Manchester. This was the arrangement of Cobden's business during the period of the Anti-Corn Law League. Unfortunately, it was not a good one, for as Cobden's political career developed he left direction of the firm too much in the hands of his brother, who had little business capacity. As a result, by the time of repeal of the Corn Laws in 1846 Cobden's company was near bankruptcy. His solvency was only saved by means of a public subscription in recognition of his services for free trade and repeal, which totalled over £76,000. Cobden was conscious that in accepting this money he was exposing himself to the charge of being a paid agitator, a charge often levied during these years against O'Connor and other Chartist demagogues. He would have preferred to refuse the money or to use it as an endowment for a college. 'But as an honest man, and as a father and husband, I cannot refuse to accept.'[17]

With part of the sum thus given to him Cobden wound up his Lancashire business. He then sold his Manchester home, bought the farmhouse and estate, Dunford, in Sussex, where he had been born, and went to live there. Soon after repeal of the Corn Laws Cobden therefore ceased to be a Manchester manufacturer or to live in the cotton district. He retained many links of memory and of friendship with the North, notably of course with John Bright, who lived all his life in Rochdale. Nevertheless, Cobden's readiness to leave Lancashire and the cotton trade underlined how untypical a cotton master he had been. He rejoiced in returning to the lovely Sussex countryside of his ancestors, far from the world of industry. In 1854 the old family farmhouse was pulled down and replaced by a pleasant medium-sized country residence, which still stands.[18]

Most of the money remaining after this house-buying and building was invested by Cobden in the Illinois Central Railroad. This venture quickly proved another mistake in business, though one which reflected Cobden's attractively sanguine and forward-looking temperament. A railway in the American Middle West was bound to prosper as the area developed, and Cobden rightly pictured millions of immigrants from Europe flocking to the rich lands of the Mississippi through which it ran. The potential was there, but Cobden was over-optimistic in expecting it to be realised in his lifetime. He made an investment likely to be profitable in the next generation when his need was for immediate income to support a young family. Instead of income he received calls upon his shares in the late '50s which he could not meet. Once again he had to be assisted by a large subscription of money from friends and admirers, totalling over £40,000.[19]

During the 1840s and '50s Cobden was becoming the father of a growing and therefore increasingly expensive family. This came upon him rather late in life, since he was nearly thirty-six before he married in May 1840. His wife was a Welsh school-friend of one of his sisters, Catherine Anne Williams, known to Cobden as 'Kate'. She survived him by some twelve years, dying in 1877. Cobden's wife does not seem to have been well-suited as the helpmate of a dedicated politician. She married Cobden at a time when he had not yet become a full-time public figure; probably she would have preferred him to remain a calico printer. References to her in Morley's official life of Cobden are guarded, probably significantly so. Cobden was always a lively husband, attentive in spirit even if often absent in body; but during the early '40s he was soon sorry to find his new wife only slightly interested in his growing political enthusiasm. This made his long absences from home harder for them both to bear. Writing to his wife in 1846 Cobden revealingly described Mrs. Grote, forceful wife of a less forceful husband, haranguing a family party 'like a regular politician in breeches'. Cobden commented that he was not much attracted to 'these masculine ladies. If I was I should not love you, for you are certainly the very opposite of her.' Here Cobden was putting a favourable gloss upon his wife's lack of political interest; but at other times regret for this absence broke through even his characteristic cheerfulness. Thus during his anti-Corn Law speaking tours, whereas he wrote to her every day, her letters to him were often brief and spasmodic. 'I have your *short* letter,' he complained on one occasion,

".... but no news ... no gossip, oh fie! ... and after two days' silence!! I shall certainly resume my correspondence with old Mrs. Drummond, or some other lady who will give me a long newsy letter sometimes.'[20]

The sudden death of their only son at school in Germany in 1856, aged fifteen, was naturally a severe shock for both the Cobdens. Cobden had felt an especial affection for the boy, expressing high hopes for him. Gradually, however, he reconciled himself to his loss, asking a correspondent characteristically if it were not one of the purposes of sorrow 'to make us more amiable and just to our kind, especially to the unfortunate and unhappy'. But Cobden's wife was shocked into a complete nervous breakdown by the way the news of their loss reached Dunford. The boy was buried before his parents heard anything. More than a year later Mrs. Cobden was still prostrated. Cobden regretted her 'morbid state of grief', finding it painful 'to dwell on what I cannot justify'. Slowly thereafter her nerves did begin to mend, and in 1861 a fifth and last daughter was born to them, although certainly a son would have been preferred. To the end, Cobden's wife remained dissatisfied with the demands made by her husband's public work. In the last year of his life, when his health was failing, she complained that despite all his good work and his fame it would have been better for them both if after marriage they had settled in the backwoods of Canada.[21]

Yet whatever problems his marriage may have produced Cobden deeply loved his family and home. A neighbour remembered in her memoirs the attractiveness of the Cobden children and their father as he sat in his drawing room at Dunford, good-temperedly writing letters, his children romping about and interrupting him with their shouting and laughter. Cobden's love of the West Sussex countryside has already been mentioned. 'I should not die happy', he admitted in 1859, 'if I did not expect to be buried under the shadow of my favourite South Downs.' And there, six years later, he was to find the resting place he desired.[22]

### 4. THE PROGRESS OF THE ANTI-CORN LAW LEAGUE

We have run on more than a quarter of a century from the beginning of Cobden's national political career in 1838–9. We have previously traced the formation of the Manchester Anti-Corn Law Association during the last months of 1838. As yet, however, there was no national organisation, no League, uniting the local anti-Corn Law associations throughout the country. On January 28, 1838 the Manchester association, which had existed so far on a provisional basis, was formally constituted at a meeting held in Newall's Buildings, near the Manchester Exchange, in rooms which were to remain the headquarters of the anti-Corn Law movement throughout its career. The Manchester Association announced its aim as the total repeal of the Corn Laws by all constitutional means. Repeal was to be sought by encouraging the formation of similar associations in other places, by the distribution of tracts, by the insertion of articles in newspapers, and by the promotion of petitions. J. B. Smith was appointed president; Cobden (but not Bright) was a member of the Council, and of the finance and executive committees.[1]

At this date Smith, rather than Cobden, was taken as the leader of the Manchester repealers. He was ten years older than Cobden, and we have seen that he had been attacking the Corn Laws in Manchester before Cobden had become known as a public man. Smith led the Manchester delegation to a national anti-Corn Law conference which opened at Brown's Hotel, London, on February 4, 1839. In the words of Archibald Prentice, the delegates found 'only Palace Yard between them and the House of Commons whose proceedings they had come to watch'. On this same day the Chartist National Convention also assembled in London. Here, in short, was a significant confrontation between Parliament on the one hand, still primarily the mouthpiece of the old landed interest, and two bodies claiming to represent the new industrial employers and the new industrial workmen. Years of struggle lay ahead before these three groups were brought more or less into harmony. In January 1839 the price of wheat had reached a peak of eighty-one shillings per quarter, the highest level for over twenty years.[2]

Much cannot be claimed for the immediate influence of the first anti-Corn Law delegate meeting. The movement was not yet extensive, although it aspired to be so. Delegations attended only from Manchester, Bolton, Liverpool, Glasgow, Leeds, Stockport, Kendal, Huddersfield, Preston, Birmingham, and London. Smith optimistically hoped that this would be enough to impress Parliament with the need for Corn Law repeal. But Cobden, who was not a delegate, rightly anticipated failure, foreseeing that a long and well-organised agitation would be necessary. He wrote to Smith the day before the conference in terms which showed how he was emerging as the real force behind the movement. Cobden warned against spending too much money at this stage in agitation based upon London; the repealers should work outwards from their Manchester stronghold:

> '*My hopes of agitation are anchored upon Manchester.* We can do more there with a sovereign than a united committee in London would with two. We have money, and also business habits; but if joined with a numerous body in London, who don't understand the matter as well, we might get into scrapes, or even fall into the claws of some jackal of the ministry. They will not agree to your being heard at the Bar. Don't let us lose our time and money over the humbug of a committee. But let all our funds, and our energies be expended in working the question from Manchester as a centre.'

A few days before this Cobden had taken the opinion of Joseph Parkes about prospects for repeal. Parkes, one of the leaders of the Birmingham Political Union during the Reform Bill agitation, and afterwards secretary to the commission which prepared the Municipal Reform Act of 1835, had built up a large practice as a Parliamentary solicitor and was a knowledgeable political figure behind the scenes. 'You ask me,' Parkes had written on January 31, 1839, ' "will Ministry say anything about us in the Queen's Speech?" *No*, they won't, Mr. Cobden, or if they do it will be tantamount to *nothing*.' The Whig Government, Parkes believed, was interested in the anti-Corn Law movement only in so far as it might strengthen or weaken its uncertain hold upon office. On the whole, Ministers were glad to see it drawing the mind of Parliament and public away from their own weakness. They knew that, even if they wished, they could not change, much less repeal the Corn Laws, with the House of Commons in its present form. If they did propose a real modification, Parkes estimated that seventy or ninety so-called Liberal members would vote against them. He then went into details to prove how the Reform Act had left the landed interest in control of the Commons. One hundred and thirty-one English and Welsh boroughs returning two hundred and one members had each under a thousand electors; fifty-four of these Members represented constituencies with three to five hundred electors, forty two of them came from constituencies with under three hundred electors. 'In all these blaggard *mis*representations,' reported Parkes, the agricultural interest generally prevailed. Cobden concluded from this that repeal of the Corn Laws would not be secured quickly. The country would have to be roused, and many more genuine anti-Corn Law Members would have to be returned to Parliament. Cobden told Smith in his letter of February 3 that although he might smile 'at my venturing thus summarily to set aside all your present formidable demonstrations as useless, I found my conviction upon the present constitution of the House of Commons, which forbids us hoping for success'. Cobden suggested that on the return home of the Manchester delegates a meeting of the Manchester electors should be called at which they should pledge themselves never to vote in future for any-one who would not support total and immediate repeal:

> 'An appeal must then be sent forth to all the manufacturing and commercial bodies represented in Parliament, to adopt the same course. Wherever, as at Stroud, or Notts, or Tiverton, or North Cheshire, or south York, Cabinet Ministers, and others in the administration are returned, lectures must be delivered, and corres-pondence entered into, for the purpose more especially of operating upon those constituencies. Such an example from Manchester would, as in the case of our Chamber of Commerce petition, have immediate imitators. The plan would moreover tend to conciliate the Chartists, since it would prove to them that we were acting upon principles, and independent of the Ministry. We cannot be in a true position until we are in such opposition to the Whig-aristocratic Ministry'.[3]

The London delegate meeting had at least shown that the framework for an agitation existed. On March 20, after Parliament had rejected all demands for repeal, the delegates formally constituted the Anti-Corn Law League as a federation of their local associations. League head-quarters were placed in Manchester, and it was specifically left to the Manchester repealers to initiate and to lead future moves in the campaign. £5,000 was to be raised to meet expenses for 1839, and an *Anti-Corn Law Circular* was announced for publication, its first number duly appearing from Manchester on April 16.[4]

The League was now in formal existence, but for some two years its support was small and its influence slight. The first enthusiasm faded both in Manchester and elsewhere. During the rest of 1839 it was the Chartists, not the Leaguers, who attracted notice. Their National

Convention was followed by a National Petition to Parliament asking for universal suffrage, said to be signed by twelve hundred thousand people but rejected by the Commons in July. In August came an unsuccessful 'sacred Month' or general strike, and in December the Newport Rising, a fumbling but indisputable insurrection. All these Chartist efforts came to nothing and by the end of the year the movement was subsiding. But the Chartists had occupied the attention, not only of working men, but also of the middle classes. They caused people of property to rally round the Government rather than add to the attacks upon it by supporting the Anti-Corn Law League.

A temporary Free Trade Hall was opened in Manchester in January 1840, holding four or five thousand people; but for some time the League could not be sure of filling it. On one occasion Cobden told George Wilson, who in 1841 had become chairman of the League Council and its chief executive, that anything would be better than empty benches: 'have the side boards put up under the galleries so as to curtail the space and secure us a full meeting'. The League came near to bankruptcy about this time. The £5,000 fund for 1839 was not raised. Tours by paid lecturers had to be restricted, and in November 1839 J. B. Smith was even contemplating winding up the organisation.[5]

The League just survived, and during 1840 it slowly attracted more support and funds. This followed no doubt in part from the decline of Chartism, which left the urban middle classes free to contemplate political initiatives. Cobden explained to Smith in June 1840 the need to activate such support in the towns. While places like Liverpool or Stockport returned one or more supporter of the Corn Laws to Parliament 'the landlords can laugh at us'. Beyond this limited electoral target Cobden was cautious. 'Ultimate victory would depend upon accident or upon further political changes. But our only chance is the enlightenment of the public mind, so as to prepare it to take advantage of such an accident when it arises.'[6]

Then at the beginning of 1841 the League made an important breakthrough. It decided to nominate a free trade candidate at the Walsall by-election. The seat had been held by a free trader, but the Whigs proposed a less committed candidate as his successor. We have just seen how Cobden felt strongly that the manufacturing towns must be represented by staunch repealers, and in this spirit he persuaded the League Council to retaliate against the Whigs by running J. B. Smith

45

as a complete free trade candidate. This eventually drove the Whig nominee from the field, to the displeasure of many Whiggish members of the League itself, whose opinions were voiced in the *Manchester Guardian*. A *Guardian* editorial regretted the presence in Manchester of certain 'philosophical reformers' who refused to accept the slightest compromise in politics. Complete intransigence, claimed the *Guardian*, would merely lead to complete failure. But the *Guardian* was to be found wrong both in the long and in the short terms. In the immediate view the League's Walsall intervention proved very successful. After an intensive and unscrupulous campaign on each side, embracing both bribery and violence, the Tory candidate was elected; but only by thirty votes. This made the Walsall by-election, though technically a defeat, effectively a victory for the League. It had risked its reputation and its money on the by-election, had nearly won it, and had thereby proved that the free traders could fight an election independently. Henceforward the Whig and Tory parties in and out of Parliament were bound to take account of the League as an electoral force. A vital step forward had been taken. At the General Election in 1841, which led to Melbourne's Whig Ministry being displaced by a Tory Government under Sir Robert Peel, the Walsall seat was actually won for the League. Prominent League supporters were also elected for Bolton, Salford, Bury, Wolverhampton and Manchester. And most important of all, Richard Cobden was elected Member of Parliament for Stockport.[7]

It is natural to ask at this point why Cobden was not now chosen to represent Manchester in Parliament. A vacancy existed, but the nomination went instead to Milner Gibson, a Sussex squire and convert from Toryism. Gibson was a man of means and charm, but never the equal of Cobden. Unfortunately, Cobden's views and personality were too uncompromising for Sir Thomas Potter, doyen of the local reformers and first Mayor of Manchester, who seems to have dictated the choice. Cobden was passed over as a young man in too much of a hurry. He accepted this with equanimity in public, although in private he expressed disgust, not so much at his own exclusion, as at the incongruous choice of a landowner rather than a manufacturer. 'What wonder that we are scorned by the landed aristocracy, when we take such pains to show our contempt of ourselves.'[8]

Cobden was content to fight and to win the Stockport seat, which he

had contested unsuccessfully in 1837. More than once he had emphasised his reluctance to undertake the responsibility of membership
of Parliament, partly no doubt because he knew that it would divert
still more of his attention from business. But in his heart he realised
that it was a necessary step. He therefore first entered the House of
Commons in August 1841 as Member for Stockport. How would
he shape there? This was a vital question for him and for the League.
Some of those who had opposed his nomination for Manchester
claimed that he would be a failure. If he proved as successful in Parliament as he had already been out of it, his leadership of the anti-Corn
Law movement would be unquestioned, for J. B. Smith was now
ceasing to play a prominent role, partly because of ill-health, partly
because his reputation as a man of business had suffered by the crash
of the Bank of Manchester of which he was a director. In the event,
Cobden quickly showed his quality in the Commons, and thereby
confirmed and strengthened his position as League leader. He made
his maiden speech on August 25, the day after the Queen's Speech. It
was a decided success, introducing a new note into the House, restrained in manner yet strong in conviction. Cobden placed the Corn
Law question at the very centre of English politics. He described the
widespread distress of the people, recently elaborated at the Manchester
conference of clergymen. Englishmen, he said, felt great respect for
the aristocracy, but they exhibited still greater respect for a 'sacred
cause'. When they fully understood the fundamentally moral and
religious nature of the case for Corn Law repeal, 'you and yours', he
told the protectionists, 'will vanish like chaff before the whirlwind'.
Cobden made two more Commons speeches in September before
Parliament was prorogued. Opponents soon realised that here was a
man who could not be ignored.[9]

Cobden had begun well, but he was not yet an experienced statesman. He was still strongly inclined to think that Parliament would
respond to purely out-of-doors agitation. He had not yet realised
that he would need to convert, if not a majority of Members of
Parliament, at least a majority of their leaders, and that though
this might be begun through agitation in the country, it must be
completed through persuasive and persistent argument in Parliament.
During the winter of 1841–2 the League had mounted an intensive and
extensive petitioning campaign, and the refusal of Westminster to be

influenced by this campaign made Cobden angry. Cobden had spread League activity outside Manchester. He had asked for large demonstrations in the woollen, pottery, hosiery and iron centres, to secure an 'apparent widening of the circle of agitation from the Manchester centre'. He emphasised how the Corn Law question was not merely a cotton question, and how this needed to be demonstrated geographically.[10] But in the spring of 1842 Peel, the new Prime Minister, merely adjusted the Corn Law sliding scale, and although in his Budget he reduced a wide range of tariffs he also introduced an income tax to compensate the revenue. The League promoted anti-Peel demonstrations in northern towns at which the Prime Minister was accused of holding the people in contempt. In both Stockport and Rochdale, Cobden's constituency and Bright's home town, as well as elsewhere, Peel's effigy was carried through the streets and then publicly burned. Cobden and Bright were greatly irritated by Peel's half-measures, by what Cobden called Peel's 'homeopathic doses'. Cobden told Wilson on February 27 that he was uncertain what course the League should pursue. If only the people felt as strongly as he did himself, he could soon bring the question to an issue. During the spring and summer of 1842 we find Cobden and Bright contemplating various illegal schemes intended to coerce Parliament into conceding repeal. They toyed with the idea of a mass lock-out by millowners, or a mass refusal to pay taxes, rejecting both ideas not on moral or legal grounds but only because they would not be sufficiently supported. 'I presume, however, that our friends are not up to the mark for a general *fiscal revolt*, and I know of no other plan of peaceful resistance. . . . The idea of ever petitioning this *present* House of Commons again upon the Corn Laws should be publicly renounced.' Cobden told Bright at midsummer that although violence was a course which 'no Christian or good citizen can look at with hopes of advantage', a fiscal revolt would be a form of justified passive resistance in accord with traditional Quaker practice. Peel's income tax was necessary only because of stagnation in trade caused by the Corn Laws. Moreover, it would fall more heavily upon manufacturers than landlords. Bright told Cobden that no Government had the right to make him disclose his income; the income tax was a 'vile system of slavery', designed merely to maintain the Corn Law. How would it be, Cobden asked, if money which had been refused in taxes were paid into a fund for the

COLLEGE LIBRARY
HAMPDEN-SYDNEY, VA.

purchase of flour in bond; this flour could then be sold duty free to the poor after repeal of the Corn Laws had been forced.[11]

During this year, 1842, economic distress was at its deepest and most extensive. Although the state of trade had been generally poor since 1837, it had fluctuated considerably from time to time, place to place and industry to industry. For a time railway construction had acted as a cushion for parts of the economy, keeping the iron and coal industries busy. Even in the cotton trade many manufacturers, because of high fixed costs, seem to have preferred to run their mills at nominal profit or even at a loss rather than to close down entirely, in hopes of an economic upswing. But during 1841-2 conditions became not better but worse. Railway investment slackened, food prices remained high, and cotton mills began to close in hundreds, especially those in the old-established centres like Stockport, where machinery was obsolescent and least profitable. The joint-stock banks could not provide manufacturers with overdrafts, for many such banks had themselves suffered by the recent American repudiation or suspension of State debts. Stockport contained so many empty houses in 1841, abandoned by unemployed workpeople, that one wag chalked on the walls of the town 'Stockport to Let'. In the late '30s the handloom weavers had suffered most; now they were joined in distress by many factory workers. The *Manchester Times* reported on July 9, 1842 that hungry and half-clothed men and women were stalking the streets of the cotton towns begging for bread. A soup kitchen in Manchester dispensed a thousand gallons of soup per day to the poor.[12]

Against this grim background the Chartist movement revived. A second National Convention met in April. A second National Petition, said to be signed by over 3,300,000 people (including over 300,000 from Lancashire and Cheshire), was presented to the Commons in May. But the petition was overwhelmingly rejected by Parliament despite this unprecedented volume of support. Many workmen now turned in despair from Chartist political action to economic direct action in the form of the 'Plug Strikes' of August 1842. These strikes constituted a spontaneous movement of protest against unparalleled economic distress. Lancashire gave a name to the outbreak as cotton operatives went round such mills as were still working to pull out boiler plugs, thereby forcing closure. But the movement spread rapidly throughout the manufacturing districts, involving cotton and woollen

81085

factory and handloom workers, colliers, pottery workers, and many others. For a time in mid-August people of property were asking if this was the beginning of the English Revolution. In fact, the movement never had revolutionary intentions. Moreover, it was so unorganised that by the end of the month, in face of firm resistance from employers and Government, it was already petering out.

Tories and Chartists each claimed that the strikes had been deliberately provoked in the cotton towns by manufacturers sympathetic to the League, that this was a disguised form of lock-out, intended to frighten Parliament into repealing the Corn Laws. At a League meeting in Manchester on August 25 Cobden categorically denied the charge:

'I will venture to say in the name of the Council of the Anti-Corn Law League, that not only did not the members of that body know or dream of anything of the kind such as has now taken place,—I mean the turnout for wages—not only did they not know, conceal, wish for, or contemplate such things, but I believe the very last thing which the body of our subscribers would have wished for or desired, is the suspension of their business, and the confusion which has taken place in this district. (Loud applause.) And I pledge my honour as a man, and my reputation as a public man and a private citizen, that there is not the shadow of the shade of a ground for accusation.'

Unfortunately, this was not entirely true. In his anxiety to dissociate the League from this threatening outbreak Cobden was glossing over what he and Bright had been writing to each other earlier in the summer. The idea of a mass lock-out was certainly canvassed by the League then, and not only by Cobden and Bright in private but also by the League's lecturers in public. But when the stoppage came of its own accord the two men were alarmed. 'Suffering *caused by law*', wrote Bright, 'has made the whole population a mass of combustible matter, and the spark now ignited may not be easily quenched.' Cobden urged that the Leaguers should be cautious and quiet. 'The League is at this moment under trial by the public for charges laid on by *The Times*, *Standard* and other papers. All that is necessary to rise higher than ever is for us to keep aloof in Manchester from all connection with the present commotions.' At the start of the strikes the Home Office obtained a warrant to open Cobden's letters. This was done only for a few days, and nothing incriminating was found. But if the Home Office had acted *before* the strikes we have seen what inflammatory suggestions would have been uncovered. Though Cobden, Bright and other Leaguers had certainly not encouraged the Plug Strikes in the direct sense, they had equally certainly contributed to the atmosphere of strong language and illegal projects out of which the strikes came.[13]

Cobden was never to act so recklessly again. His experience in 1842 confirmed him for life as a man of peaceful methods. Fortunately, this course soon became easier for him to follow. The harvest of 1842 was a good one, and trade revived in 1843. Yet this time in their prosperity manufacturers did not weaken. Instead, between 1843 and 1845 they poured money into the League organisation, which took on a remarkable complexity. The Anti-Corn Law League became the wealthiest, most intensive and most extensive political agitation ever seen up to this period.

Systematic, as opposed to spasmodic, agitation for political change can be traced in England back to the time of Wilkes and his campaigns against George III and Parliament in the 1760s. Petitions in support of Wilkes poured in from many parts of the country, to the alarm of Ministers who denounced such organised petitioning as an attempt to coerce Government and Parliament. Then about 1780, while the same King was losing the American colonies, came the County Association movement for Parliamentary reform. This was a movement mainly of country gentlemen, anxious to restrain the incompetence of the executive. It was led by Christopher Wyvill from Yorkshire, and the organisation and leadership of the Yorkshire Association foreshadowed in some ways that of the Anti-Corn Law League. Wyvill was chairman of the Association's committee, but as this consisted of well over a hundred members throughout three ridings, it delegated actual conduct of the agitation to a small sub-committee of members living in or near York, just as the Manchester men were left to direct the agitation of the Anti-Corn Law League. Wyvill, like Cobden, took care to secure publicity in the London and provincial newspapers for all the activities of his Association, initiating that close contact between press and people which underlay most later reform movements. The County Associations also introduced the novelty of co-ordinated action through delegate meetings in London. Ministers said that these gatherings were modelled upon the rebellious American Congress, and that they were designed to rival the authority of Parliament. Valuable techniques of extra-Parliamentary agitation were also adopted about this period from the Wesleyan Methodist movement. Methodism had first given the common people experience of open-air meetings, of tours by itinerant speakers, and of class meeting organisation. The outbreak of the French Revolution in 1789, coming at a time when the Industrial Revolution was beginning to disturb the traditional social and economic structure, led to these Methodist techniques being employed in the first urban working-class movement for universal suffrage and the Rights of Man. Class meetings were now arranged by political societies, not for religious but for political instruction. Admittedly, this first movement was not widely supported outside a few centres such as London and Sheffield, and by the mid-1790s it had collapsed before fierce Government repression. Twenty years later a second popular reform movement, culminating in the Peterloo Massacre of 1819, again failed before further repression. This second agitation, however, achieved unprecedented size and some sophistication of organisation. The working men formed themselves into classes and societies, and attended repeated open-air meetings for universal suffrage, where they heard travelling orators like Henry Hunt. Hunt spoke to at least sixty thousand people at Peterloo. His audiences were mainly working class, for as yet the new urban middle class had not become involved in systematic political agitation. People of respectability were prepared to petition spasmodically, as against the Corn Laws of 1815, but not to organise themselves for persistent campaigning. The change came with the Political Unions formed between 1830 and 1832 to support the passing of the Reform Bill. The Birmingham Political Union, led by Thomas Attwood, then stood as a model for scores of others. Nevertheless, the political organisation behind the middle-class victory in 1832 was still limited. Birmingham led by example alone; the B.P.U. was not linked by formal organisation with the Unions elsewhere. This was unnecessary in the excitement of a relatively short crisis; but six years later Cobden saw that a more carefully integrated national organisation would be needed to force the Corn Law question upon the attention of Parliament. The Anti-Corn Law Leaguers learnt here from the experience of the recent prolonged movement against colonial slavery. During the 1830s a central Agency Committee had assumed national control of all local anti-slavery efforts. This committee had engaged paid lecturers, which was a daring innovation within a middle-class movement, and nation-wide meetings addressed by these and other lecturers had been carefully publicised in the London and provincial press. Petitioning was persistent, and victory finally came for the anti-slavery campaigners just before the opening of the anti-Corn Law agitation.

The Anti-Corn Law League did not immediately build up its machinery of agitation to that high level of efficiency which was to make it the archetype among political organisations. During its first two years it was very short of funds, and its central organisation was neither elaborate nor especially efficient. By the end of 1842, however, thanks to changes of personnel and to a great inflow of money the League organisation behind Cobden and Bright had been transformed. In 1841 Joseph Hickin became secretary to the League, and he quickly put the central offices in Newall's Buildings upon a more businesslike footing. He introduced efficient scrutiny of accounts and quick handling of the League's correspondence. This correspondence reached large proportions as the League developed throughout the country, proportions only recently made practicable by the new penny post. The offices of the League were themselves expanded, and from October 1842 weekly meetings began to be held in a former picture gallery, a useful device for attracting steady publicity. This improvement at the centre was paralleled by a reorganisation and expansion of work outside Manchester. When J. B. Smith virtually retired in 1841 his place as chairman of the League Council was taken by George Wilson. Wilson possessed a genius for chairmanship, being able to control meetings of all sizes effectively yet good-humouredly. His work extended far beyond this, however, for he was the chief executive officer of the League. Wilson put the schemes of Cobden and other leaders into execution. He communicated their views to supporters throughout the country, and also channelled the opinions of the rank and file up to the leadership. With these ends in view he divided the whole of England in 1842 into twelve League regions, each with its own regional secretary.

This regional reorganisation was completed by October 1842, and it was now possible to promote a great increase and redirection of the League effort, turning away from the dangerous courses of the summer. Press activity was intensified. From December the *Anti-Bread-Tax Circular*, the official League organ, began to appear weekly instead of fortnightly. And to reach many who did not see the *Circular* the League decided to send a packet of anti-Corn Law tracts to every Parliamentary elector. This was a remarkable publicity move, even allowing for the relative smallness of the early-Victorian electorate, under a million voters in all. But to maintain this and other ventures during 1843 the League needed a great deal of money, and so an appeal was launched for the large sum of £50,000. In support of the £50,000 fund, and of the League cause in general, Cobden and Bright now began to undertake long speaking tours to all parts of the United Kingdom. Paid lecturers had been touring from the start, but it was another League innovation for men claiming the character and status of gentlemen to itinerate as political speakers. Cobden and Bright were fortunate in being able to speed to many parts of the country by the new railway network. As early as December 1842 Cobden could report that the country was responding from all directions to the League's call for funds. The very process of raising money, Cobden added shrewdly, would spread knowledge of the movement, while spending this money upon the distribution of anti-Corn Law tracts would put the landlords upon the defensive even in their own localities. When the League Council met for the first time in the new Free Trade Hall on January 30, 1843 George Wilson was able to announce that the subscription lists already stood at over £40,000. Clearly, a new spirit had come into the agitation.

At this same Council meeting the League decided to move into London, which had so far given only feeble support to the cause. The League began the practice, which it continued to the end of the agitation, of hiring the Theatre Royal, Drury Lane, Covent Garden, and other London theatres for great meetings. These demonstrations received national publicity, and Cobden and Bright took care to deliver some of their most telling speeches from these theatrical platforms. By November 1843, *The Times*, always a mirror of upper-class feeling, was conceding that the League had become a 'great fact'. While explaining its dislike of 'gregarious collections of cant and cotton men' it had to concede that a new power had arisen in the state, and that to hear its voice 'maids and matrons flock to theatres, as it were but a new "translation from the French".' Such theatre hiring was expensive, but

the League could now always afford to do what it wanted. The
£50,000 fund for 1843 was followed by a £100,000 fund for 1844 and
another for 1845. The resources of the League had at last come to
match the resource of its leader.

In support of the assault upon London opinion League headquarters
were nominally moved to the capital. In fact, effective control remained
throughout in Manchester, where the executive committee of the
Council met daily at Newall's Buildings. Council membership was ✳
open to all who had contributed at least £50 to League funds, nearly
five hundred people by 1845. But the League was really directed by the
small number of Manchester enthusiasts who comprised its executive
committee. One observer remarked how these men conducted the
work of agitation 'with the same precision in the minutest details as
they do in the work of cotton spinning'. They gladly accepted Richard
Cobden as their leader, but Cobden had always to be careful in his
relations with them. On the one hand, he had to restrain the extremist
wing which sought to go too fast, and on the other he had to encourage
those moderates who were half-inclined to accept less than total repeal.
In addition and at the same time, he had to keep these two wings of the
movement in tolerable harmony. His technique was typically conciliatory yet effective. When a resolution was proposed with which he did
not agree he rarely opposed it by a direct negative; instead he preferred
to amend its language and tone, seeking if possible to avoid a vote.
In this way the Anti-Corn Law League was kept in satisfactory internal
harmony throughout its seven years of fluctuating fortune.[14]

Cobden's mild manner did not prevent him when occasion required
from being firm, even tough, physically as well as mentally. The anti-
Corn Law meetings which he and Bright addressed were often noisy
affairs. The Chartists frequently disturbed early League meetings in
Lancashire on the ground that the cry for repeal was only a middle-
class trick to divert the attention of working men from universal
suffrage. At one Manchester meeting the Chartists stormed the platform, and Cobden's head was almost split open by the leg of a stool.
After this, the League organised its own Manchester Operative Anti-
Corn Law Association to protect its meetings against Chartist intruders,
using their own strong-arm methods against them. By 1842 the League
had acquired enough support and experience in Lancashire not to fear
the Chartists. In the country districts, on the other hand, anti-Corn

Law meetings always remained noisy and even potentially dangerous ventures for League speakers. Undeterred by this, during 1843 Cobden and Bright set out to convert the farmers, speaking at many meetings in the country towns. But they could make no real impact, and by April 1844 Cobden was instructing Wilson to 'abandon the counties and farmers as hopeless'.[15]

Cobden did not intend, however, that the League should abandon those counties which contained large urban populations, notably Lancashire, the West Riding, south Staffordshire, north Cheshire, Middlesex and Surrey. During 1844-5 the League began to encourage its middle-class and artisan supporters in the counties to buy freeholds or rent charges and thereby to qualify as county voters. Cobden had great faith in this scheme. If enfranchised in sufficient numbers, he believed that these supporters could win seats for the League at the next election. The League developed an efficient office system in support of this scheme, enabling a prospective freeholder to secure a vote with only the trouble of finding the necessary £50 or £60. In January 1845 Cobden guessed that up to half a million pounds had been invested by the League in this way. How many votes were created before the victory of repeal in 1846 is uncertain. Probably not enough to make much difference in most counties. The general threat was still prospective in 1846. But Cobden believed that the prospect alone had been influential. He told Smith in March 1846, while Peel's repeal measure was going through Parliament, that but for the League, its powerful organisation, 'and especially its powerful 40s. freehold bludgeon', the protectionist landlords in Parliament would have dismissed Peel with as little ceremony as they dismissed their grooms or gamekeepers. By 1861 he was regretting that the protectionists, instead of yielding at the mere prospect of their county electorates being swamped by reformers, had not resisted repeal for three or four more years while many further votes were created. Numerous other reforms could then have been secured in addition to repeal of the Corn Laws. 'But our governing class and their leaders do not wait for a complete revolution, if they can get off at half price.'[16]

By the time of the repeal of the Corn Laws significant numbers of working men had become League converts. The rival appeal of Chartism had now become much weaker. Large numbers of hard-core Chartists in chronically depressed trades like handloom weaving and framework knitting did remain faithful to Feargus O'Connor for several more years. But the factory workers, whose economic fortunes were more variable, tended to support extreme politics only when trade was bad and they were on short-time or unemployed. And for two years until 1845 trade prospered. Many factory operatives now seem to have come out in support of the League, drawn by Cobden's promise of cumulative prosperity after repeal of the Corn Laws, and influenced also by a new spirit of reconciliation with employers. In this spirit the secretary of the Lancashire cotton spinners' union declared in 1844 that his union was not anxious to continue that bad feeling which had formerly existed between masters and men. In Bolton in August 1845 a public tea-party was held by the operatives to which employers were invited with the hope of establishing better relations. A similar party was held in Preston in November, followed a few days later by a public meeting at which, in the words of one operative, 'all political and sectarian differences seemed to be forgotten and swallowed up in the all-absorbing question of cheap food'. Cobden exclaimed a few weeks later how League meetings were everywhere 'gloriously attended'. 'There is perfect unanimity among all classes; not a syllable about Chartism or any other *ism* and not a word of dissent.'

This was an exaggeration, but certainly Cobden could now claim substantial progress in gaining acceptance for his argument that prosperity would be cumulative. Events had proved that the damaging cheap labour charge was unsound. This had assumed that the level of wages was linked to the price of bread. Yet during the prosperity from 1843 to early in 1845, although bread prices were low in Lancashire, wages were high. Conversely, as trade fell off during 1845 bread prices rose, and wages, far from rising in step, now declined because of the falling demand for labour. It seemed, as Cobden had always argued, that the price of labour really was regulated, like the price of apples in the market, by the demand for it. The cheap labour cry against Corn Law repeal had been discredited. By December 1845 the *Manchester Guardian* was able to write with satisfaction of the 'great alteration' which had taken place in the minds of the workers. A speaker at a repeal meeting in Stockport explained how he had once been a Chartist; but now he had accepted the League claim that most of the suffering of the people stemmed from the Corn Laws.[17]

The climax of the repeal agitation was now near. Peel, the Conservative Prime Minister, was about to announce his conversion to support for Corn Law repeal. He had never been a theoretical protectionist, having been educated in the political school of Lord Liverpool and William Huskisson, who were themselves pupils of the Younger Pitt. Following the example of Huskisson, Peel set out on taking office in 1841 to rationalise and to reduce import duties so as to stimulate trade and to overcome distress. In 1842 the duties on over three-quarters of the twelve hundred articles then subject to tariff were reduced. Within three years the increase in consumption had almost balanced the loss in revenue. Before his defeat in 1846 Peel had abolished the duties on over six hundred articles and had reduced the rate on most of those which remained dutiable. The frequency and intensity of trade depression in the new industrial districts had greatly alarmed him. He saw this not only as unacceptable on humanitarian grounds but also as dangerous in social and political terms. He had closely studied the social origins of the French Revolution, and he was determined to avert any attempt at a similar outbreak in England, stemming from the Industrial Revolution. And by the end of 1845 he had decided that repeal of the Corn Laws would significantly reduce this risk.

Peel was the son of a pioneer master cotton spinner, but he was himself a large-scale agricultural landlord, and during these crisis years he was as much concerned to improve the state of agriculture as of industry. By 1845 he had become convinced that the Corn Laws brought little benefit even to agriculture, that they exerted little effect upon prices despite the fact that both opponents and defenders usually assumed this. Many agriculturalists were complaining of distress even under the supposed protection of the Corn Laws, and Peel had come to see that the pressure upon them came not from foreign rivals, from whom they needed protection, but from more efficient British competitors who had adopted new techniques of scientific high farming. Peel therefore proposed repeal of the Corn Laws in terms intended not only to satisfy the aspirations of industry, but also to encourage many more landlords and farmers to adopt new high farming techniques. In the same speech of January 27, 1846 in which he outlined his Corn Law scheme he also announced proposals designed to help agriculturalists to seek profits through prosperity instead of through protection. Repeal of the Corn Laws itself was not to take full effect for three years, whereas these other provisions were to come into force as soon as accepted by Parliament. The duties on grass and clover seeds, on linseed cake and rape cake were to be reduced. Maize and buckwheat, then coming into wide use as cattle fatteners, were to be admitted at nominal duty. Ways were also proposed in which the burden of rates might be reduced, particularly in the countryside. In addition, Peel outlined an important Poor Law reform to prevent those born in the country but working in the towns from being so easily returned to their parishes of birth in times of urban trade depression. And most important of all, he proposed a drainage loan as a measure specifically designed to encourage high farming. All these measures were to be added to Corn Law repeal as part of what Peel called his 'general scheme'. The crisis of the '40s has often been described in terms of a duel between landlords and manufacturers; but it was not so regarded by the man who proposed repeal of the Corn Laws. Peel sought to serve not one interest, but both.[18]

Richard Cobden adopted a similar attitude. Although famous as the spokesman of the manufacturers, he never forgot the importance of agriculture. Born in rural Sussex, yet in business in industrial Lancashire, he was able to see the Corn Law question from both sides, and from both points of view he was convinced that repeal would bring great advantage. He told one anti-Corn Law meeting in Manchester in 1843 that the Leaguers were the 'great agricultural improvers of this country'. Amongst the glories attached to the name of Manchester would be the fact that Manchester men 'not only brought manufactures to perfection, but that they made the agriculturalists also, in spite of themselves, bring their trade to perfection'. Two of Cobden's best and most telling House of Commons speeches were delivered while debating the effects of the Corn Laws upon agriculture, the first in March 1844 when he moved for a select committee to inquire into the effect of protective duties upon tenant farmers and farm labourers, and the second a year later when he moved for a committee to inquire into agricultural distress. Cobden pointed out to the landlord majority in the Commons how distress was widespread among tenant farmers and farm labourers: 'your boasted system is not protection but destruction to agriculture'. He was always careful to separate the position of tenant farmers and farm labourers from that of landowners. Even if, as landlords wrongly believed, the Corn Laws protected their rents, Cobden emphasised how the laws did not thereby assist farmers or labourers. 'You do not want Acts of Parliament to protect the farmer—you want improvements, outlays, bargains, leases, fresh terms.' In the conclusion of his speech in March 1844, however, he made it strikingly clear how he saw no need for irreconcilable conflict even with the landlords. He knew that many representatives of land in Parliament were in fact uncertain on the repeal question. He promised the landowners a continuance of that traditional deference which had always been shown to them if they showed themselves still worthy of it by embracing free trade:

> 'You, gentlemen of England, the high aristocracy of England, your forefathers led my forefathers; you may lead us again if you choose. ... But this is a new era. It is the age of improvement, it is the age of social advancement. You live in a mercantile age, when the whole wealth of the world is poured into your lap. You cannot have the advantages of commercial rents and feudal privileges; but you may be what you always have been if you will identify yourselves with the spirit of the age. ... If you are indifferent to enlightened means of finding employment to your own peasantry; if you are found obstructing that advance which is calculated to knit nations together in the bonds of peace by means of commercial intercourse; if you are found fighting against the discoveries which have almost given breath and life to material nature, and setting up yourselves as obstacles of that which destiny has decreed shall go on,—why, then, you will be gentry of England no longer.'

Cobden always afterwards believed this to be the best speech that he ever made, a speech, be it noted, advocating repeal of the Corn Laws in the interests of agriculture. Peel followed it closely, and at length crumpled up his notes, saying to Sidney Herbert who sat next to him, '*You* must answer this, for *I* cannot.' Peel's conversion to support for Corn Law repeal in the interests of both agriculture and industry was now virtually complete.[19]

By 1845 Peel was therefore waiting only for a suitable moment to tell his party of his conversion. But events forced his hand. In the late summer came news of a potato blight threatening famine in Ireland alongside a bad corn harvest and renewed trade depression in England. Peel decided that the barrier against easy importation of foreign corn must be quickly lowered. Early in November he told his Cabinet of his readiness to propose first suspension and then repeal of the Corn Laws, both on general grounds of economic policy and as a means of facing the immediate crisis. Peel's Government eventually broke up, and Lord John Russell, the Whig leader, who had also announced his conversion to support for complete repeal, tried to form a Ministry. Because of differences within the Whig ranks he failed, and Peel therefore returned to office, determined to recommend repeal of the Corn Laws. On January 27, 1846 he introduced his proposals in the Commons. We have already outlined his scheme for agricultural improvements. Peel advocated entire abolition of the Corn Laws from 1849; before that date colonial corn was to be admitted at a nominal duty, but foreign corn was to be subject to a new sliding scale of duties. This was not therefore the 'total and immediate' repeal for which the League had campaigned, although it was to become total in three years. 'Peel is at last delivered,' wrote Cobden to his wife, 'but I hardly know whether to call it a boy or a girl. Something between the two, I believe.' Cobden thought that Peel's plan would mean effectively a fixed duty of four shillings a quarter, 'more than was expected from him, and *all but* the right thing'. The left-wing members of the League Council were not at first satisfied, and with a view to conciliating them Cobden encouraged Villiers to introduce in February his annual motion for immediate repeal. When this had been defeated, Cobden was able to persuade League opinion to accept Peel's plan as sufficient and as much as Parliament could conceivably countenance.[20]

The final battle in Parliament was bitter. Disraeli and Lord George Bentinck led the protectionists in fierce and sharply personal attacks upon what they regarded as Peel's betrayal of interests which he had promised to defend. Peel made five great speeches on the corn question before repeal of the Corn Laws passed the Commons by a majority of ninety-eight on May 15, 1846. The Lords accepted repeal on June 25. But on the same night Peel's Government, which now lacked a solid majority, was defeated in the Commons on an Irish coercion bill. Peel thereupon resigned. In his resignation speech he paid a remarkable tribute to Cobden:

'There has been a combination of parties, and that combination of parties together with the influence of the Government has led to the ultimate success of the measures. But, Sir, there is a name which ought to be associated with the success of these measures . . . the name of a man who, acting, I believe, from pure and disinterested motives, has advocated their cause with untiring energy, and by appeals to reason, expressed by an eloquence, the more to be admired because it was unaffected and unadorned—the name which ought to be and will be associated with the success of these measures is the name of Richard Cobden. Without scruple, Sir, I attribute the success of these measures to him.'[21]

Peel here generously underestimated the significance of his own part in the victory of repeal. Even so, we may notice how, while praising Cobden's persuasive eloquence as a Member of Parliament, he made no reference to the agitation of the Anti-Corn Law League in the country. Peel was very much a high Parliamentary politician, reluctant to admit that public opinion could influence him except when conveyed through the representatives of the people in Parliament. He had told the Commons in 1841 that it was dangerous to set up 'supposed opinions of the constituencies against their declared and authorised organ, the House of Commons'. But Peel had become increasingly impressed by the arguments of the leader of the Anti-Corn Law League as a member of the House of Commons.[22] The influence of the League upon Peel was thus indirect. The League made Cobden, and Cobden in Parliament played an important, though not exclusive, part in converting Peel. Looking back in 1856, Cobden himself modestly but accurately assessed the nature and extent of the influence exerted by the League and himself upon Peel. Cobden remembered how Peel had always been a theoretical free trader. 'But he never believed that absolute free trade came within the category of practical *House of Commons* measures. The League helped the time forward a little; and I have reason to believe that some discussions I raised in the House with the view of proving that the agriculturalists themselves were as a whole injured by protection gave him some confidence as to the practicability of the change of policy.'[23] The conversion of the Whigs in the Commons to support for complete repeal perhaps owed rather more to the campaign of the League in the constituencies. Up to the beginning of the final crisis in November 1845 many Whigs still wanted to maintain a moderate fixed duty

*The Progress of the Anti-Corn Law League*

upon imported corn. Then at the end of November came Russell's 'Edinburgh Letter' announcing his conversion to support for complete repeal. The Opposition in the Commons, comprising Whigs, Liberals, Radicals and Irish, now became almost unanimous for abolition. Such Opposition support proved vital for Peel. Twice as many Opposition Members voted for him on the third reading of the corn bill in May, as did Peelite Conservatives, two hundred and thirty-five to one hundred and fourteen. These two hundred and thirty-five Opposition repealers balanced the two hundred and forty-one Conservatives whom Peel could not carry with him, and who voted against him.

Cobden had long realised that it was votes in Parliament which ultimately mattered, and that he alone could not influence them. He knew that one of the two high political leaders, either Peel or Russell, would have to be converted before repeal could become practical Parliamentary politics. And he had long held greater hopes of Peel, the Conservative leader, than of Russell, the leader of the supposed reform party. Russell, explained Cobden in 1845, lived in a narrow aristocratic circle, and knew far less of the force of public opinion than Peel. 'The thing is going fast, and *Peel is the man to give us Free Corn*.' When in office up to 1841 the Whigs had refused to adopt repeal. Melbourne, the Whig Premier, had disgusted Cobden by his superficiality, and the League leader was not sorry to see Peel displace such a man, despite the former's protectionist connections. 'I say give me Peel, a fellow with ambition, talent, and insincerity, if you like, for an object of attack. We shall extort something from his hopes or fears, profit in some way from his likes and dislikes.' Cobden was here alluding to, and hoping to exploit, Peel's reputation for untrustworthiness, stemming from his sudden acceptance of Catholic Emancipation in 1829. As yet, Cobden had little respect, still less liking for Peel. In 1843 they quarrelled fiercely in the Commons. Cobden told the Prime Minister that he held him 'individually responsible' for the prevailing distress. Peel construed this charge as holding him personally to blame beyond his official responsibility as head of the Government. Cobden quickly repudiated such an interpretation, but the tone of his remarks had certainly been over-strong. He himself admitted this three years later when, just before Corn Law repeal began to go through Parliament, the two men were persuaded privately to express a new respect for each other. After repeal Cobden received a letter from Peel regretting that, as the League leader was leaving London immediately, they would have no early opportunity of becoming better acquainted. In the event, although their names are linked in history, Peel and Cobden never became on close personal terms.[24]

Cobden did not himself aspire to take office in order to repeal the Corn Laws. He knew that the Parliamentary system of the 1840s must operate through politicians with the traditional social background. He emphasised many times how the League leaders were not general politicians. They had been drawn unwillingly from their businesses, and they wanted their work completed by 'men having established character as statesmen—men to whom privileges appertain, and to whom the people are inclined to look as leaders, statesmen, and politicians'. Cobden readily accepted that he must give place in the end to a high politician, a 'Moses to conduct us through the desert to the land of promise'. Cobden's lack of personal ambition made this attitude easy for him. Moreover, he was glad to set himself and his cause above the Whig–Tory party political struggle. This befitted his elevated view of the whole case against the Corn Laws. 'We care nothing for political parties. . . . Let a statesman of established reputation, of whatever side in politics, take the step for perfect freedom of trade, he shall have the support of the League.'[25]

In the last months before repeal the League had to wait while the party leaders in Parliament speechified and manœuvred. Its role was now a minor one. There were no General Elections as during the Reform Bill crisis, and the League could not busy itself with electioneering, unlike the Political Unions of 1831–2. As a Conservative, Peel was well pleased that the primacy of Parliament was not compromised by any open or implied appeal for extra-Parliamentary support. Melbourne had refused to advocate repeal of the Corn Laws in 1839 partly because he believed that it could be carried only by the same clamour outside Parliament as had carried the Reform Bill. Peel successfully secured repeal without such clamour. The League did launch a final campaign to raise a quarter of a million pounds, lest the Lords should reject the Bill and force Peel to go to the country. But the Lords gave way, and during the vital first six months of 1846 the League found itself playing the part of a chorus without any decisive share in the action.[26]

When victory came in June 1846 celebrations were widespread

throughout the industrial districts. In Lancashire flags were flown from mill tops and church bells rung. 'My dearest Kate,' exclaimed Cobden writing to his wife in Manchester, 'Hurrah! Hurrah! the Corn Bill is law, and now my work is done. I shall come down tomorrow morning by the 6 o'clock train in order to be present at a Council meeting at 3, and shall hope to be home in time for a late tea.' The Anti-Corn Law League dissolved itself at a celebration meeting in Manchester on July 2. Only a standing committee remained in nominal existence until the final extinction of the Corn Laws. Cobden told the meeting why he believed repeal to be the most important event in history since the coming of Christ:

'There is no human event that has happened in the world more calculated to promote the enduring interests of humanity than the establishment of the principle of free trade,—I don't mean in a pecuniary point of view, or as a principle applied to England, but we have a principle established now which is eternal in its truth and universal in its application . . . it is a world's revolution and nothing else.'[27]

Cobden was here looking beyond the economic aspect to the moral aspect of free trade. In purely economic terms Peel's free trade Budgets, which swept away hundreds of tariffs, probably brought much greater benefit to working men than did repeal of the Corn Laws. Peel's tariff relaxations greatly stimulated overseas trade and helped to provide a basis of prosperity for both employers and employed in the 1850s and '60s. The old system of high protective import duties had worked to the disadvantage of the United Kingdom. Although Britain was a major importing country, in times of trade depression high import duties permitted foreigners to sell to us only at low prices to themselves. Yet the same high duties prevented these low prices being transmitted to British consumers. Meanwhile, foreigners were left with little sterling for the purchase of British manufactured exports. Peel's bold policy of abolition and reduction broke this log-jam, producing a huge upsurge of both exports and imports. After only slow growth for a generation, the official value of domestic exports almost doubled between 1841 and 1851 (£102·2 m. to £190·7 m.), while imports in the same period increased from £64·4 m. to £110·5 m.

Free trade could not claim sole credit, however, for this new prosperity. The Californian and Australian gold discoveries of 1848 and 1851 made important contributions to mid-Victorian well-being. Because of her advanced industrial system and large merchant fleet Britain was able to supply goods to the expanding gold-producing territories more cheaply than any other country. Cobden himself warned George Wilson in 1852 not to allow free traders to take too much credit for recent affluence. 'There is no doubt but that good seasons, railways, and gold discoveries have had much to do with it. France, the United States, and other countries have had their prosperity at the same time, without any alteration in their tariffs to account for it.'[28]

How far then was Cobden's anti-Corn Law cumulative prosperity argument borne out in its economic aspects by events after 1846? There was widespread prosperity, as Cobden had promised, but neither especially cheap bread nor a great influx of foreign corn. The prevailing well-being did encourage many working people to think that, in fact, they were enjoying cheap bread and that the Corn Laws had produced this. In reality, during the 1850s and '60s wheat prices remained about an average of fifty-three shillings per quarter, a moderate but not a low figure, only five shillings a quarter less than the average during the last twenty-six years of protection. This proved that the Corn Laws had not been forcing up prices in 1830s and '40s. Yet this meant in turn that they had not been protecting British agriculture from the effects of prospectively ruinous foreign competition. In truth, during normal years in the 1840s home production was still supplying 85 or 90 per cent of home demand. Moreover, as Cobden himself was sometimes ready to admit, European producers did not hold large extra supplies ready for export, particularly not in years of poor harvest in Britain when European harvests were usually also poor. On the other hand, if corn prices did not fall especially low after repeal of the Corn Laws, at least they did not rise especially high. Under the old sliding scale, and with continuing rapid increase in population they would often have done so after 1846. 'Let us be thankful for what we have escaped,' exclaimed Cobden in 1852. In short, repeal of the Corn Laws brought some direct economic gain, but not as much as Cobden and the Anti-Corn Law League had prophesied.

The damaging effects of the Corn Laws had really been more

psychological than economic, and on this level the fervour and arguments of Cobden and the League were amply justified by the improvement which occurred after 1846. The laws had made both industrial employers and workmen feel that Government and Parliament existed to serve only the interests of agriculture. Here was an attitude full of potential danger, the possible basis of revolution. In 1846 Peel set out to overcome this psychological problem. We have already noticed his plan with respect to agriculture. In relation to industry he laid heavy emphasis upon the need to convince masters and men that Government and Parliament could respond to their needs and wishes. In his final speech in the Commons on the corn question he stressed how his 'earnest wish' during his tenure of office had been 'to impress the people of this country with a belief that the legislature was animated by a sincere desire to frame its legislation upon principles of equity and justice'. In the famous peroration to his resignation speech he hoped that his name might be remembered by working men as they enjoyed abundant and untaxed food 'the sweeter because it is no longer leavened by a sense of injustice'. Peel was particularly impressed that in uniting to demand Corn Law repeal masters and men seemed to have abandoned their fierce class antagonism. Here was a novel 'union of sentiment', a 'common conviction' which, in the interests of social harmony, should not be denied.

In these terms, therefore, Peel offered repeal of the Corn Laws to the industrial population. And he struck a remarkable response. The workers were deeply impressed that a Prime Minister had made a dramatic intervention on their behalf. Middle-class employers, for their part, were attracted by Peel's determination and success in forcing the landlords who predominated in Parliament to surrender their favourite policy of protection. Here was ample demonstration, in the words of a Manchester journalist a few years later, that 'the owner of ten thousand spindles' was now the political equal of 'the lord of ten thousand acres'. With the repeal of the Corn Laws, reinforced by the Ten Hours Factory Act in 1847, and also by abolition of the Navigation Acts in 1849, of sugar preference in 1854, and of the timber duties in 1860, the danger of a French Revolution in England springing out of the Industrial Revolution passed away for ever. Economic protection and privilege had given way to freedom and equality of economic opportunity. Cobden himself closely related Corn Law repeal to the

Industrial Revolution. Writing to Francis Place a few days after repeal, he congratulated the veteran reformer on living through fifty years 'more fertile in great and enduring incidents than any five centuries I could select. Bless yourself that you live in times when Reform Bills, steamboats, railroads, penny postage and free trade, to say nothing of the ratification of civil and religious liberties, have been possible facts.'[29]

After repeal of the Corn Laws what Cobden described as 'Peel fever' continued very strong among the industrial middle classes. They felt as much gratitude to the man who had responded to their demand as to Cobden who had voiced it. And among the industrial workers Peel was decidedly more popular than Cobden. The standing of the latter among the operatives was weakened by his opposition to factory legislation; Peel was more easily recognised as sincerely anxious to serve and to reconcile all classes and interests. When he died in 1850 mourning was general among all classes in the industrial districts. Subscriptions were quickly started to erect statues and other memorials to Peel. Working men contributed their pennies as eagerly as their masters contributed their pounds. Cobden was deeply shocked by his death. Peel, he wrote, was a martyr for free trade, whose health had been undermined by the unsparing hostility of the protectionists. A great Prime Minister was dead, but so were the Corn Laws. Peel and Cobden between them had changed the course of British history.[30]

# II

## *Bright*

### I. BACKGROUND

JOHN BRIGHT was born at Rochdale, Lancashire, on November 16, 1811. His birthplace, a small redbrick house named Greenbank, stood by the side of the cotton spinning mill which his father, Jacob Bright, had opened two years earlier. The name of Bright, destined by mid-century to become closely involved with the fortunes of Lancashire, was still very new to the county at that century's beginning. The Brights came from Wiltshire, where they can be traced back to the seventeenth century and probably earlier. John Bright's grandfather moved from Wiltshire to Coventry, and there his father was born in 1775. The Brights were Quakers, so young Jacob was sent to the famous Quaker school at Ackworth in Yorkshire. He was then apprenticed to a farmer at New Mills on the Derbyshire fringe of the rapidly developing cotton district. This farmer worked a few hand-looms, and at these Jacob Bright learned cotton weaving. So began the connection of the Brights with the cotton trade. In 1802 Jacob made his vital move to Rochdale. He went as book-keeper and salesman in a new cotton spinning factory established by the sons of his old master. Finally, in 1809 he set up on his own, with the financial backing of friends in Manchester who had been impressed by his business acumen. Their confidence was well founded, for the Bright mill gradually became one of the most important in Rochdale. The town was growing rapidly into a major woollen and cotton spinning centre. By 1825 over 90 per cent of its population of about fifty thousand was connected with the textile trades. Into this busy expanding town John Bright was born, into a family growing and prospering within its growth and prosperity. After fourteen years Jacob Bright was able to end his connection with his original backers, and to stand on his own as an independent master cotton spinner.[1]

The Brights did not prosper at the expense of their workpeople. Jacob Bright was outstanding for his paternalism as an employer. He did not allow children in his mill to be beaten for breaches of discipline. He also employed an old man in his warehouse to teach them the rudiments of reading, writing, and arithmetic during working hours, and eventually he built them a schoolhouse. Jacob Bright's interest in working-class education eventually made him known to young Richard Cobden. A letter to the elder Bright from Cobden has survived from 1837, asking for permission to add Jacob's name to a committee being formed to promote mass education. This letter was written only a few weeks before Cobden's first contact with Jacob Bright's son, John. The good name of the father no doubt helped to recommend his son to Cobden.[2] Jacob's paternalism encouraged him to give material as well as educational assistance to his workers. When they grew up and married he increased their wages by two or three shillings a week to help them bear their new responsibilities. Such good human relations produced good work, and Bright's cotton twist soon became noted on the Manchester market. Old Jacob retired in 1839, leaving his sons to carry on the business under the name of John Bright and Brothers. He died in 1851.

As his first wife Jacob Bright took a daughter of his old master; but she died without children. Then in 1809, the same year as he set up independently and moved to Greenbank, he married Martha Wood, a Quakeress from Bolton. Two years later she became the mother of the future politican. Family tradition held that John Bright inherited many qualities from his mother. Jacob Bright was a straightforward hard-working businessman; his wife probably thought more deeply and sensitively. If John Bright's bluntness came to him from his father, his intellectual power probably stemmed from his mother. She died in 1830, aged forty-one. She bore seven sons and four daughters. A first boy died at the age of four, leaving John Bright, the second-born, as the eldest of the family. One younger brother, Jacob, was to make something of a name of his own in late-Victorian politics.

The Brights were a strong Quaker family, without being a narrow one. They attended the meeting house in Rochdale regularly every Sunday. During the early nineteenth century the Quakers were not numerous either in Rochdale or in the country at large. The forty thousand adherents attracted by George Fox, their founder, had been reduced by half, and numbers were still falling despite the rapid growth of population. In Bright's boyhood the Rochdale meeting numbered less than a hundred; in 1860 only fifty-nine. The sect had become ingrown and over-meticulous. When, for example, Bright's sister married a non-Quaker in 1849 she was immediately disowned despite her good character. Bright denounced this tendency to attach as much weight to mere forms as to genuine Christian feeling, and he himself always concentrated upon the essential Quaker virtues. He gave up wearing Quaker dress, and ceased to speak or write to non-Quakers in the second person singular, or to use Quaker forms for days and months. Yet, while abandoning these outward peculiarities, he remained a convinced member of the sect to the end of his life. Not that his conviction led him to speak often of religion. He played a prominent part at Quaker business meetings, both local and national, but he never spoke at the religious meetings of the society. This may at first seem strange, but Bright was never a man for wasting words on matters not in dispute. He was a convinced Quaker; he assumed that his fellow Quakers were equally convinced; and this left him satisfied that there was nothing he need say. Bright saved his eloquence for politics. To the end of his life he was sure that Quaker practice was best, as for example in refusing to employ clergy. On a visit to Gladstone's home in 1879, where he found himself meeting five clerics in three days, he still bluntly announced that 'as a rule' he disliked all clergymen.[3]

Bright received all his education in Quaker schools. His first school was a local one. Then in the summer of 1821 he was sent to a school near Warrington. A year later he went, like his father before him, to Ackworth School in Yorkshire. There he suffered some of the then almost customary rough treatment and neglect, although not nearly so much as Cobden had borne a few years earlier in another Yorkshire school. In 1823 he moved to Bootham School in York. His health, which had been delicate from birth and which had been further undermined by semi-starvation at Ackworth, did not improve in the damp atmosphere of the cathedral city. So in 1825 he was moved to a rural school at Newton-in-Bowland, high among the hills on the Lancashire–Yorkshire border. Here he developed a lifelong love of the countryside, and thanks to the fresh air and a not over-intensive course of instruction his health so improved that he left the school in February 1827 with a strong constitution, which was to serve him well during the first half of his political career.

The formal education which Bright had received at these Quaker schools was patchy, but he had been encouraged in the Quaker belief in the equality of all men, the irrelevance of worldly distinctions, and the supreme importance of good moral conduct. Like Cobden, Bright set out in the years after leaving school to fill some of the gaps in his formal knowledge by earnest self-education. After getting up at five o'clock each morning to hand over the keys of the mill, he used to study before breakfast in a room over his father's counting house. He began to read political economy and politics, perusing for example the *Spectator*, a Radical organ started in 1828 and an early opponent of the Corn Laws. He also read widely in history and poetry, favourite subjects throughout his life. The works of Milton, and especially *Paradise Regained*, gave Bright especial pleasure. He once reminded his wife how reading Milton seemed to raise him 'above the disappointments of the world'. Cobden remembered in 1856 that Bright loved to read Milton 'aloud for hours together'. Bright's Quaker education, Cobden continued, had discouraged interest in painting. Four years later Bright did go to see Holman Hunt's new 'Christ Found in the Temple,' finding it 'as fine a picture . . . as had ever been painted'. But Bright was more stirred by the subject of the painting than by the art form in general. 'I do not believe in the regeneration of a people, or the saving of a country by pictures, or statues, or by any amount of fiddling', he had bluntly written of the Manchester Art Treasures Exhibition in 1857.[4]

Of course, most of Bright's time after leaving school at the age of fifteen was spent helping his father to run the family mill. He came to understand all its workings from first-hand experience, driving its machinery as readily as he drove a pen in the counting-house. This close knowledge was the foundation of his delight in the power of the new industry. Bright took pride in being a master spinner. Yet his pride was not constricting. His experience of his father's benevolent methods as an employer ensured that he never felt separated from the operatives. His early religious experience and his early business experience both taught him to believe in the essential equality of men.

In order to protect themselves from worldly corruption the first

Quakers had traditionally stood aside from politics. They regarded politics as fundamentally the expression of violence in a concealed form. By Bright's young days, however, the philanthropic zeal of the Quakers was bringing them into increasing contact with politics and politicians, notably in the campaigns for the abolition of the colonial slave trade and then of colonial slavery. In 1832 the legal barriers to Quaker membership of Parliament were removed when Joseph Pease was allowed to take his seat without swearing the oath. This trend was highly congenial to young John Bright, who saw no reason why his religion should bar him from politics and many reasons why it should lead him into it as a reformer of abuses and inequalities.[5] We first hear of Bright on a public platform speaking in a cause which, like that of slavery abolition, was on the borderline between philanthropy and politics, the cause of temperance. In 1830, aged nineteen, in support of this cause he first addressed a Rochdale audience. He apparently began nervously, but grew increasingly effective as his speech proceeded. Both Bright and Cobden were virtual teetotallers throughout most of their lives, partly as an example at a time when working-class drunkenness was a major social problem, partly because they found that alcohol reduced their stamina as political campaigners.[6]

John Bright came of age soon after the crisis of the Reform Bill. The Brights were keen supporters of the Bill. It seemed natural to them to support reform, bearing in mind the persecution which Quakers had suffered under the old constitution. Bright read out news of the progress of the Bill to his father from the columns of the *Manchester Guardian*. The moderate liberalism of the *Guardian* was, however, already too qualified for young Bright. At the end of 1830 he had heard with satisfaction of the Preston by-election victory of Orator Hunt, the working-class Radical, over Edward Stanley, heir to Lord Derby, the great Lancashire landlord. In April 1832, while the Reform Bill crisis still continued, Bright made his first visit to London. On the way his coach met expresses carrying the glad news that the House of Lords had passed the second reading of the Bill.

Under the Reform Act Rochdale was granted its first Member of Parliament. Bright hoped that this constitutional reform would permit the introduction of many other reforms, and his views in this direction were beginning to be noticed in Rochdale. In 1833 he played a leading part in forming the Rochdale Literary and Philosophical Society.

Though only twenty-one, he presided over its first meeting. In the discussions of the society during the next few years we find him supporting, among other things, a system of limited monarchy and the provision of universal education, while opposing in the Quaker tradition the injurious moral tendencies of the theatre. At one meeting the society was unanimous in the belief that 'laws for restricting the importation of grain are impolitic'.[7]

In the summer of 1833 Bright first travelled abroad, the year also of Cobden's first foreign journey. Cobden, seven years older, had been compelled to wait until he had acquired money for foreign travel; Bright was more fortunate in his family circumstances. Bright was never to become as far-reaching a traveller as Cobden, but he came to know well much of the Mediterranean and Western Europe. In 1833 he toured Belgium and the Lower Rhine, returning home speaking better French, impressed by the architecture of Brussels cathedral but aghast at the ignorance of Roman Catholics who maintained (so he believed) two thousand priests to serve it. From August 1835 to April 1836 he went round the Mediterranean, visiting the parts associated with Lord Byron, one of his favourite poets, and reaching as far as the Holy Land. A year later Cobden took a similar tour. Cobden found much evidence on his travels to support the view of foreign affairs given in his first pamphlets. Young Bright had not yet appeared in print, but his background knowledge was expanding.[8]

On his return home Bright came right to the front as a Rochdale politician. At a by-election in April 1837 he seconded the nomination of the Liberal candidate, John Fenton. Bright's long speech was reported in the *Manchester Guardian*. He declared that, like Fenton, he viewed politics as 'the science of human happiness', and human happiness required further extension of the suffrage and vote by ballot. Bright told the electors that, although he had formerly believed that the £10 householder franchise of the Reform Act might be broad enough, experience had taught him otherwise. 'I am sorry to say that the present constituency does not fulfil those ends which I expected to be accomplished by that measure.' He had found that the £10 electorate showed no more honesty, knowledge and independence 'than might be found amongst many of those who work for their livelihoods with their own hands'. Bright then went on to attack the Corn Laws. Taxation should fall on those most able to bear it, and it should not impede commerce. The Corn Laws were unsound on both counts. The poor probably consumed as much bread as the rich, and therefore paid equal bread taxes with the rich, which was unfair. The ill effect of the Corn Laws on commerce had been given local demonstration when Britain's refusal to allow importation of American corn had caused the Americans to retaliate with their tariff, which 'half ruined' the woollen trade of Rochdale. Bright concluded by looking at religion and politics. The day of complete religious equality had not yet come, but (he announced with a turn of phrase anticipating his future quality as an orator) 'the dawn of its light has come, and I hope that it will soon blaze in full meridian splendour'. In immediate political terms this meant equal rights for Catholics and Protestants in Irish municipal corporations, and abolition of compulsory church rates in England.[9]

This activity in the cause of reform politics was in the background of the historic first meeting between Bright and Richard Cobden. Since publication of his first pamphlet in 1835 Cobden had become increasingly known among Lancashire reformers. In July 1837 he had stood for Parliament. He knew Bright's father, and he must have read of the political activities in Rochdale of young Bright himself. Cobden and Bright were bound to meet sooner or later, if only by chance. But Bright did not wait upon chance. In December 1837 he decided to invite Cobden to speak in Rochdale at an education meeting, the cause about which Cobden had written to Jacob Bright in October. We have a conflict of evidence, however, as to the manner of Bright's invitation, a conflict which, as well as being of importance in terms of detail, casts light upon the image of the Cobden–Bright relationship in history. The British Museum possesses what was apparently the first-ever letter from Cobden to Bright, dated December 14, 1837. In this note Cobden agreed to attend an education meeting at Rochdale on December 21. Cobden referred to a letter of invitation from Bright dated the previous day. However, at the unveiling of the Cobden statue in Bradford in 1877, Bright gave a less prosaic account of this first contact, claiming that he went over to Manchester to deliver the invitation to Cobden verbally,

'to ask him if he would be kind enough to come to Rochdale, and to speak at an education meeting which was about to be held in the schoolroom of the Baptist chapel in West Street of that town. I found him in his office in Mosley street. I introduced myself to him. I told him what I wanted. His countenance lit up with pleasure to find that there were others that were working in this question, and he, without hesitation, agreed to come.'

The effect of this passage was to encourage the idea in Bright's old age that he had been on a level as a politician with Cobden from the very first, that he went over to Manchester and met Cobden face to face as his equal. The odd claim that Cobden did not previously know of the education efforts of others (including the Brights, father and son) contributed to the impression that Bright had as much to give to Cobden at this stage as Cobden had to give to Bright. This was the over-simplified late-Victorian image of the partnership, of an immediate, continuous and equal union. It may be significant that in an earlier version of this story, given at Rochdale in 1859 before Bright had lapsed into his reminiscent old age and when Cobden was still alive, Bright did not give this impression:

'I dare say there are many now present who recollect his attending a meeting in this town, which was held in the schoolroom of the Baptist Chapel, in West Street . . . for the purpose of promoting education in connection with the establishment or the support of British schools. It was in connection with that question, about that time, that I became acquainted with Mr. Cobden, and he spent the night at my father's house after that meeting was held.'

In this earlier version Bright was not claiming to have enlightened Cobden about the education movement while delivering an invitation face to face. What probably happened was that Bright went to see Cobden in Manchester *after* he had accepted the written invitation. In his letter of December 14 Cobden had invited Bright to 'look in upon me' on the following Tuesday, two days before the meeting. But a first encounter on these terms does not sustain the overtones of Bright's 1877 version. The prosaic evidence of Cobden's acceptance by letter of Bright's invitation also by letter cannot be gainsaid.

Notwithstanding these qualifications with respect to Bright, the Rochdale education meeting remains an historic, even though modest, occasion. Both Morley and Trevelyan fulfilled their functions as biographers inadequately in merely dating this key event 'some time in 1836 or 1837', and in finding no contemporary account of it. It was reported in the *Manchester Times*, Cobden's local mouthpiece, though only briefly.

## ROCHDALE

### BRITISH AND FOREIGN SCHOOL SOCIETY

A numerous and highly-respectable meeting of the friends and supporters of the British and Foreign School Society in this town was held on Thursday evening, at the school room in Baillie-street, to witness an examination of the boys taught there. About 270 persons afterwards partook of tea together in the Wesleyan-Methodist Association school room, when John Fenton, Esq., M.P., was called to the chair, and the assembly was addressed by Richard Cobden, Esq., and Lieut. Fabian, agent of the British and Foreign School Society. At seven o'clock the company adjourned to the chapel, the doors having been thrown open to the public. John Bright, Esq., and other gentlemen subsequently addressed the meeting in able and energetic speeches, in support of an enlightened system of education. We are glad to learn that the Rochdale school is in a most prosperous state. The girls' school is to be opened shortly.

Years later Cobden recalled Bright's address on this occasion, the first speech he ever heard from his future friend. 'It was highly rhetorical and declamatory, all about Rome and Palmyra, but there were evident indications of his natural aptitude for oratory.' Cobden told Bright's father that, with encouragement and practice, his son could become an orator. ' "Oh, no, no, no," said the old gentleman, shaking his head, "he must attend to business, he has got to look after the mills." '[10]

It could be argued that the meeting of December 21, 1837 was not the one referred to by Bright in 1877, that he may have gone over to Manchester, as he claimed, to invite Cobden to speak at a meeting at some earlier date in 1836 or 1837. Such a verbal invitation would not then have left correspondence behind it as evidence. But the whole tone of Cobden's letter of December 14 implied that he and Bright had not met up to this time. Nor is there any report of an earlier Rochdale education meeting in the *Manchester Times* for 1836 or 1837. Moreover, in the same Bradford speech of 1877 Bright went on to give what can certainly be proved to be a misleading account of the significance of his meeting with Cobden at Leamington in September 1841 after the death of his first wife. If Bright could distort the one story, he could distort the other.

For this Leamington meeting we again have two versions from Bright, one from the Bradford speech, one from a speech at Rochdale, though both in this case were delivered after Cobden's death. Bright suggested that his serious work for the Anti-Corn Law League only began after the inspiration of this meeting, at which he and Cobden made (in Bright's phrase) 'a solemn compact'. The Bradford version ran as follows:

'Mr. Cobden called upon me as his friend, and addressed me, as you might suppose, with words of condolence. After a time he looked up and said, "There are thousands of houses in England at this moment where wives, mothers, and children are dying of hunger. Now," he said, "when the first paroxysm of your grief is past, I would advise you to come with me, and we will never rest till the Corn Law is repealed." I accepted his invitation. I knew that the description he had given of the homes of thousands was not an exaggerated description. I felt in my conscience that there was a work which somebody must do, and therefore I accepted his invitation, and from that time we never ceased to labour hard on behalf of the resolution which we had made.'

Once again Bright was giving in retrospect an impression of equality in political status between Cobden and himself, an equality which did not in fact exist at the time, but which was accepted on his testimony by late Victorians glad to simplify and to romanticise the relationship. Bright's Rochdale version put a still more marked emphasis upon what 'we', Cobden and Bright as partners, achieved together after the Leamington 'compact':

'Mr. Cobden called upon me the day after that event so terrible to me, and so prostrating. He said, after some conversation, "Don't allow this grief, great as it is, to weigh you down too much; there are at this moment in thousands of homes in this country wives and children who are dying of hunger, of hunger made by the law. If you will come along with me, we will never rest till we have got rid of the Corn Law." We saw the colossal injustice which cast its shadow over every part of the nation, and we thought we saw the true remedy and the relief, and that if we united our efforts, as you know we did, with the efforts of hundreds and thousands of good men in various parts of the country, we should be able to bring that remedy home.'

As with his version of the 1837 encounter, Bright's version of the Leamington conversation in wrongly estimating the significance of the event also fell into error in detail. In fact, Cobden visited Bright not the next day after, but three days after the death of Bright's wife. Here was a small indication of how Bright's memory could wander in seeking to heighten the effect of his narrative. But more important in contradicting Bright's account was the certain fact that he had been working hard for the League for some months before his wife's death. For a time afterwards, far from increasing his efforts as a result of a pact with Cobden, he had to reduce his work for the League partly in deference to the strict Quaker feelings of his wife's family. A letter from Bright to Cobden a month after his wife's death, although showing Bright heavily dependent upon Cobden's moral support, revealed him still reluctant to return to his previous activity:

'As to myself during the winter, recent events have somewhat impaired my elasticity, and nothing but the consciousness that we are in a struggle where we must either win or be destroyed with multitudes of our fellow countrymen would induce me to take any public part at present, and it would be much more agreeable to spend a few months in quiet retirement. Sometimes we lose correspondents from neglecting them. I fear I shall lose thee by writing so tediously. May I have a line to say where and when I can see thee.'

The evidence makes it clear that Bright had come to the fore as a League speaker by the spring of 1841, six months before the loss of his wife. In May, for example, Cobden was pressing Bright to join him in speaking at a Liverpool meeting: 'we can't do without *your* assistance. So no excuses will do.' A month later Cobden was again urging Bright to go with him to speak at Bristol. Bright was always much inferior to Cobden, as an organiser, but by the spring of 1841 Cobden had clearly come to regard him as his chief speaking lieutenant.

In his old-age reminiscences Bright was probably not aware how he was subtly inflating the image of his own position during these first days of his friendship with Cobden. He actually began his Bradford speech by a request for indulgence lest he might appear 'to speak in terms of praise even of myself as having been connected with him in much of his work'. Yet even this disclaimer suggested closeness and equality. We can see how Bright was led into distortion by a wish to heighten the emotional effect of his narratives. He was anxious to present Cobden and himself starting their crusade together for good against evil in the most effective and therefore simplest terms. He had no room for qualifications. He and Cobden became partners; they remained partners to the end of Cobden's life. It would have spoiled the effect to dwell upon any inequalities of status or differences of view between them. Late-Victorian audiences found this simplified version highly convincing. Bright's account of the Leamington conversation especially moved them, for they revelled in deathbed scenes. Even the newspaper reporters shed tears when Bright told this story at Bradford. Robertson, Bright's leading hagiographer, claimed of this speech that 'these strong impressions cannot be conveyed to the minds of others, except when the mind producing them is face to face with truth and nature'. Late Victorians believed this, and many historians have accepted Bright's evidence as if they believed the same. In fact, 'strong impressions' are often produced by adjustment of, rather than fidelity to, truth and nature.[11]

Before 1841 Bright had been active in support of the anti-Corn Law movement in Rochdale, but he had spoken only occasionally elsewhere. In Manchester in the first stages of the agitation the repealers were glad to use his name on the list of the provisional committee of the Manchester Anti-Corn Law Association, but they were not yet aware of his potential as a speaker. Bright was not a member of the Manchester Chamber of Commerce at the time of its two important meetings in December 1838. At the beginning of February 1839, however, Cobden invited him to join, offering to pay his guinea subscription. 'We want your aid', explained Cobden, 'at the annual meeting of the Chamber on Monday next.' Clearly, Cobden already thought well of Bright. Though not yet intimate friends, their friendship was developing.

What really showed Bright's quality, however, was his part in the church rate crisis at Rochdale in the summer of 1840.[12]

During the early nineteenth century many Nonconformists had become increasingly hostile to paying the rate traditionally levied for the upkeep of the local church. Rochdale was one of the strongest centres of anti-church rate feeling, and the Brights were among its leaders. Jacob Bright was served with many distress warrants for non-payment of rates, and goods to the value of over £100 were taken from him in distraint of payment. Church rate disputes poisoned the social atmosphere of Rochdale throughout the 1830s. Then in 1840 came the final crisis, provoked by J. N. Molesworth, the new vicar, a man as stridently anxious to assert his right to levy a compulsory rate authorised by parish meeting as John Bright was keen to deny that right. When one parish meeting declined to impose a compulsory rate, Molesworth boldly called another. This second meeting in the parish churchyard proved to be a turbulent occasion. John Bright mounted a tombstone and forcefully exposed the un-Christianity of all attempts to exact compulsory church rates:

> 'the New Testament teems with passages inculcating peace, brotherly love, mutual forbearance, charity, disregard of filthy lucre, and devotedness to the welfare of our fellow-men. In the exaction of church rates, in the seizure of the goods of the members of his flock, in the imprisonment of those who refuse to pay, in the harassing process of law and injustice in the church courts, in the stirring up of strife and bitterness among his parishioners—in all this a clergyman violates the precepts he is paid to preach, and affords a mournful proof of the infirmity or wickedness of human nature. I believe that in these contests for the iniquitous exactions of the church, more mischief will be done, and more strife engendered, than will be atoned or compensated for by all the preaching of the clergy of the parish during the rest of their lives.'

This speech marked a stage in the development of Bright's speaking manner. He had not yet developed the polished style of his prime, but he was now master of the attacking style which served him well as Cobden's chief support during the anti-Corn Law campaign.

Despite Bright's fierce opposition another poll was taken in Rochdale.

Troops had to be called out while it was in progress. This time a majority was claimed for levying a compulsory rate. In the event, however, it could not be collected, and by 1841 it was clear that John Bright had led the Dissenters of Rochdale to a notable victory.[13]

Bright fought this church rate battle only a few months after his first marriage. On November 27, 1839 he married Elizabeth Priestman, gentle daughter of a Newcastle Quaker family. The couple settled at a new house which Bright had built above the family mills, named One Ash. This remained his home for the rest of his life. In October 1840 a daughter was born, but soon afterwards Bright's wife began to show signs of consumption. This grew steadily worse, and she died at Leamington on September 10, 1841. Bright wrote on the same day to Cobden. 'I know thou wilt sympathise with me in this very deep trial, and it is therefore I write to inform thee of it.' Three days later Cobden was at his friend's side, full of understanding but full of plans for future agitation, which he unfolded to Bright so as to draw his mind away from his sorrow. Such was the true character of the conversation which, as we have seen, Bright misinterpreted in his old age.[14]

By the spring of 1842 Bright was back hard at work as the League's second speaker. The loss of his wife at least made it easier for him to travel constantly about the country. By contrast, we have seen how Cobden's wife regretted the time and energy which he devoted to the League. In business circumstances, too, Bright was more fortunate than Cobden during their years as League orators. Cobden's brother, when left in charge of his firm, allowed it to head towards bankruptcy. Bright, by contrast, during his League days and throughout his life was able to leave the family business under the competent direction of his brother, Thomas. Indeed, his brother's acumen eventually brought great profit and secured Bright a comfortable income during the second half of his life.

On June 10, 1847 Bright married again. His second wife, Margaret Elizabeth Leatham, was the daughter of a Quaker banker from Wakefield. Two of her brothers eventually became Liberal Members of Parliament, and she always took an interest in her husband's political work. She also brought a considerable dowry which, at a time when the Bright business had not yet grown to its later prosperity, helped Bright to continue in Parliament despite the growing demands of an

increasing family. Seven children were born to the Brights, four sons
and three daughters. In 1864 their third son died suddenly of scarlet
fever while on holiday, aged five. Bright wrote a letter to his elder
children away at school which deserves quoting at some length to
show the tender side of his character, a side rarely shown in his pugnacious political speeches:

'The grave was not deep, not more than five feet deep, the little
coffin was let down into it and Mama and I stood by, looking down
upon it, our eyes running with tears and our hearts ready to break.
The day was fine—the sea perfectly calm—there were several vessels
in sight, some very near; on the mountain there were sheep, and we
heard the bleating of one of them as tho' seeking for companionship
and comfort. The wildness and desolation of the place were relieved
by the calm and mildness of the day, and we thought that but for
the distance from home, there could be no more desirable place for
the remains of our precious child to rest in. We were a small party—
very lonely—we remained but a few minutes looking down upon his
last resting-place, who, not a week ago, was apparently full of life
and health—and then we turned away with a wish to bow to the
dispensation of God, which had taken from us the sweet and
precious child we loved so tenderly.'

Bright was deeply attached to his children. Cobden, after the death of
his own son in similar circumstances eight years earlier, had described
his friend as 'one of the tenderest-hearted creatures I know'.[15]
Bright's second wife died on May 13, 1878, while Bright was in
London. The marriage had been an increasingly happy one. They had
written to one another almost daily when separated during the long
Parliamentary sessions. 'Thy daily notes', Bright had admitted on one
occasion, 'are a sort of daily bread.'[16] After his wife's death Bright
found himself at heart a lonely man, although, during his remaining
eleven years he could still be lively in company. His constitution was
now gradually breaking up as he moved into his seventies. From his last
schooldays into middle-age he had enjoyed good health. Then early
in 1856 he suffered a severe nervous breakdown, brought on by the
strain of his unsuccessful opposition to the Crimean War. He had never
liked to be opposed even on small things, least of all to be opposed
successfully. A few weeks before the war began he admitted to his wife

that he might 'sustain an injury to my temper from the disgust with which I am filled'. The chief symptoms were great physical weakness, frequent severe headaches, and inability to undertake mental work. Cobden and others long doubted whether Bright would ever be able to return to politics. Cobden's affection for Bright was shown at its most intense and engaging at this period. We find him solicitously urging Bright to rest his brain as he would do a sprained ankle, to eat less meat and more fish and vegetables (Bright tended to overweight), and to go abroad away from familiar haunts. 'I am afraid you are not like me a good sleeper. You are often perorating in bed when you ought to be in a state of oblivion. Now there is no rest for your brain like sleep, and for this you must take exercise in mountain regions.' 'Eschew politics,' Cobden advised a fortnight later, 'political economy, and peace and war.' Bright eventually went to Algiers, then to the South of France and Italy. Slowly he recovered, but not until 1858 did he return to politics.[17] Thereafter he was never far from another breakdown, especially after 1865 when Cobden's support had gone and when he was involved in the agitation for a Second Reform Act. To avoid another collapse Bright had to spend several quiet months each autumn fishing and recuperating in Scotland and Wales. Even so, in 1870 the long threatened second breakdown overtook him, still more serious than that of 1856. For a time he was unable to walk or to read. Once again it took some three years before he was better. Thereafter he never risked over-stretching himself. During his last fifteen years he enjoyed long periods of quiet, rousing only occasionally to make a speech or to write a public letter. The hectic days of the campaign against the Corn Laws, when year after year he shared platforms as Cobden's lieutenant, were already history, history for which, as we have seen, Bright's speeches from these last years provided not always accurate evidence.

## 2. COBDEN'S LIEUTENANT

John Bright was striking in appearance, in personality and in his oratory. Each was forceful, and each supplemented the other. Bright's appearance was unmistakable to the Victorian public. A large head boldly set on a sturdy body, a flowing mane of hair merging into side whiskers, first black, then grizzled, finally white, a challenging eye which occasionally could soften with emotion or twinkle with humour, a stern square mouth and jaw, a beautiful clear voice of wide register without accent, likened by a contemporary to an organ, 'at once strong and harmonious, which swelled but never screeched'. The total effect, especially in his prime in the 1850s and '60s, was formidable. As early as 1842 Gladstone was impressed when young Bright in dark Quaker costume came to the Board of Trade as a member of an anti-Corn Law deputation. Bright sat forward on his seat and intervened vigorously in the discussion. 'He seemed to me rather fierce,' remembered Gladstone, 'but very strong.' He was then only thirty; by middle age he had assumed that patriarchal appearance which redoubled the effect of his earnestness. He looked and sounded, as was often said, like an Old Testament prophet.

One discerning observer remarked that the nobility of Bright's upper face contrasted revealingly with the perverse curve of the mouth and the strong, heavily moulded jaw. In private, when not thinking of politics, Bright was ready to show that noble gentle side of his character which we have already noted in the mourning letter to his children. He once said that his greatest pleasure in life was playing with little children, and his second greatest was reading poetry. In talking of music or of poetry he could display animation without that taint of asperity which coloured all expression of his political opinions. But once drawn on to politics, his temper became as fervent in private as it was on the platform. A Liberal lady who met Bright at dinner in 1866 found him 'certainly as violent and one-sided in his execration of Tories as any of them say'. One hostess admitted that she only invited 'congenial spirits' to meet him, with the result that he once told her how he enjoyed her parties more than any others because 'he knew that no one there would ever rouse the evil passions which had taken possession of him'. Another lady who knew Bright in private society described him indulgently in 1861 as 'great fun, always ready for a chat and a fulmination'. She liked to have his opinion on men and things because it was 'strong, clear and honest, however one-sided'. Up to 1865 Bright directed his fiercest fulminations against Lord Palmerston. Revealingly, whereas Cobden came to accept Palmerston's sincerity, Bright never did. He dubbed Palmerston 'the Feargus O'Connor of the middle classes', meaning thereby that the old Prime Minister played unscrupulously upon popular passions merely to maintain himself in office and power, regardless of the consequences. Even after

Palmerston's death Bright could find nothing charitable to say about him, remarking that he had 'played solely for himself'. Not surprisingly, Palmerston, who did not dislike Cobden, vigorously reciprocated Bright's hostile feelings.

We have already seen how, towards the end of their partnership, even Cobden liked to indulge Bright by not opposing him. 'Our friend Bright is so abused by other people that I never find it in my heart to tell him even when I differ from him.' Of course, unlike some society hostesses, Cobden was not afraid of Bright. He understood both the gentle and the rough sides of his friend's character. He loved the former, and was satisfied that Bright's roughness was employed only for good purposes, for fighting abuses and for promoting reform. He was delighted in October 1857 to find Bright so recovered from his breakdown that he 'talked incessantly, quite in his old way, taking everybody to task in his most pungent style'. Cobden regarded Bright's vituperative political manner not as a fault, but merely as a virtue sometimes carried to excess. During the Crimean War he was sorry to find Bright concentrating his attacks too much upon Ministers, who had been reluctantly led into hostilities by public opinion. He told a mutual friend that he had often tried to persuade Bright to rely less upon criticism of Ministers, 'and more on the enforcement of sound principles upon the public'. But, added Cobden indulgently, 'his pugnacity delights in a knockdown blow at something as visible and tangible as a Minister of State'.[1]

Bright's greatest gift was his power of oratory. It was deliberately simple in form, both in gesture and in language. He always stood firmly before his audience, sometimes with his right arm half raised, his notes held in his left hand, dropping them one by one into his hat beside him. The effect of this immobility was to concentrate attention upon his face. Like Coleridge's Ancient Mariner, explained one admirer, 'he holds us with his glittering eye'. Bright's simple choice of words concealed much careful preparation, even though most of his matter was not written down but stored in his brain. His notes contained only a carefully arranged sequence of heads of argument and key phrases, plus a peroration with the main sentence written in full. Bright's description (quoted on p. 75) of his first dealings with Cobden as given in his Bradford speech of 1877 was extemporised from just four phrases in his notes: 'First interview—Mozley St.—West St

Plate II

Bright in his speaking pose

Chapel—Education.'* In his prime in the 1850s and '60s, free from distractions of office, Bright was able to spend weeks preparing his ✳ speeches, coining striking phrases, <u>choosing precise adjectives</u>. During his League years perforce he spoke too often, but after 1846 he appeared only at intervals, sometimes of months. A speech from Bright was then ⟨ a great event, in Parliament and out, because of its quality and relative rarity, and because of the Victorian lack of much counter-attraction to politics. The newspapers reported every word. Bright's denunciations and forecasts were eagerly read by all classes except the lowest. Only the unskilled workmen, who read little but sensational Sunday newspapers, were not reached by him, and we shall see how his view of suffrage extension did not include them.

Bright's speeches for the Anti-Corn Law League did not match those of his prime when he spoke against the Crimean War or in support of Parliamentary reform. Bright's League manner was too vituperative. In his defence it must be said that the circumstances of his early partnership with Cobden tended to encourage this. When they appeared together on League platforms <u>Cobden normally spoke first</u>, making his usual persuasive appeal. Bright was then left (in his own phrase) to do the 'prize fighting', to exploit the effect made by Cobden to expand dawning conviction into active enthusiasm. Bright's speeches of the '50s and '60s, when he had matured and when he often spoke without Cobden, were at least a little less fierce and crushing. Nevertheless, as late as 1869 a reviewer of his first volume of collected speeches complained of <u>the 'total scorn' which Bright</u> poured upon his <u>opponents, denying them any reason and often any honesty</u>. These speeches were published just before the 1868 General Election, the first after the passing of the Second Reform Act. The tone of Bright's editor in his introduction was in keeping with Bright's strong matter. He claimed that Bright's speeches would be valuable in an election 'where the broad principles of truth, honour, and justice are arrayed on one side, and their victory is threatened by those false cries, those reck-

---

* Bright's account in the same speech of his Leamington conversation with Cobden after his wife's death in 1841 (quoted on p. 78) was anticipated slightly more elaborately: 'Condolence—invitation—Thousands of homes in England where mothers and children are perishing of hunger—come with me, and we will not rest till Corn Law is abolished—I went with him—we did not rest—not we alone—we were joined by scores—hundreds—thousands.'

less calumnies, those impudent evasions which form the party weapons of desperate and unscrupulous men.'

Cobden never published a collection of speeches, but had he done so, he would never have allowed his editor to print such a partisan preface. Robertson, Bright's most admiring Victorian biographer, rightly described Cobden as of a sensitive nature, 'as careful of other men's reputations as of his own'. Even Robertson could not claim that Bright showed a similar care. He and other Victorian biographers listed many examples of Bright's humour. Some sallies were permissible political badinage, like the comment upon members of the aristocracy who took pride in claiming that their ancestors came over
> with the Conqueror—'I never heard that they did anything else'; or the suggested motto for the aristocratic, office-loving Whigs—'A place for everyone, and everyone in his place'. But much of Bright's humour was sharply sarcastic, of a kind which, as Robertson admitted, Cobden did not usually employ. Robertson even cited one jibe by Bright against Cobden himself, an anecdote probably only repeated because it had been supplied by Gladstone. There was discussion of some religious matter in the Commons; someone pleaded with Bright that Cobden was favourable to the Anglican view. 'Oh, yes,' replied Bright, 'Cobden is turned Puseyite.' Gladstone added in explanation that Bright did not of course mean this to be taken literally. Cobden could never be suspected of Puseyism. But Bright did mean his remark to be taken as an irritated and sarcastic hit at his friend.

Bright entered Parliament in 1843, but his breakthrough into the first rank of Parliamentary speakers did not come until a speech on Irish distress in April 1849. This finally convinced the Commons that, although Bright was over-fond of vituperation, he was much more than a mere ranter. Thereafter he was always heard in the House with respect for his views and with admiration for his oratorical skill, even though he was usually arguing against the opinion of the majority. Here is the peroration to Bright's 1849 speech:

'I met an Irish gentleman the other night, and, speaking upon the subject, he said that he saw no remedy, but that it seemed as if the present state of things were the mode by which Providence intended to solve the question of Irish difficulties. But let us not lay these calamities at the door of Providence; it were sinful in us, of all men, to do so. God has blessed Ireland—and still does bless her—in position, in soil, in climate; He has not withdrawn His promises, nor are they unfulfilled; there is still the sunshine and the showers; still the seed-time and the harvest; and the affluent bosom of the earth yet offers sustenance for men. But man must do his part—we must do our part —we must retrace our steps—we must shun the blunders, and, I would even say, the crimes of our past legislation. We must free the land, and then we shall discover, and not till then, that industry, hopeful and remunerated—industry, free and inviolate, is the only sure foundation on which can be reared the enduring edifice of union and of peace.'

This was characteristic of Bright's best manner. It is difficult to appreciate such language today. The choice of words seems at the same time too obvious and too careful; the simplicity is seen to be contrived. But mid-Victorian audiences were not so sophisticated as those of today. Moreover, the Victorians shared an active religious faith not widely shared a century later, so that Bright could gain many of his best effects by referring (as here) to the Almighty, to the Bible, or to religious writers such as Milton. Bright was an earnest Quaker, and he sincerely believed himself to be the voice of God. 'I consider that when I stand upon a platform, as I do now, I am engaged in as solemn a labour as Mr. Dale when he addresses his congregation. It is not only upon the affairs of the other world that men must be true to themselves and to their consciences.' This Quaker conviction constituted the very heart of Bright's power as a speaker. One shrewd observer noted how it meant that in effect Bright was not only claiming possession of an inner light which told him the truth: he was also telling his hearers, 'you have the same inner light which tells you the truth, and you are sinning against it'.

In the following passage we can see how in 1865 Bright delivered this message to the electorate over the heads of Ministers and Members of Parliament, who were holding back on the question of Parliamentary reform:

'I speak not the language of party. I feel myself above the level of party. I speak, as I have ever endeavoured to speak, on behalf of the unenfranchised, the almost voiceless millions of my countrymen. Their claim is just, as it is constitutional. It will be heard. It cannot be rejected. To the outward eye monarchs and Parliaments seem to rule with an absolute and unquestioned sway, but—and I quote the words which one of our old Puritan poets has left for us—

"There is on earth a yet auguster thing,
　　Veiled though it be, than Parliament or King."

That auguster thing is the tribunal which God has set up in the consciences of men. It is before that tribunal that I am now permitted humbly to plead, and there is something in my heart—a small but an exultant voice—which tells me I shall not plead in vain.'

In terms of factual argument, as opposed to moral assertion, Bright did not often penetrate deeply in his speeches, especially in those out of Parliament. He saw issues simply, and he stated them simply. He himself contrasted his approach with that of Gladstone. 'When I speak, I strike across from headland to headland. Mr. Gladstone follows the coast-line; and when he comes to a navigable river he is unable to resist the temptation of tracing it to its source.' In his powerful speeches in Parliament against the Crimean War Bright did go more into detail, citing the Blue Books, and this extra depth helped to make them his most successful Parliamentary orations.

The 'Angel of Death' excerpt from one of his Crimean speeches became Bright's best-known piece of oratory (see p. 130). Quiller-Couch found a place for it in the *Oxford Book of English Prose*. Quiller-Couch was a late Victorian, of a generation which still found Bright's manner moving and exciting. As late as 1907 a selection of Bright's speeches was felt appropriate as an early title in the Everyman Library, reprinting in 1910 and 1914. But since 1914 Bright's oratory has seemed out of date. We cannot now rate it in the first rank. Despite its literary pretensions its success seems to have depended more than with most orators upon seeing and hearing the speaker. All Bright's early biographers were agreed upon this. Robertson remarked that the difference between seeing and hearing and merely reading Bright was the difference between the House of Commons in daylight under the studious contemplation of a solitary visitor, 'and the same edifice beheld lighted up, when thronged by excited members listening in breathless silence'. In summing up Bright's oratory in the official *Life* Trevelyan referred despairingly to 'some emanation of personal power which only those who have been subjected to its influence can realise, and which even they can neither describe nor define'. We have stressed the blemishes in Bright's character and oratory more than these earlier biographers, but this is not to deny his great impact upon the Victorian public which saw and heard the man in the flesh.[2]

Bright's virulent political tone sprang from his temperament, but his temperament had been stimulated from his earliest days by a sense of exclusion, religious exclusion as a Quaker, social and political exclusion as a new manufacturer. Bright's Quaker sense of religious penalty was especially strong. Opposing the Government scheme of educational reform in 1847, which he believed would further extend the privileges of the Church of England, Bright reminded the Commons how his forefathers had 'languished in prison by the acts of that Church which you now ask me to aggrandise'. He brought this sense of past Quaker suffering and deprivation even into his advocacy of political reforms which might seem to contain no religious element. He saw religious and political privilege as parts of one exclusive system in-tended to advance the interests of the Anglican landed aristocracy. In the mid-seventeenth century the first Quakers had fought against oppression and privilege in Church and State: in the mid-nineteenth century Bright was consciously continuing this fight. During the Reform crisis of 1866 he wrote to a fellow Quaker: 'I know where I am, I try to know it, and that in the midst of a great war, blows must be struck. Our forefathers thought so also two hundred years ago.' It was no accident that Bright's favourite period in history and in litera-ture was the seventeenth century. Cobden felt the same sense of ex-clusion, but not to the same degree. He had been born with a different disposition from Bright. He had also been born an Anglican. In his Cobden biography John Morley perceptively observed how those brought up in an Established Church 'escape one source of a certain mental asperity and the spirit of division'. Cobden was not much dis-turbed that he and Bright and other political representatives of the new industry could not yet expect to form Governments or to control Parliament. He accepted that the power of the aristocracy in politics and in society excluded the possibility of a Cobdenite Government. As we have seen, Cobden found genuine advantage in standing above party battles. But Bright found such acceptance hard to make. As late as 1859 Cobden had to remind him that he must 'accept certain conditions of things as a part of our English political existence during your time'. For instance, the Church and aristocracy were 'great realities, which will last for your life and your sons'. To ignore them or despise them is equally incompatible with the part which I think you have the ambition to play.'³

The tone of this passage showed how Cobden remained the senior partner to the end of his life. In 1860 Bright wrote to Cobden, who was wintering in Algiers, admitting his sense of isolation without his friend beside him in the Commons. In reply, Cobden tried to encourage Bright, then in his fiftieth year, to come forward on his own account. 'You do not do justice to yourself. You are the natural and necessary leader of a large body in the House.' During the League period Cobden's seniority had been very clear. Thus in October 1842 we find Bright admitting with regard to a suggested speaking tour that, while he would gladly go 'to play *second*' with Cobden or Colonel Thompson, 'with any other I don't feel very willing to go out, the responsibility being more upon myself than I should like'. Three years later when the bad state of Cobden's business seemed likely to compel his retirement from politics, Bright was very despondent at the prospect of losing Cobden's guidance. He told Cobden that his departure 'would be tantamount to a dissolution of the League—its main spring would be gone. I can in no degree take your place—as a second I can fight, but there are incapacities about me of which I am fully conscious which prevent my being more than a second in such a work as we have laboured in.' Money was found by a few friends to tide Cobden over his immediate difficulties, and he did not retire. He remained the leader, Bright his lieutenant. This letter was printed in full in Morley's biography of Cobden, published in 1881, but was glossed over by late Victorians anxious to equalise the roles of Bright and Cobden. 'I hope you will come to the House as soon as you can,' pleaded Bright to Cobden in 1860, 'for I am alone and helpless without you.'⁴

Cobden found Bright's assistance valuable in League journalism as well as in League speech-making. Bright wrote frequently for the *Anti-Bread-Tax Circular*, later *The League*, and also for other journals favourable to the cause. Cobden sometimes suggested subjects to Bright. For example, in May 1842 he wrote urging an article on the Queen's letter to the Anglican clergy which had ordered Church collections for the distressed. Here, explained Cobden, was a 'good opportunity for doing justice to the dissenting Ministers who met last year to proclaim the miseries of the people and to propose a better remedy than almsgiving'. Through their collection of tithes the Anglican clergy, claimed Cobden, shared an interest in maintaining the high price of bread through the Corn Laws. Cobden suggested that Bright should also emphasise the impossibility of subsidising the wages of the cotton workers through charity, when these wages amounted to £20 millions per year. 'If you have also leisure for another article, make a swingeing assault upon the corruptions of the last General Election, and argue from the disclosures made by the House of Commons itself that we, the anti-Corn Law party, were not defeated but virtually swindled and plundered of our triumph at the hustings.' With such vigorous advice Cobden helped Bright to write articles which he could not find time to compose himself.[5]

In August 1842 in the middle of the Plug Strikes Bright published a powerful *Address to the Working Men of Rochdale*. It was phrased in plain, candid language characteristic of his writing at its best. He expressed deep sympathy with the sufferings of the people, but regretted their drift into direct action and urged them to combine not against employers but against the Corn Laws:

'Your sufferings have naturally produced discontent, and you have turned eagerly to almost any scheme which gave hope of relief. . . . Many of you know full well that neither Act of Parliament nor act of a multitude can keep up wages. . . . What are you to do then? RETURN TO YOUR EMPLOYMENT. . . . Your first step to entire freedom must be *commercial* freedom. We must put an end to the partial famine which is destroying trade, the demand for your labour, your wages, your comforts, and your independence. The aristocracy regard the Anti-Corn-Law League as their greatest enemy. That which is the greatest enemy of the remorseless aristocracy of Britain must almost of necessity be your firmest friend.'[6]

In July 1843 Bright was returned as Member of Parliament for Durham City. Two elections proved necessary, the first won by the Tory candidate who was then unseated for bribery, the second by Bright with a majority of seventy-eight. The Anti-Corn Law League claimed this as a great victory for its principles; but the League leaders knew privately that Bright really owed his victory to a shift in the Londonderry interest to Bright when the Marquess quarrelled between the two elections with the local Tory leadership. Be this as it may, Bright was now available to act as Cobden's lieutenant at Westminster as well as in the country.[7]

Bright was not so quick as Cobden in making his mark in the House of Commons. His language was too strong. Cobden was just as bold in principle, but he was usually more conciliatory in manner. Bright's maiden speech, delivered on August 7, less than a fortnight after his election, although not a failure was not a complete success. His second attempt a week later was reported by Cobden to be much better. Real success, however did not come until 1845 when he succeeded in securing a select committee to inquire into the working of the Game Laws. The League regarded the Game Laws as an important part of the structure of landed aristocratic oppression. They compelled farmers to suffer continuous damage to their crops and pasture by game birds and animals preserved by law for the sport of the aristocracy and gentry. During the winter of 1844–5 Bright collected a mass of detailed evidence, which he deployed in his speech of February 27, 1845. For once Bright deliberately abandoned the tone of high denunciation which he used against the Corn Laws, taking the quieter and more conciliatory line of retailing facts, figures and stories. He realised that only in this way could he hope to persuade a majority of the landlords who dominated the House to admit that he had a case. He ended by pointing out how he had brought the question forward 'without using a single word or a single expression of harshness towards any human being'. This unusual moderation won him his committee and much pleased Cobden, who wrote to Wilson telling him how Bright's speech had taken the squires 'quite aback'. His success had put him 'in a right position—shown that he has power'.[8]

With the onset of the Corn Law crisis at the end of 1845 excited League meetings were called all over the country, and Cobden and Bright were invited to most of them. 'Bright and I are almost off our legs', admitted Cobden to his wife on December 4, 'five days this week in crowded meetings.' Bright described in Quaker language the sequence of their meetings to his sister-in-law. 'On 2nd day we go to Gloucester, 4th day to Stroud, 5th day to Bath, 6th day to Bristol, on the 8th of the month to Nottingham, 9th to Derby, 11th Stockport. Everywhere our meetings are greater than ever.' In little over a fortnight the pair appeared at meetings in nine counties.[9]

On December 19 Bright spoke after Cobden at one of the last great League demonstrations in Covent Garden Theatre. A revealing contrast emerged there between the attitudes of the two orators. Bright was consciously much less conciliatory than Cobden. Cobden emphasised how he had never attempted to make repeal of the Corn Laws a class question, setting the manufacturing middle and working classes against the landed aristocracy:

> 'I have preached from the first that we would have the co-operation of the best and most intelligent of all ranks in life—working, middle, and upper classes. No, no; we will have no war of classes in this country . . . we will save the Duke of Richmond's order from the Duke of Richmond. We have got Lord Morpeth, and we have also Lords Radnor, Ducie, and Kinnaird, and a good many more; and among the rest Earl Grey, our earliest and most tried champion of the aristocracy. This is one proof that ours is not a class question, and that we are not at war with the whole landed aristocracy.'

But Bright began by brushing aside Cobden's emphasis upon harmony.

> 'Notwithstanding the hope that my friend who has just addressed you has expressed, that it may not become a strife of classes, I am not sure that it has not already become such, and I doubt whether it can have any other character. I believe this to be a movement of the commercial and industrious classes against the lords and great proprietors of the soil.'

Bright reflected the prevailing feeling among League stalwarts in Lancashire. The opening address of the new *Manchester Examiner* on January 10, 1846, a paper in which Bright held shares, exulted in Manchester's 'victorious conflict with the spirit of feudalism. . . . The great dynasty of idleness is shaken to its foundations—the men who make the country, and keep it, have effectually vindicated their right to rule it.' Bright was interested in Corn Law repeal mainly for two purposes, firstly to promote industrial progress, but secondly to overthrow the power of the landed aristocracy. In July 1846 Cobden described Bright's 'champion-like feeling for the interests and honor of his order'. By contrast, we have seen how Cobden himself was interested in Corn Law repeal as a means of benefiting agriculture as much as industry, and we have also seen him assuring the landlords in Parliament that if they accepted repeal they could expect their social and political power to remain intact. These were important differences of emphasis and expectation behind the partnership of Cobden and Bright against the Corn Laws.

These differences can be partly explained in terms of the different backgrounds of the two men. Cobden had lived in both the agricultural society of the South and the industrial society of the North. He could look at national problems from both points of view. He never advocated repeal of the Corn Laws, or any other reform, simply in the interest of one economic or social sector, always because he believed his reforms to be in the interests of the nation as a whole. Bright, on the other hand, spent all his days in Rochdale. He had no contrasting experience to set beside his industrial knowledge. At the final Manchester meeting of the Anti-Corn Law League he showed very plainly how he saw the repeal victory as a victory for the North:

'it is to this and a neighbouring county that the great element of power in this country is henceforth to be found. Lancashire, the cotton district, and the West Riding of Yorkshire, must govern England. I don't mean that they must of themselves assert a superiority over other parts of the kingdom, like that which the rural and agricultural counties have asserted over us in times past; but I say that the vast population of those counties, with their interests, their morality, their union, that all these must exercise an immense influence upon all future legislation in this kingdom, and that the direction of legislation must be in accordance with the prevailing sentiments of the population of those two counties.'[10]

Bright's work for the Anti-Corn Law League was recognised after repeal with a public subscription of over £5,000. This was spent upon a library of twelve hundred volumes, all handsomely bound and housed in a special bookcase at One Ash. Its uprights were elaborately carved with sheaves of corn and fruit, and a relief on the cornice showed a vessel homeward bound with a quayside loaded with barrels of flour and bales of cotton. The books were chosen by Bright himself, chiefly history, biography and English literature. His favourite English poets were given pride of place on the shelves. Bright was to turn to their works many times for inspiration and quotation while preparing his speeches during the next forty years.[11]

## III

# Cobden and Bright

### 1. THE PARTNERSHIP AFTER 1846

DIFFERENCES in attitude between Cobden and Bright even over Corn Law repeal underlined the inaccuracy of the late-Victorian view of the pair as almost always in agreement. Genuine friendship did not require this. Yet John Morley, in his official biography of Cobden which Bright vetted, encouraged this idea. Morley quoted part of a letter written in great concern by Cobden to Joseph Parkes at the height of Bright's illness in November 1856, when it seemed doubtful if Bright would make a full recovery. The important part of the letter ran as follows:

'You bring me back to my old fears that he will never be again equal to his former part in public life. I have always had a sort of selfish share in his career, for I have felt as though when passing the zenith of life I was handing over every principle and cause I had most at heart to the advocacy of one not only younger and more energetic but with gifts of natural eloquence to which I never pretended. For the last two or three years I have made him my mouthpiece on many important questions, and have given him budgets of facts and arguments upon the war, newspaper stamp and other debates which he has always hurled about him with his usual force. He had a good deal of Hume's breadth and genial aptitude for bringing out in his speeches (though with far different effect) ideas or facts with which he was prompted. I remember on one occasion upon an ecclesiastical debate remarking to him that "if Oxford could have it's way unchecked England would have been ere now Austrian in politics and Roman Catholic in religion", and out it came with tremendous force upon Gladstone and Co. These are little secrets known only to you and him and myself. But perhaps there never

⁎ were two men who lived in such transparent intimacy of mind as
Bright and myself. Next to the loss of my boy I have had no
sorrow so constant and great as from his illness.'

The genuine affection shown here is not to be doubted. Nevertheless,
Morley encouraged an over-simplified view of the friendship by partly
quoting this letter without allowing for its emotional, almost mourning tone. This was not a time when Cobden would be likely to
emphasise differences between Bright and himself. Even so, he did
indicate how he had still been supplying Bright with ideas at this late
stage in the partnership, just as we have seen him doing at its beginning.
This again showed how much Cobden remained the senior partner.
Yet Morley cut this passage, and also the next passage dealing with
Bright's assault upon Gladstone, then Member of Parliament for
Oxford University. To omit these revealing middle sentences while
quoting the earlier and later passages flattering to Bright, amounted to
distortion of evidence, an instance of *suggestio falsi* if not of *suppressio veri*.[1]

Morley was subscribing to the late Victorian idealisation of the
partnership as continuously warm and equal. In reality, within weeks
of the repeal of the Corn Laws it entered a period of relative coolness,
which lasted for some seven years up to the Crimean War. During
this time Cobden and Bright were still friends, but they were not
intimates. In July 1846 Cobden stopped signing his letters to Bright
'yours truly', and for over two years lapsed into 'yours faithfully'. The
initial reason for this was the way in which Bright became a candidate
for the representation of Manchester at the 1847 General Election.
Even before repeal of the Corn Laws Bright had made known his
keenness to become a Liberal candidate. This move, however, met
strong resistance from the *Manchester Guardian* Liberals, who regarded
Bright as too extreme in manner and views. These moderates would
have been content with Cobden and tried hard to persuade him to
stand, but Cobden was anxious to remain Member for Stockport,
where his constituents made few demands upon his time and left him
free to concentrate upon national objects. Initially, Cobden seems to
have encouraged Bright in his hopes of the candidature, but Cobden
became increasingly concerned at the strength of the opposition to
Bright. Then a few weeks after the victory of repeal, while preparing to
take a long recuperative holiday on the Continent, Cobden was made

angry by Bright's plainly self-interested attempts to hurry him into a final declaration that he would not stand for Manchester. Cobden still genuinely hoped that Bright would be nominated, but he thought that his friend had unwisely provoked local feeling against himself by his brusque manner. On July 17, 1846, Cobden wrote in confidence to the town clerk of Stockport, emphasising how he was 'most anxious' to remain the representative of that town. But, went on Cobden, a 'strenuous effort' would probably be made to return him for Manchester:

'I will tell you very confidentially what is at the bottom, to some extent, of this movement. Bright has been named as a proper person to represent Manchester. And I joined a year ago in expressing an opinion that he ought to be the candidate to succeed Mark Philips. I thought his talents, his large stake in the staple trade of the town, his thorough honesty, and his champion-like feeling for the interests and honor of his order qualified him to represent Manchester. It is now evident that, however high he may stand with the ten-pounders, he is not exactly approved by the influential men. In fact, he takes no pains to conciliate people of his own rank, and if they do not know him thoroughly, as I do, they think him arrogant and supercilious. The leading men say there would be a contest if he stood, and that if he were returned, it might probably be at the risk of Gibson's seat. I am inclined to think Bright would be returned easily and Gibson with him, but it would probably make the seats less secure permanently than if I and Gibson sat. . . . Both on Bright's account and my own, I should regret being placed in a situation to be in a manner forced to accept the seat.'

On July 29 Bright sent Cobden a long and obviously carefully worded letter which hardly concealed his own ambition. Bright admitted that the whole Manchester Liberal Party would be glad to accept Cobden as a candidate, but if Cobden refused to stand a large section (claimed Bright) would want him to do so. Even those Liberals who did not like this would probably acquiesce in it. Bright asked Cobden not to go abroad without having decided for or against nomination for Manchester:

'Now we have, I believe, always dealt honestly with each other, although perhaps some other parties may not have dealt honestly with either of us, and it is in an honest spirit that I write first to put these things before you and to ask your opinion. I have always thought the representation of Manchester would become you, and have always approved of the looking towards you which has been evident for several years past, and now if you will consent to stand you will gratify the great body of the constituency and take a position to which you of all men have the first claim. I am free to confess that, although until you suggested it, I had never thought of it, the representation of Manchester is a very proud position, and one which any man of active mind and willing to work would prefer to any other, and therefore if it were probable that I should be invited to stand I would keep myself free from any other Borough till the question were decided—not that I have any claims as against you, or if I had that I would prefer them.'

Bright concluded this tense letter by saying that he had spoken frankly and expected 'equally frank candour' from Cobden. He wanted to avoid misunderstanding, inconvenience, 'and a diminution of that mutual good feeling which has existed between you and me'.

Cobden was much annoyed by the tone of this letter. He could see, as we can see, that Bright protested too much. Bright did *not* want Cobden to stand for Manchester: he very much wanted to stand himself. Cobden replied the next day (in a letter signed for the first time 'faithfully yours') coldly referring Bright to his letter to the town clerk of Stockport already quoted. 'You will perceive at a glance that the communication was not intended for *your* eye. But it is on that account that I wish you to peruse it—for it will satisfy you perhaps more completely as to my real feelings upon the matter in question than a more lengthened explanation made to yourself.' This suggested that Bright might not believe Cobden if he repeated the gist of this letter directly, that only sight of a letter not intended for Bright's eyes would convince Bright of Cobden's good intentions towards him. This was clearly a low point in the friendship. A meeting a few days later between Cobden and Bright seems to have eased the tension. Cobden wrote to Wilson on August 3 that he had held a very long conversation with Bright on the Manchester question. Cobden asked Wilson to persuade their Manchester friends not to keep urging him to stand; he explained how he found the pressure hard to resist, although he found it equally hard to accept the nomination. 'How truly it is to be desired', concluded Cobden, referring to Bright, 'that he should have his obvious ambition to sit for Manchester gratified.'

Cobden now went to the Continent, where he remained from early August 1846 to October 1847. On September 17 he wrote to the President of the Manchester Reform Association finally refusing to stand for the local seat. He explained that he would have stood only to advance some public principle, and he could not see that any such principle was involved. With the vital assistance of George Wilson, Bright now redoubled his efforts. The *Manchester Guardian* party, denouncing Bright as 'an extravagant political theorist' who favoured universal suffrage and opposed the Church, the Crown and the aristo-cracy, desperately tried to promote the candidature of Lord Lincoln, Peelite son of the Duke of Newcastle. The incongruous prospect of the son of a duke as a representative of Manchester understandably made Bright still more anxious to secure the nomination. At the end of November he sent a long letter to Cobden in which he claimed that if it had not meant handing over the seat to the *Guardian* group he would have withdrawn. In the circumstances, however, he was determined to remain in the field, and he asked Cobden to write a public letter in his support. Cobden replied from Genoa six weeks later firmly refusing to do this, saying that he could not involve himself in Manchester politics from such a distance.[2] In the event, Bright secured the nomina-tion, and at the General Election in July 1847 he and Milner Gibson were returned unopposed. We shall see, though, how ten years later what Cobden had shrewdly forecast came about when both Bright and Gibson were rejected by the Manchester electorate. In the 1847 election Cobden himself was returned in his absence for the great West Riding constituency. He felt bound to accept the honour, and so after all he did reluctantly leave his comfortable Stockport seat.[3]

The 1847–52 Parliament saw a continuation of the relative coolness between Cobden and Bright begun by the Manchester episode. Important differences emerged between them on the question of Parliamentary reform which we shall discuss in due place. In the summer recess of 1851, and again a year later, we find Cobden ad-mitting that he had 'lost sight of Bright'. They were still friends, but not at this time friends in continuous or intimate contact.[4] Their friendship was restored to its former level by the unpopularity which both, and especially Bright, incurred through their opposition to the Crimean War, which started in 1854. Two years later came Bright's breakdown, which as we have seen, brought out Cobden's warmest feelings. Nevertheless, important differences of ends and means persisted between Cobden and Bright throughout the 1850s and '60s, and we must now turn to their partnership during these years in its many-sided but not always united reality.

## 2. THE MANCHESTER SCHOOL

By the time of repeal of the Corn Laws the wide range of political views and activities linked especially with the names of Cobden and Bright was becoming known as the work of 'the Manchester School'. This term was coined by Disraeli in the Commons in February 1846 as 'a homage to their deleterious but well-disciplined doctrines'. Cobden and Bright readily adopted it. At the Manchester Free Trade Hall in 1852 Bright exclaimed that the hall was the 'schoolroom of the Manchester School . . . I do not repudiate that name at all. I think it is an honour to ourselves—an honour to you—that by your own intelligence, your sacrifices, your combinations, your intrepidity, you have actually marked the impression of your mind and your convictions upon the policy of the greatest empire of the globe.'

Bright was here flattering his audience by equating the Manchester School with the city of Manchester. In fact, the School embraced elements which had little to do with Manchester itself. It included merchants, manufacturers and businessmen from all parts of the country, who supported free trade because it seemed to offer them profit; it included Philosophic Radicals, centred in London, who supported free trade on abstract grounds of political economy; it included pacifists, especially Quakers, who advocated free trade for moral and religious reasons. Finally, it included middle-class Radicals who had entered politics under the influence of mixtures of all three motivations. At the head of this last group, and at the head of the Manchester School as a whole, stood Cobden and Bright. The various elements were held informally together only by a general, though never total, acceptance of their leadership. No one line of thought or action followed by Cobden or Bright was necessarily accepted by all members of the School. At times, notably over the Crimean War, the pair differed completely from the majority. The Manchester School was never more homogenous than this. It never seemed likely to become an organised national party. Only in Manchester itself for some ten years after 1846 did the League machine under George Wilson operate as an organised force in politics.[1]

Cobden, as leader of the School, was no party leader, manœuvring for office and power. Several times between 1845 and 1859 he rejected actual or prospective offers of office such as no party leader could have refused. During the Corn Law crisis of December 1845 he declined an invitation from Lord John Russell to serve as Vice-President of the Board of Trade, outside the Cabinet, in the Government which the Whig leader was then attempting to form. In July 1846 after Peel's resignation when the Whigs at last did form an Administration, Russell again wrote to Cobden holding out the prospect of Cabinet office after his return from his long Continental tour. When, however, in October 1847 Russell raised the matter with the Queen she vetoed the idea of Cobden's elevation to the Cabinet 'direct from Covent Garden'. This would be a 'dangerous example to agitators in general': Cobden should serve an apprenticeship in lesser office first. Five years later when the Aberdeen Government was being formed Cobden's name was again canvassed for office, but Cobden once more discouraged the idea. Finally, in 1859 came the most determined attempt to enlist Cobden. Palmerston called him for interview, and pressed him hard to become President of the Board of Trade. But again Cobden refused, despite strong pressure from all elements within the Manchester School, 'everybody, Radicals, peace men, and all'. Cobden was able to hold firm on his last line of argument, that it would have been improper for him to serve under a Prime Minister who was known to be the foremost advocate of a foreign policy which he had consistently and strongly denounced. If Russell had been making the offer, Cobden subsequently admitted that he would have been unable to refuse to complete a strong mixed Liberal Ministry.

As it was, both Milner Gibson and Villiers joined Palmerston's Cabinet. Cobden welcomed this, since he felt it important for the political influence of the Manchester School in Parliament that some of its members should be individually available for office. Cobden reminded Bright at the end of 1859 that, at least in times when opinion outside Parliament was quiet, 'we are comparatively powerless if we can be assumed to be excluded from the Government by either our own will, or that of the ruling class'. In different political circumstances Cobden himself would have been glad to take office to promote the cause of reform. His refusals were the outcome of contemporary political circumstances, not of an inherent indisposition. Admittedly, in 1860 he did write of his 'insuperable repugnance' to office. But by this time his health was breaking up. Five years earlier he had confessed to Bright that by nature he was not without aspirations. Had he been born in the United States, with its free institutions and absence of aristocratic control, 'I should have set no bounds to my ambition'; but his judgement had told him at the beginning of his political career that if he aimed at office in this country 'it must lead either to disappointment or an abandonment of objects which I cherish far before official rank, and therefore I preferred pioneering for my convictions to promotion at the expense of them'.[2]

Cobden ruled out office for himself in the England of the 1850s, but not for his leading supporters in Parliament, certainly not for Bright. The idea, encouraged by Trevelyan and other biographers, that Bright was always reluctant to take office is a misconception which Cobden would not have countenanced. Cobden was well aware that Bright in his prime was very interested in office. In refusing for himself during his interview with Palmerston in 1859, Cobden urged that an offer be made to Bright. Palmerston resisted by saying that Bright 'in his attacks on *classes*' had given too great offence to powerful groups in politics. Palmerston did try to arrange a Privy Councellorship for Bright, but the Queen objected that this might seem to condone his attacks upon national institutions.

This bandying of his name was wounding to Bright's always prickly pride. He **could** not help comparing the consideration shown to Cobden with his own treatment. In the '50s he very much wanted at least the *offer* of office (such as Cobden had received), so that at least like Cobden he could refuse it. In 1852 he wrote to his wife that he presumed that Lord Aberdeen would approach Cobden for office, 'who will not accept—and as for me, they say I am a republican!' By 1859 however, Bright did not merely want to refuse an offer of office. It was possible that, like Milner Gibson and Villiers, he would have joined Palmerston's Cabinet, if given the chance. A year earlier he had complained in revealing terms to his wife of the frustrations of his role as an outsider in Parliamentary politics, 'having a very advantageous position in the House, and yet unable from my opinions on certain subjects to avail myself of the rewards which meet other men in their political careers. Never mind, I hear thee saying, perhaps all is for the best.' This was not the language of a man who was glad to be excluded from official positions. We have already seen how at this time Cobden was writing to Bright of 'the part which I think you have the ambition to play'. This part explicitly included the possibility of office for Bright: 'if you intend to follow politics, and not eschew office, you must in future be more exclusively a House of Commons man'. Cobden apparently prophesied in Bright's presence that one day he was 'certain to be a Right Honourable'. He understood Bright much better than his biographers, who allowed their accounts of Bright's attitude to office to be too much coloured by his mood in 1868 when he did finally receive and accept an offer. He then became President of the Board of Trade in Gladstone's first Ministry. All the evidence suggests that Bright was now genuinely reluctant. But by this date he was physically and mentally an old man, verging on his second breakdown. He joined Gladstone only out of personal regard and in order to make plain his support for Gladstone's new Irish policy. Bright remarked that he 'liked no part of the office except the salary'. In this spirit a story circulated for many years of a minute supposed to have been written by Bright on a memorandum submitted to him by a senior civil servant. 'I have read Mr. Giffen's very able and interesting memorandum. I do not clearly apprehend whether he approves or disapproves the proposal which he discusses, but in any case I agree with him.' Bright's breakdown forced him to withdraw from active politics in February 1870 and to resign in December. In October 1873 he rejoined Gladstone's Cabinet as Chancellor of the Duchy of Lancaster, hoping thereby to revive the fortunes of the crumbling Government. In 1880 he again became Chancellor of the Duchy in Gladstone's second Administration, finally resigning in 1882 because he could not support the bombardment of Alexandria.[3]

Cobden was much more content than Bright to acquiesce in the mid-Victorian monopoly of office by traditional aristocratic party leaders. Cobden knew that repeal of the Corn Laws had been finally secured only through the leader of the Conservative Party, Peel. Cobden reminded a staunch Leaguer in 1849 that they could 'scarcely feel too strongly the obligation we are under to him'. After repeal of the Corn Laws in the summer of 1846 Cobden hoped fervently that Peel would remain in office and continue the work of reform. On June 23, six days before Peel's resignation, he sent a confidential letter to the Prime Minister urging this. Cobden's letter was the only important step (as he afterwards told a mutual friend) which he had taken as a Leaguer without the knowledge of Bright and Wilson.

He began by telling Peel that his resignation would be a national misfortune. Peel need not bow to a 'chance medley of factions' in the House of Commons, for he was the idol of public opinion. 'I will not speak of the populace, which to a man is with you; but of the active and intelligent middle classes, with whom you have engrossed a sympathy and interest greater than was ever before possessed by a minister. . . . *You represent the Idea of the age, and it has no other representative amongst statesmen.*' Cobden underlined this last sentence, and double-underlined the word 'idea'. This idea was free trade, not only in corn, but in sugar, coffee and all articles of exchange. By developing this policy in its full domestic and international applications Peel could achieve 'the greatest triumph of a century'. Cobden advised an immediate dissolution of Parliament, with the cry at the hustings 'Peel and Free Trade'. Many old protectionists would be defeated in the elections, and many new middle-class free traders would be returned:

'Do you shrink from the post of governing through the bona fide representatives of the middle class? Look at the facts, and can the country be otherwise ruled at all? There must be an end of the juggle of parties, the mere representatives of traditions, and some man must of necessity rule the state through its governing class. The Reform Bill decreed it; the passing of the Corn Bill has realized it. Are you afraid of the middle class? You must know them better than to suppose that they are given to extreme or violent measures. They are not democratic.'

Democracy was not an issue in politics. There was no demand for further organic reform. 'Practical reforms are the order of the day, and you are by common consent the practical reformer. *The Condition of England question—there is your mission.*' The Irish question was likewise an urgent practical problem. Peel should deal as firmly with the

Irish landlords as he had dealt with their English counterparts, and then the Irish people would be satisfied.

Peel replied the next day in a letter, scribbled from his seat in the House of Commons, which bypassed Cobden's main argument. He refused to accept the need to continue in office. The country needed 'repose' after the turmoil of the corn crisis, rather than a fiercely contested General Election. Peel was not certain that he would win any such election, and even if he could be certain of victory he was sure that the electorate ought not to be asked simply to decide a 'personal question between myself and inflamed Protectionists'.

Peel clearly thought that Cobden's view of affairs was too narrow, too dependent upon Peel himself, and too much linked with the middle class. One modern historian has described Cobden's argument as a kind of middle-class Marxism. His letter taken by itself can certainly be so interpreted. But was this really what Cobden meant to convey? We have seen how he was careful in his League campaigns to appeal not merely to the middle classes but also to the workers and even to the landed aristoctacy. We have seen how this emerged in his important Commons speech of March 1845 on agriculture in relation to the Corn Laws, and in his Covent Garden speech of December 19, 1845. It was Bright who on this last occasion, in explicit contradiction of Cobden, dwelt upon rivalries between interests and classes. Cobden's letter to Peel really did not do justice to the breadth of his vision. 'I do not like classes', he had told a League audience in 1844; the Anti-Corn Law League, he claimed, happily comprised 'the best of all classes'. What Cobden intended to say was that Peel might rule *through* the middle class, as the core of his electoral support. Such rule was to be on behalf of all classes and interests, not just for the manufacturing middle class. Cobden used the word 'through' twice in this intended sense in the key passage already quoted. Unfortunately, his language was over-compressed. It could read as if Cobden was urging Peel to initiate a period of narrow middle-class rule, as selfish as the landlord control which it displaced. Peel would have been much more impressed if he had understood that Cobden wanted class union after repeal, since this was the basic aim of his own policy in office. But even so, Peel could probably not have been persuaded to attempt to retain power through an immediate dissolution. If Cobden had indeed moved Peel to fight such an election, he would probably have

won it, and the years after 1846 might have been years of great progress in Britain.[4]

### 3. INTERNATIONAL BEARINGS

During the years after 1846 the British people and their Governments turned away from the possibility of social progress at home to a
noisy interest in foreign affairs. During the 1850s and early '6os the
names of Cobden and Bright were before the public much more in
connection with foreign than with domestic questions. We have
already seen how the creed of free trade, which in its domestic application made the pair famous in the 1840s, also contained an equally
important international aspect, seeking the establishment of world
peace through the spread of commerce. How far, then, was the free
trade cumulative prosperity argument influential after 1846 in international affairs? In the short term, the answer must be hardly at all.
As early as 1848 we find Cobden complaining that the Corn Laws
seemed to have been repealed 'by accident without knowing what we
were about. The *spirit* of free trade is not yet in us.' British foreign
policy in the 1850s and early '6os, associated especially with Lord
Palmerston, Foreign Secretary 1846–51 and Prime Minister 1855–8
and 1859–65, was not devoted to promoting peace through the world-
wide spread of free trade, but to vigorous promotion of British interests. With these interests in mind Palmerston was always busy seeking
to maintain an elusive balance of power and to support liberalism and
nationality in Europe and beyond.

Cobden's international ideas were stated early and clearly in his two
pamphlets of 1835 and 1836, *England, Ireland and America*, and *Russia*.
In his later writings Cobden varied little from the principles laid down
in these two works. His pamphlet *1793 and 1853*, published in the latter
year, showed how the long period of war with Revolutionary France
had been unnecessary, and how a fresh war, which threatened in 1853,
would be equally misguided. *What Next—and Next?* (1856) discussed
the Crimean War, which Cobden and Bright had staunchly opposed.
Finally, *The Three Panics* (1862) demolished the unfounded French
invasion alarms which had seized the British Government and people
three times since 1848. Cobden believed that such foolish scares were
caused by too intense a British interest in the affairs of foreign states.
Our Foreign Ministers were always meddling. Cobden wanted non-

involvement and non-intervention. All would be well if only the power of diplomats and soldiers in shaping the foreign policies of their states could be minimised. 'I believe the progress of freedom depends more upon the maintenance of peace, the spread of commerce, and the diffusion of education, than upon the labours of Cabinets or Foreign Offices.' International contacts through diplomatic channels should be reduced at the same time as contact through commercial channels under free trade should be increased. 'As little intercourse as possible betwixt the *Governments*, as much connexion as possible between the *nations* of the world!' Such would be the best safeguard against unnecessary wars and against the vast waste of life and resources which wars produced. In particular, international businessmen, prospering through free trade, would oppose war as damaging to commerce. 'Commerce is the grand panacea which, like a beneficent medical discovery, will serve to inoculate with the healthy and saving taste for civilisation all the nations of the world.'

The practical basis of this argument, emphasising profit and prosperity, will be apparent. Cobden was himself an international businessman, selling his calicoes. He was also a shrewd judge of the public mind. He knew that a practical approach was more likely to attract interest than one couched in terms of abstract high moral principles. Discussing privately his plan for international arbitration of disputes in 1849, he explained that he was well aware of the moral arguments in his favour, but that he had deliberately chosen to present his case to the Commons in cool practical terms to counter in advance the charge of being a mere visionary. Fortunately, God had contrived that peace-keeping could be made not only morally right but also materially advantageous. Men could be led via materialism to morality.

Here we are reminded of the strong Christian feeling behind Cobden's free trade vision. This vision was also in tune with the growing scientific spirit of the first half of the nineteenth century. Cobden regarded free trade as a law of economic science as 'natural' as the laws of physical science. He was also influenced by the failure of successive attempts in his youth to secure international co-operation through diplomatic or military action. The ancient Holy Roman Empire finally expired two years after his birth; Napoleon's empire collapsed during his boyhood; the post-war Congress System and Holy Alliance rose and fell during his adolescence. If politicians, diplomats and soldiers had failed, could businessmen do better? Kant in his essay on *Everlasting Peace* (1795) had argued that 'the commercial spirit cannot co-exist with war'. Young Cobden may have read this essay during his years of self-education in the 1820s. Very likely he studied some earlier writers who had propounded systems for maintaining world peace, Rousseau, the Abbé de St Pierre, Sully, Grotius, Erasmus. He certainly discovered the free trade views of Lord Shelburne, Prime Minister 1782–3. Shelburne was the mentor of the Younger Pitt, who himself became Premier at the end of 1783; but Pitt's liberal economic and diplomatic policies had unfortunately collapsed after 1793 under the pressure of war with Revolutionary France, a war which Cobden always regarded as unnecessary.

These influences contributed to the shaping of Cobden's international ideas, but the most important influence upon him was contemporary. Cobden could see the Industrial Revolution progressing all around him, transforming the economic and social life first of Britain and then increasingly of much of the Western World. He believed that this economic and social change required corresponding political and diplomatic change. At home and abroad the old order based upon ownership of land would have to surrender its monopolies of power. Cobden and Bright noted how everywhere the diplomats and soldiers were relatives of the landed aristocrats and squires. In a long-remembered passage from a speech of 1858 Bright claimed that Palmerston's foreign policy, his regard for 'the liberties of Europe', his concern for the balance of power, was 'neither more nor less than a gigantic system of outdoor relief for the aristocracy of Great Britain'. A large diplomatic service, an inflated army and navy, were each maintained to provide employment at national expense for members of the aristocracy, while our interfering foreign policy was pursued in order to justify these overgrown establishments. English landlords had abandoned their outdated Corn Laws: their sons and brothers and cousins in the diplomatic and military services must also abandon their equally outdated and unsuccessful system of foreign policy. On his Continental tour in 1846 Cobden wrote home to Bright in terms which showed how closely his mind linked reform of foreign policy with reform of domestic policy. He admitted 'an instinctive monomania against this system of foreign interference, protocolling, diplomatising, etc. . . . oppose yourselves to the Palmerston system, and try to prevent the

Foreign Office from undoing the good which the Board of Trade has done to the people.'

British foreign policy was supposedly designed to support national interests, and peace was Britain's foremost national interest. Yet Cobden and Bright argued that under the control of the landed aristocracy our policy had plunged us into unnecessary wars for generation after generation. It was a favourite remark of Bright's that every war since the accession of William III had been unnecessary and unprofitable. Cobden pointed out how, even before the Crimean War, we had spent more than £150 m. upon wars since 1688, 'not one of which has been upon our own shores, or in defence of our hearths and homes'. Cobden opened his first pamphlet upon this theme. History, he argued, showed Britain at different periods 'in the act of casting our sword into the scale of every European state'. Yet history had also shown 'how futile must be our attempts to usurp the sceptres of the Fates. Empires have arisen unbidden by us: others have departed, despite our utmost efforts to preserve them.'

Cobden knew that British interference in the affairs of foreign states was often defended on the ground of support for liberty and nationality; but he refused to believe that these good causes could be effectively promoted through interference. Speaking against the Crimean War, he told the Commons that he would never sanction interference to establish nationality by force of arms because such a policy contravened a principle which he wished to maintain in the other direction, 'the prevention of all foreign interference with nationalities for the sake of putting them down'. Peoples, as much as individuals, should put their trust in God.

> 'Some people will say, do you intend to leave these evils without a remedy? Well, I have faith in God, and I think there is a Divine Providence which will obviate this difficulty, and I don't think Providence has given it into our hands to execute His behests in this world. I think, when injustice is done, whether in Poland or elsewhere, the very process of injustice is calculated, if left to itself, to promote its own cure; because injustice produces weakness—injustice produces injury to the parties who commit it.'

Non-intervention was the right Christian policy. Let Britain concentrate upon purifying its outdated institutions at home. She could then exert more influence through domestic good example than would ever be attained through direct involvement. A reformed Britain would both benefit the British people and serve as 'the beacon of other nations'. So wrote Cobden in his first pamphlet, and he was still saying the same in his last public speech twenty-nine years later. 'If a man is best doing his duty at home in striving to extend the sphere of liberty —commercial, literary, political, religious, and in all other directions . . . he is working for the advancement of the principles of liberty all over the world.'

Cobden deliberately avoided advocating any formal international organisation to promote and preserve peace. At first sight this might seem surprising, but it was consistent with his free trade beliefs. Cobden was suspicious of all government, even world government. He was concerned for the freedom of each state to work out its own progress. An organisation like the United Nations or the League of Nations might wish to reduce this freedom. Individual and informal contacts, especially through free trade, would foster international peace and understanding much better than international diplomatising. 'Whatever may be the future state of the world, I am quite convinced that at present it would be to the last degree inexpedient to bring the representatives of the different nations together for the purpose of inducing them to *agree to anything*. They would be far more likely to sow the seeds of war than to plant the olive tree throughout Europe.' Cobden even opposed the establishment of a permanent international high court of arbitration. He was a strong advocate of arbitration, but he wanted arbitrators appointed for each occasion. 'There would be danger of intrigue and corruption if you had a permanent Court.'

The United States stood to Cobden and Bright as the outstanding example of a nation which had made rapid progress by following their principles of foreign policy. The Americans did not involve themselves with foreign states. They did not maintain large armies or navies. They were not burdened with an aristocracy. As a result, they were developing their economic potential at a remarkable rate, and threatened to surpass in real power Britain and all the other so-called 'Great' Powers of Europe. America was both an example to be admired and a rival to be feared. To match the Americans we would need not only to develop our strength through free trade at home, but also to conserve it by following a policy of non-intervention abroad, avoiding waste of wealth and manpower upon wars or preparation for wars. 'In that portentous truth, *the Americas are free,*' exclaimed Cobden in his second pamphlet, 'teeming as it does with future change, there is nothing that more nearly affects our destiny than the total revolution which it dictates to the statesmen of Great Britain in the commercial, colonial, and foreign policy of our Government.'

In a letter to Bright during the Crimean War Cobden conveniently restated the essence of his views upon foreign affairs. At this time the public mood was totally against them. Cobden mournfully forecast that if we continued to be dragged down by foreign entanglements the United States, Canada, and Australia would overtake us:

'The more I reflect on such matters the greater importance do I attach to that principle of competition which God has set up in this wicked world as the silent arbiter of our fate, rewarding the industrious, frugal, and honest, and punishing by the very process of such recompense the wasteful and the wicked. And this law operates in nations as well as individuals. The effect of it will be visible some day in the superior condition of those countries which have no faith in Eastern Questions, in the balance of power, and which content themselves with minding their own business and leaving the rest of the world *free* to do likewise, or to find out from their good example the evil effects of following an opposite course. But the danger is that *we* shall only find this out when it will be too late. In the meantime you and I may be stoned or burned in effigy for not prophesying smooth things.'

Five weeks after repeal of the Corn Laws Cobden had set off for the Continent. Nominally he went for recuperation, but from the start he was thinking in terms of a free trade propaganda tour. 'I am possessed with an idea, and can't help myself.' He described himself as 'the first ambassador from the people of this country to the nations of the Continent'. He felt confident that the case which he would present to the protectionist nations of Europe was even stronger than the one which had successfully overturned protection at home. From August 1846 to October 1847 he ranged through France and Spain, Italy and Germany, until finally he reached Russia. He met people of all ranks from rulers to peasants, talking to them with his customary enthusiasm and being everwhere welcomed as a great man. But he soon came to realise that he had started out too confident of the instant persuasiveness of his case. The Europeans were courteous but not convinced. Writing home to Bright in October 1846 and to Wilson six months later, Cobden began to warn them not to expect quick success for free trade principles overseas. How should it be otherwise, he concluded realistically, remembering the degree of ignorance shown 'even in the land of Adam Smith upon the question only a few years ago'? Nevertheless, Cobden was still confident for the long term. He was planning, he admitted, to make his son as fluent in French as in English, in the hope that the boy would live to see communication between European countries as free as it now was between the provinces of France.

Cobden was prepared to wait a long time for the Europeans to appreciate his message, but after 1846 he grew increasingly disappointed at the slowness of the British people, who had adopted free trade at home, to accept its corollaries in foreign policy. 'You ask me when *our* turn will come,' he answered Bright during the Crimean War. 'When common sense and honesty are in the ascendant, a day for me not very likely to be realised, as I am fifty, and not of a long-lived family. You may have a better chance, but don't be too sanguine.' As early as June 1847 Cobden was regretting that repeal of the Corn Laws had not been 'the prelude to a wiser foreign policy'. If only the English could understand how little their £200 m. National Debt, acquired through constant intervention in European wars, had improved the condition of the people of Europe, and how little those people felt grateful to us for our sacrifices. During his travels in Spain and Italy, countries for which much British blood had been spilt, Cobden commented that he had found no portrait of a British general or admiral in any private or public house, Yet under the influence of Lord Palmerston the British people seemed to be growing still more willing to involve themselves in Europe and elsewhere. Cobden warned Bright in 1847 to admit that public opinion supported Palmerston, and that therefore their task was the large one of transforming the public mind. 'You must not disguise from yourself that the evil has its roots in the pugnacious, energetic, self-sufficient, foreigner-despising and pitying character of that noble insular creature, John Bull.'

In this knowledge Cobden set out on his return home in 1847 to convert public opinion. He explained in his 1853 pamphlet that he did

not expect our aristocratic rulers to reduce expenditure upon armaments 'until impelled to it by public opinion. Nay, as in the case of
repeal of the Corn Law,—*no Minister can do it, except when armed by a
pressure from without.*' Free traders must therefore agitate 'in the manner
of the League, and preach common sense, justice, and truth, in the
streets and market places'. But whereas seven years of agitation proved
enough to precipitate repeal of the Corn Laws, seven years of foreign
policy agitation by Cobden and Bright was to find the British people
embarking enthusiastically upon the Crimean War. Triumph and
popularity for the League leaders in 1846 was to be followed by failure
and repudiation in 1854. Cobden admitted in that year how large
numbers of Radicals had become even more warlike than many
Tories. The old progressive cry, 'Peace, Retrenchment and Reform',
dating from the great days of the Reform Bill crisis, seemed to have
been totally forgotten. 'The Radicals have cut their throats before
Sebastapol.'[1]

#### 4. PEACE AND WAR

Cobden and Bright tried hard in the 1850s to gather support for all
three traditional Radical demands. 'I walk in the old ways', Bright
told his constituents in 1859. 'I am for "Peace, Retrenchment and
Reform", the watchword of the great Liberal party thirty years ago.
Whosoever may abandon the cause, I shall never pronounce another
shibboleth.' The novelty of the approach of Cobden and Bright lay
not in these objectives but in their use of the all-embracing free trade
formula to link them together. Retrenchment required peace, reform
required peace, retrenchment would make possible reform, each and
all were best attainable under free trade. After 1846 Cobden and Bright
campaigned for all three demands simultaneously, sometimes emphasising one more than another, but never losing sight of the overall
unity of their programme. In this section we will study their presentation of the 'Peace' call, and in the subsequent section their handling of
the call for 'Retrenchment and Reform'.

The campaign of Cobden and Bright after 1846 for a new attitude in
foreign affairs never became as systematic as their campaign against the
Corn Laws. More than once they sent out a call for money and tracts
and lecturers, but they found little response from the general public.
This was the result in part of the diffuseness of the free trade peace

message compared with the simple once-for-all negative demand for Corn Law repeal. Peace could never be secured and maintained through one dramatic measure of repeal legislation. It required many changes in public and diplomatic attitudes, in diplomatic practice, and in international law. The public mind likes simplicity, even over-simplicity. Cobden himself admitted in 1853 that the peace movement had 'not the same clear and definite principle on which to take our stand that we had in the League organisation'. Significantly, the peace views of Cobden and Bright were quickly distorted in the public mind into the simple cry of 'peace at any price', a phrase which first became current at this time. Such distortion could be easily understood; their real views could not.

Cobden and Bright were not in fact pacifists, although they often worked with pacifists. In the 1830s there is some evidence that Cobden may have been a complete non-resister, but by the '50s he and Bright often explained their readiness to accept the use of force for self-defence. 'I am no Quaker in the physical force non-resisting sense', stated Cobden explicitly in 1853. If the British Isles were invaded, he was ready to fight; but we should not meddle and fight overseas. In 1848 when the French Revolution brought alarmist fears of another general European war such as had stemmed from the first French Revolution, Cobden came forward with the message 'neutrality and isolation unless attacked'. While demanding large reductions in naval and military expenditure incurred only for the sake of overseas inter-vention, Cobden accepted the need for a small standing army at home as a nucleus 'around which the people might rally to defend their country'. Bright's attitude was the same as Cobden's. He was not a total pacifist, unlike many Quakers, as his staunch support for the North was to show during the American Civil War. 'I have never advocated the extreme peace principle, the non-resistance principle, in public or in private.' So Bright told Sturge, the Quaker pacifist, some two years after his famous series of orations against the Crimean War. 'I opposed the late war as contrary to the national interests, and the principles professed and avowed by the nation, and on no other ground. It was because my arguments could not be met that I was charged with being for "peace at any price", and by this our opposition to the war was much damaged.'[1]

In the period between his return from Europe in 1847 and the outbreak of the Crimean War Cobden played a leading part in the work of the Peace Society. This body (its full title was the Society for the Promotion of Permanent and Universal Peace) had been formed as early as 1816, mainly by Quakers; but it did not attract much interest until the late '40s. In 1849 Cobden was one of its representatives at an international peace congress in Paris. This congress affirmed the duty of all Governments to submit mutual differences to arbitration; it emphasised the need for disarmament, condemned all loans and taxes to finance aggressive wars, urged all friends of peace to campaign for a conference to revise international law and to institute a tribunal for the settlement of disputes between states, and called upon the press and the clergy to speak out strongly in support of world peace.

In June 1849 Cobden proposed in the House of Commons a resolution suggesting the negotiation of arbitration treaties with foreign states for the peaceful settlement of differences. Because he was anxious to counter the 'peace at any price' slur, Cobden avoided taking any high ground in his speech, talking simply of the material benefits of peace. Despite this restraint, Palmerston successfully carried the previous question against him by a majority of nearly a hundred. Europe was at this date in turmoil, and Cobden had chosen a bad time for trying to persuade Members of Parliament that wars could be things of the past.

Cobden none the less persisted with his efforts, in and out of Parliament. In June 1850 he spoke alongside Peel, Gladstone and Disraeli against Palmerston in the famous Don Pacifico debate. On Palmerston's initiative a British fleet had called at Athens to enforce the dubious claims for compensation of a Portuguese Jew who, as a former resident of Gibraltar, was entitled to British citizenship. Greek ships were seized and a general blockade proclaimed, eventually forcing the Greek Government to agree to our demands. Cobden wrote to Bright that this was the very type of dispute which, instead of turning into an international incident, could have been quietly settled by arbitration. They decided to vote against Palmerston, even though this might bring down the Liberal Government of which he was a member. Many other Radicals, by contrast, determined to support the Foreign Secretary. Bright noted in his diary how some of them 'at first looked at the dirty work they are to do with wry faces, but are gradually coming round to a stout defence of what they know is wrong but have not the courage to resist'. Cobden asked these Radicals in his speech whether they could truly say that Palmerston had followed the policy which Grey had laid down in 1830. Grey had then deplored the burden of the £800 m. National Debt incurred through foreign wars, and had pledged himself 'that peace, non-intervention, and retrenchment should be the watchwords of the Whig party'. But in answer to his critics Palmerston revived the cry, 'Civis Romanus sum', meaning thereby that any British subject had the same unqualified right to protection throughout the world as Roman citizens had enjoyed within the Roman Empire. And this new Palmerstonian cry overshadowed the old slogan of 'Peace, Retrenchment and Reform' for the rest of the decade. The Don Pacifico vote marked the beginning of that cleavage between Cobden and Bright on the one hand and many Radicals, in and out of Parliament, on the other, which was to become complete with the outbreak of the Crimean War in 1854. In a letter written after that war Cobden again referred to Grey's policy, regretting that it was now 'useless to utter their old shibboleth'.

Up to 1854, however, Cobden and Bright still continued to hope that they might successfully counter the Palmerstonian trend. In 1851 came the Great Exhibition, for which Cobden was one of the Royal Commissioners. The exhibition showed what the world could produce through peaceful enterprise, but Cobden was not deluded into thinking that such a display could itself do much to ensure continuing peace. Peace would have to be promoted and protected through fundamental changes in the principles and conduct of foreign affairs. The year 1853 saw the final efforts of Cobden and Bright to attract support for their peace views. First, they opposed a French invasion scare; then later in the year they denounced the drift towards the Crimean War. Cobden still put his faith in the dissemination of sound information and argument. To this end in January 1853 he published his pamphlet *1793 and 1853*, dismissing the French danger. In June he attended another international peace congress, held on this occasion in Manchester. Cobden called upon the Mancunians to give a fresh lead to the world in promoting the principles of free trade, this time in their diplomatic application. He asked for money to support an army of lecturers and a deluge of tracts to counteract 'the poison that was being infused into the minds of the people'.

Yet in the next year the people of Manchester and of England entered willingly, even jubilantly, into the Crimean War. Cobden and Bright were shown to have failed completely in educating public opinion in the peace policy of free trade. In September 1856, after the end of the war, Cobden admitted this to George Wilson of Manchester. Many former Leaguers, like Baines, editor of the *Leeds Mercury*, the most influential newspaper in Cobden's West Riding constituency, had supported the war. 'I will never again be a party', wrote Cobden, 'to the old movement, carried on in such a way as to allow everybody, *Baines* included, to join in the "hallelujahs" for *peace*, and nine-tenths of them to run off and cheer any Minister who will offer to make war with any people on earth.' Cobden was particularly disappointed at the attitude of Manchester. Up to 1853 he had still been hopeful that it might again lead the country. But when in November 1856 Sturge wanted to restart the peace movement Cobden was both doubtful about the wisdom of this and certain that Manchester was not the place to begin it. 'Manchester has never been more than a ghost of its former self in the agitations that have been attempted since the League shut up shop.' People in Lancashire were growing prosperous and conservative.' London in my opinion would be more likely to turn up new blood.'[2]

In 1849 first the Austrian and then the Russian Governments had floated loans on the London market. They had just ferociously put down the Hungarian revolution, led by Kossuth, and Cobden strongly opposed what he saw as an attempt to use British money to finance oppression. Cobden's sympathy for Kossuth even drew him into regret that on this occasion we had not tried to use diplomatic means to check Russian intervention in Hungary. Similar sympathy with European nationalism was soon to lead many Radicals into virtual repudiation of Cobden's doctrine of non-intervention. When Kossuth visited England in 1851 Cobden and Bright welcomed him warmly, but (as Bright warned Cobden) many other Radicals were excited beyond this into thoughts of '*fighting* for Hungary'. Bright described a lively discussion in the League rooms in Manchester for and against a punitive war with Russia. Bright deplored this desire 'to become knight-errants in the cause of freedom to other nations'. Although tempted into advocacy of diplomatic support for Kossuth, Cobden and Bright never wavered in their belief that we should not become militarily involved in support of national movements, in Hungary or elsewhere. Equally, they opposed financial involvement in support of Governments which oppressed nationalities. Britain should remain detached. Cobden argued that the whole European system of large armaments was based upon borrowed money, 'and thereby there are concentrated into one generation those evils of war, which would not have been suffered except successive generations were called upon to pay for them'.[3]

The most expensive war of Cobden's adult lifetime was the Crimean War of 1854–6. It cost France and Russia over a hundred thousand men, Turkey about thirty thousand, and Britain some twenty-three thousand. It also cost Britain £50 m. Yet the British public, stirred up by the press, entered the war enthusiastically in the belief that it was necessary, firstly, to punish Russia for her oppression of nationalities like the Hungarians and Poles, and, secondly, to prevent Russia from dismembering the Turkish Empire and thereby dominating the eastern Mediterranean to the injury of British trade and also of the route to India. Russia's ambition was in fact much less fervent than the British people imagined. It was the Turks, supposedly the injured party, who finally precipitated the conflict. Their action was unexpected, for a compromise settlement of the Russian claim to rights of protection over all Greek Orthodox Christians within the Turkish Empire had seemed near. The Turks declared war in October 1853, but at first the British public did not demand outright hostilities in support. Then in December came news of the total defeat of the Turkish fleet at Sinope, which was regarded quite wrongly in Britain as a treacherous 'massacre'. Britain and France finally declared war in March 1854. Prince Albert described what passed for justification in the mind of the British public. 'The Emperor of Russia is a tyrant, and the enemy of all liberty on the Continent, the oppressor of Poland. He wanted to coerce the poor Turk. The Turk is a fine fellow; he has braved the rascal; let us rush to his assistance.'

Kossuth now again toured Britain encouraging his audiences in the belief that the Crimean War could secure independence for Hungary and Poland. Cobden and Bright knew that this would not be possible, that the British and French armies in the Crimea could inflict no mortal injury upon Russian despotism, safe in its vast land mass. At the end of 1854 Cobden foretold that history would describe the expedition to the Crimea 'as almost the wildest and most irrational undertaking in our annals'. He and Bright were especially irritated to think that the enthusiasm for the war, and the wealth behind it, had come from prosperity brought by free trade. He reminded J. B. Smith of the jingle,

> 'Peace makes riches flow
> Riches make pride to grow,
>      Pride brings war:
> War brings poverty,
> Poverty brings peace:
>
> Peace makes riches flow, etc., etc.

And so we go round in the circle of blind instincts.' And so we would continue to go until the people understood the message of free trade in relation to foreign affairs.

At first Cobden hoped to continue to teach this message even during the war. He told Bright that he was willing to incur any obloquy in telling the people bluntly of their blame in pressing an uncertain Government into war. 'It is better to face any neglect or hostility than to allow them to persuade themselves that anybody but themselves are responsible for the war.' To this end in January 1855 Cobden went to Leeds to face his West Riding constituents. He shared the platform with Edward Baines. Baines told the audience that the conflict had been forced upon us by Russian aggression against Turkey. Cobden demurred, emphasising the monstrosity of a war in which we had not only a despot for an enemy (Russia) but also a despot for an ally (France) and a despot for a client (Turkey). Notwithstanding this truth, resolutions in favour of the war were carried against Cobden, and he soon came to the conclusion that it was pointless trying to spread the free trade message until the war fever had passed. A year later he told J. B. Smith that he had no plans to visit the North of England again, because it gave him pain to see even old Leaguers whom he respected 'suffering under the war madness, for it is madness'.

As early as 1835 Cobden had foreseen the danger of war with Russia. Already Russophobia was growing strong in Britain, fanned most actively by David Urquhart, whose suspicions amounted to monomania, but who exerted considerable influence upon British opinion from the '30s to the '50s. Cobden's 1835 pamphlet began by criticising a pamphlet of Urquhart's. Russia rather than France, wrote Cobden, was now 'the chimera that haunts us in our apprehension for the safety of Europe; whilst Turkey for the first time appears to claim our sympathy and protection against the encroachments of her neighbours'. Hostility towards Russia was so strong that 'with but few additional provocatives administered to it by a judicious Minister through the public prints, a conflict with that Christian Power in defence of a Mahommedan people more than a thousand miles distant from our shores might be made palatable, nay popular, with the British nation.'

This passage made clear Cobden's dislike of the Turks. Without wishing in any way to encourage Russian aggression, he was prepared to accept Russian occupation of Constantinople rather than to fight for the maintenance of the corrupt and decaying Turkish Empire. 'To assert that *we*, a commercial and manufacturing people, have an interest in retaining the fairest regions of Europe in barbarism and ignorance—that *we* are benefited because poverty, slavery, polygamy, and the plague abound in Turkey—is a fallacy too gross even for refutation.' His own observation during his Mediterranean tour of 1836–7 confirmed Cobden in this view of Turkish decadence, which he retained throughout life. He reminded the House of Commons during the Crimean War that 'the whole gist of the Eastern Question lies in the difficulty arising from the prostrate condition of this race'. Britain had only become involved because of the anarchy and barbarism that reigned in Turkey. Yet if Turkey were fit to survive, argued Cobden, she would do so without our help.

Cobden gave up speaking against the Crimean War in the country, but he was not entirely silent in the Commons. In June 1855 he delivered a speech in his best style, putting his case moderately yet trenchantly, and holding the attention of the House despite its opposition to him. He began by emphasising the practical nature of his arguments, again trying to remove the impression that he was an unrealistic pacifist. 'I am prepared to assume that wars may be inevitable and necessary, although I do not admit that all wars are so.' But this war was foolish for entirely practical reasons. The British public had entered upon it in arrogance and ignorance. 'I rest my case entirely upon your infatuation in invading Russia with a land force.' This invasion was undertaken 'in blind obedience to a cry out of doors, against and over which the statesmen of this country ought to have exercised a counteracting influence and control'. Cobden ended by yet again explaining that he opposed the war not on abstract pacifist grounds but on the ground that it was against British interests.

'If the Russians were besieging Portsmouth, I should not talk about what was to be done; and if I could not work in the field, I would do so in the hospital. I should not then ask for any one to allay the excitement of the people; but I now repeat—and I have repeated it again and again—you have undertaken a war with an empire of sixty million people, three thousand miles away, and the people of this country, and those who guide them, do not fully appreciate the importance, the magnitude, and the danger of this undertaking.'

Six months later, when peace was at last becoming a possibility, Cobden published in his pamphlet *What Next—and Next?*, a five-point policy for ending the war:

(1) British soldiers to be withdrawn from Russia, 'the invasion of which was a heedless blunder, both in a political and strategical point of view'.

(2) Russia to be offered terms consistent with her honour as a Great Power.

(3) Prussia and Austria to be encouraged to keep watch on Russia's western frontier as a shield against Russian aggression.

(4) The states of Europe to be invited to form a defensive alliance against Russia. If they refused to join such an alliance, this would show that our fears of Russian hegemony in Europe were exaggerated, since the Europeans themselves did not share them. We could then 'forgo the quixotic mission of fighting for the liberties of Europe', and concentrate upon reform at home.

(5) No more lives or money to be wasted in the attempt to extract worthless pledges from the Russians to give up their Black Sea fleet. Instead, the powers of Europe should agree to a general reduction of naval armaments, not least because the present great size of the British and French navies might provoke the United States, with its huge economic potential, to outbuild all other nations. If such a general reduction of naval armaments could be achieved some good would have come out of the evil of the Crimean War.[4]

Up to the time of the Crimean War Bright had been generally overshadowed by Cobden. Now, through his famous speeches against the war, he came into equal prominence with his friend, although in private always remaining Cobden's pupil. Bright's campaign against the Crimean War was not conducted in the elaborate manner of the anti-Corn Law agitation. In the face of widespread public hostility a campaign of this type could not have been mounted. Bright formed no organisation, but depended solely upon speeches in and out of Parliament and upon public letters, both his speeches and his letters receiving widespread press publicity. His speeches were not numerous, but their relative fewness was probably an advantage, for if he had spoken more often he might have been less fully reported and less noticed.

The day after the Turkish declaration of war in October 1853 Bright replied by letter to an invitation to a Manchester meeting in support of Turkey. The division between Bright and a majority of the Manchester electorate was becoming plain, but Bright's language was even plainer. 'War will not save Turkey if peace cannot save her; but war will brutalise our people, increase our taxes, destroy our industry, postpone the promised Parliamentary reform.' A week later he developed this theme at an international peace congress at Edinburgh. He pointed out that £11 m. had been spent in the past year upon war preparations, while £28 m. had been paid in interest upon the National Debt created by former wars. These sums amounted together to more than half the annual value of British exports. Such was the enormous cost of war. An expensive new war to preserve the decrepit Turkish Empire would be an especial crime. 'If you want war, let it be for something that has at least the feature of grandeur.' As for the supposed Russian threat to India, Bright contended that in the light of past history we were more likely to attack Russia from India than the Russians to attack us there, for our Asian policy had been much more aggrandising than Russia's. Even though he was addressing a peace congress most of Bright's speech was devoted to such practical points. Like Cobden, he usually avoided a high moral line in explaining the international peace aspect of free trade.

In January 1854 at a meeting of Liberals in Manchester Bright again made clear his readiness to incur unpopularity rather than support a war against Russia. On March 13 in the House of Commons he denounced the arrogance and levity of speeches about the war delivered at a banquet by Admiral Sir Charles Napier, British naval commander in the Baltic, and Sir James Graham, the First Lord of the Admiralty. Palmerston himself was in the chair at this gathering. War, Bright reminded the Commons, was not a fit subject for arrogance or levity. Yet when Palmerston rose to answer Bright's criticisms he began in terms which seemed intended to continue the irresponsible mood: 'If the hon. and *reverend* gentleman. . . .' At this, Cobden sprang to the defence of his friend, attacking Palmerston in restrained but effective terms for using an inappropriate epithet in a 'flippant' manner. Palmerston answered with more irritation than effect that he would not quarrel about words, telling Bright that he treated his opinion as fit only for contempt.

War came in March, and on the last day of the month Bright made the first of his four famous Commons speeches in opposition to British involvement. He began by explaining that he opposed the war on practical grounds, not because he was for 'peace at any price'. 'I shall maintain that when we are deliberating on the question of war, and endeavouring to prove its justice and necessity, it becomes us to show that the interests of the country are clearly involved; that the objects for which the war is undertaken are probable, or, at least, possible of attainment; and, further, that the end proposed to be accomplished is worth the cost and the sacrifices which we are about to incur.' To underline the practical nature of his approach, Bright then launched into an analysis of the recent foreign policy Blue Books. He showed how the Government had allowed the Turks to drag us into the war, although in his anxiety to prove the folly of our policy he inclined to exaggerate the peaceful tendency of Russian policy. As A. J. P. Taylor has pointed out, this bias was an almost inevitable effect of the British Parliamentary party system. A critic may achieve some effect in the Commons by attacking the British Government, whereas he will achieve little by attacking foreign Governments.

But Bright spent only part of his speech analysing the Blue Books. This was simply a *tour de force*, intended to show that he could meet Ministers on their own ground. In fact, he and Cobden did not accept that ground. They rejected the basic assumptions of traditional British diplomacy, and wanted to substitute for them the principles of free trade. We have seen how Cobden remarked in 1856 that he had given

Bright 'budgets of facts and arguments' for his war speeches. Thus Bright's remarks about the balance of power in relation to the United States were probably inspired by Cobden.

'There is, indeed, a question of a "balance of power" which this country might regard, if our statesmen had a little less of those narrow views which they sometimes arrogantly impute to me and to those who think with me. If they could get beyond those old notions which belong to the traditions of Europe, and cast their eyes as far westward as they are now looking eastward, they might there see a power growing up in its gigantic proportions, which will teach us before very long where the true "balance of power" is to be found.'

Bright asked members if they had read the Reports of our Commissioners to the New York Exhibition, which had revealed the great material progress being made by the United States in manufactures, trade and transport. 'There has been nothing like it under the sun. The United States may profit to a large extent by the calamities which will befall us; whilst we, under the miserable and lunatic idea that we are about to set the worn-out Turkish Empire on its legs, and permanently to sustain it against the aggressions of Russia, are entangled in a war.' Here were characteristic Cobden sentiments presented in characteristic Bright language. In dealing with the economic damage done by the war Bright probably needed little prompting from his friend. He told the Commons that Lancashire's Russian trade was lost, its Levant trade almost gone, and its German trade much damaged. 'All property in trade is diminishing in value, whilst its burdens are increasing.' Bright then moved into his peroration.

'I believe, if this country, seventy years ago, had adopted the principle of non-intervention in every case where her interests were not directly and obviously assailed, that she would have been saved from much of the pauperism and brutal crimes by which our Government and people have alike been disgraced. This country might have been a garden, every dwelling might have been of marble, and every person who treads its soil might have been sufficiently educated. We might have had neither Trafalgar nor Waterloo; but we should have set the high example of a Christian nation, free in its institutions and just in its conduct towards all foreign states, and resting its policy on the unchangeable foundation of Christian morality.'

Bright's speech was immediately repudiated in his constituency by the *Manchester Guardian*. The *Guardian* claimed that Bright reduced every question to a matter of pounds, shillings and pence, whereas Manchester itself was 'guided by the dictates of justice and patriotism'. This hostility to Bright was shared by a majority of the Manchester electors; but the Bright minority there was still well organised by George Wilson, and a fortnight later Bright sent a letter to a public meeting which his Manchester supporters had called against the war. The time would come, wrote Bright, when history would record how much was wasted upon an object in which we had no real interest and in which we could not succeed.

In November 1854 Bright issued a public letter that attracted widespread national and international attention. It was addressed to Absalom Watkin, one of his Manchester constituents, a veteran middle-class reformer, who had written to Bright arguing that the Crimean War could be justified by reference to the law of nations, notably as laid down by Vattel, the eighteenth-century jurist. Bright began by repudiating the authority of Vattel. He noted how there had even been writers on international law who had attempted to show that private assassination and poisoning of wells was justified. Bright then divided the question of the Crimean War into two parts. Firstly, was it necessary for us to interfere in a dispute between Russia and Turkey? And secondly, having decided to interfere, why was not the whole issue terminated when Russia accepted the Vienna Note? Bright concentrated upon this second question. After detailed references to the Blue Books, he concluded that the Turks had rejected the note even though it had been drawn up by their own negotiators and accepted by the Russians. 'The Turks having rejected it, our Government turned round, and declared the Vienna Note, their own note, entirely inadmissible, and defended the conduct of the Turks in having rejected it.' The Turks declared war against the advice of the English and French Governments, 'but the moment war was declared by Turkey our Government openly applauded it'. Bright concluded by restating the principle of non-intervention.

'My doctrine would have been non-intervention in this case. The

danger of the Russian power was a phantom; the necessity of permanently upholding the Mahometan rule in Europe is an absurdity.
Our love for civilisation, when we subject the Greeks and Christians
to the Turks, is a sham; and our sacrifices for freedom, when working
out the behests of the Emperor of the French and asking Austria to
help us, is a pitiful imposture.'

On December 17, 1854 Bright attended a noisy public meeting in
Manchester Town Hall, called to discuss the views which he had put
forward in his letter to Watkin. A resolution was presented saying that
Bright's opinions were not those of Manchester. Bright attempted to
speak, but he could not be heard against a background of cheers and
groans. Watkin claimed in his diary that the Bright party had mustered
'all the blackguards whom they have in their pay', although he admitted disingenuously that on his own side 'Dr. Hudson had intimated
to the Protestant Association that their presence was desirable'. In
his short, unheard speech Bright reiterated that he did not intend to
change his views simply because these did not please many of his constituents. Five times the mayor called for a show of hands for and
against the motion. Finally he decided, amidst uproar, that the numbers
were so even that he could not make a decision.

On December 22, 1854 came the second of Bright's four major anti-
war speeches in the House of Commons. This was delivered in the same
debate as a speech by Cobden, and we find the pair working together
as in the days of their speaking tours for the Anti-Corn Law League.
Cobden's speech had provided plain, anti-war argument; Bright
followed with rhetoric. One passage brought the House to a hush,
causing Ministers on the Treasury bench evident embarrassment.
Bright avowedly built this passage upon what Cobden had already
said less emotionally about the wretched state of the British army in the
Crimea. Keeping characteristically close to facts, Cobden had quoted
from a letter sent to him from the front. Here was how Bright took up
the theme:

'My hon. friend, the Member for the West Riding, in what he said
about the condition of the English army in the Crimea, I believe
expressed only that which all in this House feel, and which, I trust,
every person in this country capable of thinking feels. When I look
at the Gentlemen on that bench, and consider all their policy has

brought about within the past twelve months, I scarcely dare trust myself to speak of them, either in or out of their presence. We all know what we have lost in this House. Here, sitting near me, very often sat the Member for Frome (Colonel Boyle). I met him a short time before he went out, at Mr. Westerton's, the bookseller, near Hyde Park Corner. I asked him whether he was going out? He answered, he was afraid he was; not afraid in the sense of personal fear—he knew not that; but he said, with a look and a tone I shall never forget, "It is no light matter for a man who has a wife and five little children." The stormy Euxine is his grave; his wife a widow, his children fatherless.'

In January 1855 both Cobden and Bright attended a Liberal soirée in Manchester where Bright again spoke against the war. In February he described its serious economic effects to the Manchester Chamber of Commerce, emphasising the spread of unemployment and poverty. Then on February 23 he delivered the third of his major Commons orations. His first two anti-war speeches had been denunciatory; now Bright changed to conciliation, even towards Palmerston. He declared that, just as Ministers had possessed the power to make war, so they held the power to make peace, especially now that the Aberdeen Government which entered the war had been displaced by a new Palmerston Administration. Bright's speech did not succeed in persuading Palmerston to consider peace, for the Premier was determined to await the fall of Sebastapol, but this oration became the most famous of all Bright's utterances. It was the more effective for being quite short, building up steadily to its climax.

'I don't suppose that your troops are to be beaten in actual conflict with the foe, or that they will be driven into the sea; but I am certain that many homes in England in which there now exists a fond hope that the distant one may return—many such homes may be rendered desolate when the next mail shall arrive. The Angel of Death has been abroad throughout the land; you may almost hear the beating of his wings. There is no one, as when the first-born were slain of old, to sprinkle with blood the lintel and the two side-posts of our doors, that he may spare and pass on; he takes his victims from the castle of the noble, the mansions of the wealthy, and the cottage of the poor and the lowly, and it is on behalf of all these classes that I make this solemn appeal.'

This 'Angel of Death' speech attracted much praise, especially in Parliament where war fever was not so virulent as in the country.

On March 6, 1855 Bright once more spoke against the war at Manchester Liberal headquarters, and a month later at Manchester Town Hall. On June 7 came the last of his four major House of Commons orations. This was a long speech, dealing first with the diplomatic aspects of the war after the failure of peace negotiations at Vienna, and then with its economic cost. Bright was often charged with viewing the whole war in cash terms, as if money were the sole standard. *Punch*, for example, a fierce critic of Bright throughout the mid-Victorian years, ascribed to him, under the heading 'Manchester Peace-Goods', the motto: 'There is but one Manchester, and the whole world is its profit.' This interpretation of Bright's attitude was most unfair, as can be seen from a passage in his June 7 speech. Bright compared the good effects upon the physical and moral condition of the people of the gradual reduction of taxation since 1842 with the likely damaging effects of the reimposition of taxation to support the war. 'Hon. Members may think this is nothing. They say it is a "low" view of the case. But, these things are the foundation of your national greatness and of your national duration; and you may be following visionary phantoms in all parts of the world while your own country is becoming rotten within.' Discontent would grow as trade continued to suffer from the war, and presently Ministers would find themselves 'pointed to as the men who ought to have taught the nation better'. Bright appealed to the House to revolt against Palmerston and Russell and against the bellicose press which supported them because war increased newspaper sales. He described Palmerston as 'a man who has experience, but who with experience has not gained wisdom—as a man who has age, but who, with age, has not the gravity of age, and who, now occupying the highest seat of power, has—and I say it with pain—not appeared influenced by a due sense of the responsibility that belongs to that elevated position.' Then came Bright's peroration.

'The House must know that the people are misled and bewildered, and that if every man in this House, who doubts the policy that is being pursued, would boldly say so in this House and out of it, it would not be in the power of the press to mislead the people as it has done for the last twelve months. If they are thus misled and bewildered, is it not the duty of this House to speak with the voice of authority in this hour of peril? We are the depositories of the power and the guardians of the interests of a great nation and an ancient monarchy. Why should we not fully measure our responsibility? Why should we not disregard the small-minded ambition that struggles for place? and why should we not, by a faithful, just, and earnest policy, restore, as I believe we may, tranquillity to Europe and prosperity to the country so dear to us?'

Bright thus concluded his series of major orations against the Crimean War. In September he spoke at Hulme, and in October at Rochdale. Finally, at Manchester on January 28, 1856 he made his last speech before his breakdown, when he was already obviously unwell. He described the balance of power as 'precisely one of those things that lasts forever—that is, until you grow wiser, and find that there is nothing whatever in it—like hunting for the philosopher's stone, or perpetual motion'.⁵

Peace finally came in March 1856. It was made when Ministers decided upon it, not because of pressure from Cobden and Bright. Bright's speeches did not end the war a single day sooner than it would have ended if he had never delivered them. Cobden and Bright could only find satisfaction that they had acted rightly. 'As for you and me', Bright told Cobden in January 1855, 'we never occupied a position of which we might be more satisfied.' They had sacrificed all their former popularity to oppose an unnecessary war. In the Commons after Bright's death in 1889 Gladstone was to remember the nobility of the <  pair at this time. Their sacrifice of popularity was the more striking because they were politicians whose hopes of influence wholly depended upon the backing of popular opinion.⁶

Unfortunately, Bright could never really rest satisfied with his isolated position. He clutched at every hint that his speeches were producing, not merely admiration, but also conversion. He delightedly retailed to correspondents scraps of praise from various clergymen. 'All this is pleasant', he told Sturge in December 1854, 'as showing there is some response, and bye and bye there may be some reaction.' But about this very time Bright was being burned in effigy by the mob in his Manchester constituency. The effigy, wearing a Quaker hat with a twelve-inch brim and bearing a placard 'Bright, the Friend of Nicholas', was paraded through the town before being lit. The placard carried the doggerel,

> To brighten up the Quaker's fame,
> We'll put his body to the flame,
> And shout in mighty England's name
> Send him to old Nicholas

Everywhere Cobden and Bright were regarded at least as 'peace at any price' men (hence the heavy emphasis upon Bright's Quakerism), at worst as traitors. Feeling was as strong in the drawing rooms as in the streets. Even Tennyson, the Poet Laureate, joined in the prevailing attacks in his poem *Maud*. In the days of the Anti-Corn Law League Tennyson had entertained hopes of universal peace:

> Till the war-drums throbb'd no longer, and the
>   battle-flags were furl'd
> In the Parliament of man, the Federation of the world.

Now he accepted that this had been the false teaching of a commercial pacifist:

> This broad-brim'd hawker of holy things,
> Whose ear is stuff'd with his cotton, and rings
> Even in dreams to the chink of his pence.

In the face of hostility like this Bright was forced to admit by the summer of 1855 that his oratory had achieved nothing in immediate terms. After his last major anti-war oration in June he complained frustratedly to Wilson that there still seemed not the smallest hope of peace. 'My speech pleased my friends here, but the best arguments seem lost under the pressure of events and passion.' In September he asked Cobden despairingly 'can men be very useful without popularity, and is popularity compatible with doing right?' Cobden had soon realised that speeches, however powerful, could not overcome popular passion. Yet Bright was right to risk his health in strikingly publicising the free trade peace message at this time, for his speeches were to achieve influence in the future even if not in the present. Cobden was equally right in saving his strength to continue the struggle after the return of peace. Bright was then away ill, and Cobden carried the burden alone.7

By February 1857 the mood in Parliament had changed, albeit uncertainly, in favour of restraint in the conduct of foreign affairs, and Cobden was able to secure the defeat of Palmerston's Government. In October 1856 the Chinese authorities at Canton had boarded the *Arrow*, a British-registered lorcha from Hongkong, claiming that the crew included a notorious pirate and that the vessel was probably a pirate ship. This may have been the case, but the British Consul felt bound to demand the return of the crew and an apology. When an apology was refused a British naval squadron bombarded the Chinese forts in the Canton river. All this was in the Palmerston manner, although Palmerston could not be held directly responsible for the action. Chief responsibility lay with Sir John Bowring, Governor of Hongkong, who, curiously enough, has already been noticed as one of the inspirers of the Anti-Corn Law League and a staunch free trader. But this did not prevent Cobden from leading an attack upon both Bowring and Palmerston for supporting violence in the Far East. Even in purely material terms, argued Cobden, such a policy was bad because it was likely in the long run to damage our trade. ' "*Civis Romanus sum*" is not a very attractive motto to put over the door of our counting-houses abroad.' In any case, the Chinese deserved respect and fair dealing. Cobden's characteristically temperate and practical speech made a great impression upon the Commons, and Gladstone believed that if a vote had been taken at once Palmerston would have been defeated so overwhelmingly that he would have been forced to surrender office. But there was a delay of five days, and the eventual majority of fourteen against Palmerston was small enough to give him grounds for appealing to the country. A jingoistic General Election therefore took place, conducted round the cry 'For or Against Palmerston'.

The British electorate proved to be still strongly in Palmerston's favour. Bright and Milner Gibson were both defeated at Manchester, and Cobden lost at Huddersfield. Cobden's Huddersfield candidature had been only hurriedly arranged, and his defeat there was much less dramatic than Bright's at Manchester. This was the main event of the whole election. It was not, however, entirely the outcome of the

*Arrow* affair. Bright's defeat can be clearly linked with his first election for Manchester in 1847. We have described the strong opposition to Bright at that time from Manchester Whigs and Conservatives. Bright had overcome this, but Cobden had shrewdly forecast that Bright's occupancy would make the seat less secure for the Radicals in the long term. This danger had been glossed over at the 1852 General Election, which had fought under the threat of a return to protection under a Conservative Government; but soon afterwards Bright's opposition to the Crimean War had separated him markedly from a majority of the Manchester electors.

Bright was abroad throughout the 1857 contest, and Cobden campaigned for him in Manchester as well as for himself in Huddersfield, before finally collapsing from exhaustion. On March 18 he spoke at the Manchester Free Trade Hall, justifying the votes of Milner Gibson and himself (and the similar vote which Bright would have given) on the *Arrow* affair. Then in an emotional passage he described his friendship with Bright.

'I have lived with Mr. Bright in the most transparent intimacy of mind that two human beings ever enjoyed together. I don't believe there is a view, I don't believe there is a thought, I don't believe there is one aspiration in the minds of either of us that the other is not acquainted with. I don't know that there is anything that I have sought to do which Mr. Bright would not do in my place, or anything that he aims at which I would not accomplish if I had the power. Knowing him, then, I stand here, in all humility, as his representative; for what I have long cherished in my friend Mr Bright is this, that I have seen in him an ability and eloquence to which I have had no pretensions, because I am not gifted with the natural eloquence with which he is endowed; and that I have had the fond consolation of hoping that Mr. Bright, being seven or eight years younger than myself, will be advocating principles—and advocating them successfully—when I shall no longer be on the scene of duty. With these feelings I naturally take the deepest interest in the decision of this election.'

Cobden went on to express disgust at the attacks being made upon Bright while he was too ill to reply. 'Whilst this man is not able to use those great intellectual gifts with which God has gifted him—whilst their full activity is suspended for the day—the vermin of your Manchester press, the ghouls of the *Guardian*, are preying upon this splendid being, and trying to make a martyr of him in the midst of his sufferings.' The character of Bright would survive such attacks, but the character of Manchester would suffer if he were rejected.

The *Manchester Guardian*, for its part, defined the purpose of the election as being to destroy the 'mischievous notion that the honour and safety of England are less dear to a large and important commercial community than the profit of their industry'. The *Guardian* party had wanted Lord Lincoln as a candidate instead of Bright in 1847. Now candidates were put forward in opposition both to Bright and to Milner Gibson. Efforts were made to secure a nationally-known politician, such as Robert Lowe, but when these failed the *Guardian* group chose two local businessmen, Sir John Potter and J. A. Turner, both well known in Manchester commercial circles, Potter a former Mayor. Accounts of atrocities said to have been committed by the Chinese reinforced anti-Bright feeling in Manchester. When the result was declared he was bottom of the poll: Potter 8,368 votes, Turner 7,854 (both elected), Gibson 5,588, Bright 5,454 (both defeated). Cobden was likewise emphatically rejected at Huddersfield (823 votes to 590), and Miall and Fox, two other once popular Leaguers, lost their seats at Rochdale and Oldham.

The defeat of Bright gave Cobden much more pain than his own rejection. He deplored such 'atrocious treatment'. Prosperity based upon free trade, which had doubled cotton exports in twelve years, had converted the Manchester voters 'into little better than Tories, and now the base snobs kick away the ladder'. 'We used to boast that our big loaf had checked Chartism, but it has done more—it has in many cases converted Whigs into Tories, and turned Radicals into Whigs, nay it has even lulled many Dissenters into an oblivion of their principles.' To dismiss such a man as Bright, concluded Cobden, while broken in health in the service of the Manchester electorate, with less ceremony than would be used in getting rid of a worn-out horse, was 'the worst specimen of political ingratitude I ever knew'.

Bright in Italy took the not unexpected news of his defeat calmly. He told Cobden that he would not despair of a revolution of opinion upon foreign affairs within a few years. 'During the comparatively

> short period since we entered public life, see what we have done. Through our labour mainly, the whole creed of millions of people, and of the statesmen of our day, has been totally changed on all questions which affect commerce and customs duties and taxation. They now agree to repudiate as folly what twenty years ago, they accepted as wisdom.' Bright ended with the lighthearted comment that they had taught the truth in their 'School', but for the time being the discipline had proved a little too severe for the scholars.

Cobden and Bright had been sharply attacked in the press during the election, but afterwards the newspapers were rather abashed at the effect which their attacks had helped to create. There was a general consensus of view that the pair would, and should, soon return to Parliament. The *Manchester Guardian*, which on polling day had urged the voters to cleanse the name of Manchester from connection with 'delusive and degrading doctrines', was writing two days later that Bright's opponents would be glad to see his 'manly character and real abilities' again in the Commons. *The Times* remarked that surely the House was aristocratic enough to have found advantage from the counter-balancing presence of Bright, even though he might at times be over-assertive in attack.

In the event, Bright was not to remain out of Parliament for long. In August 1857 he was elected unopposed to represent Manchester's great rival among provincial manufacturing centres, Birmingham. Cobden was still uncertain about Bright's condition, and he was therefore doubtful at first about the wisdom of this move. But Cobden soon decided that it was hopeless to expect his friend to keep his mind off politics, and he saw that Birmingham would prove a much more congenial seat than Manchester. He explained to J. B. Smith how there was 'more social equality and a greater faith in democratic principles' in Birmingham than in Manchester.

'The latter was a good cradle for the League, for there were strong *purses*, and their owners thought they would be replenished with free trade. It was one aristocracy pitted against another, and with a good moral right on their side too. But you know we had but little sympathy from the "workers" till the work was done. The fact is there is an unhealthy disparity of condition in the factory towns, with its millowner employing his thousand hands, which will always militate against a hearty and fearless co-operation on ordinary political questions. In Birmingham where a manufacturer employs his three or four hands only, and sometimes but an apprentice or two, there is a much more cordial and united feeling among the two classes. In fact the social steps connecting one class with another are so gradual that instead of a great gulf which separates masters and workmen in Stockport or Manchester it is difficult to know where the line which divides the two is to be found.'

For this reason, concluded Cobden, he had often argued with Bright and Wilson that the cotton region could never become 'the head-quarters of a democratic movement of the rational character to be championed by Bright'. It could conceivably become the centre for an extremist, class-conscious reform movement, following some great collapse of manufacturing prosperity, but such a movement 'would not be of a character to be led by a millowner'.

Cobden seems to have been anticipating a closer identification between Bright and his Birmingham constituents than was ever actually to develop, even though Bright was to represent them for the rest of his life. Even during the Second Reform Bill agitation of 1866–7 Bright did not try to organise Birmingham opinion as Cobden had organised Manchester in the days of the Anti-Corn Law League. Bright was not an organiser, and it was largely left to Joseph Chamberlain to do this after 1867. Instead, Bright regarded Birmingham from the viewpoint of a sympathetic outsider, favouring its citizens once or twice a year with some of his most powerful speeches for which the local artisans provided a responsive audience. These occasions received national publicity, and greatly helped Bright in his attempts to form national opinion. But Bright was never 'of Birmingham' in the same way as Chamberlain, who became his colleague in its representation in 1876. Revealingly, Bright always spoke of 'your city', never of 'our city' when addressing his constituents.

Nearly a year passed after Bright's first election for Birmingham before he could resume full political work. He found himself warmly welcomed back to the Commons, and he noted how Cobden's return was also widely anticipated. Cobden, however, was enjoying his freedom from Parliamentary responsibilities. 'I am deep in mangolds and pigs', he admitted in July 1857. 'When I saw the other day that the

House sat till half-past four, I hugged myself, and looked out on the South Downs with a keener relish.' Cobden's name was linked with several possible constituencies, but finally in the General Election of 1859 he was returned, unopposed and in his absence in the United States, for Rochdale, the home town of his great political friend. During the last six years of Cobden's life the connection between Bright and himself was thus appropriately demonstrated.[8]

On his return from America at the end of June 1850 Cobden was met, first, with the offer of a seat in the Cabinet, which he refused, and then with the chance to promote a free trade treaty with France, which he eagerly accepted. Cobden had canvassed the idea of such a treaty when in Paris in 1849, but he had struck no response from the French Government at that time. Ten years later in a Commons speech in July 1859 Bright had asked why, instead of wasting money upon competition in armaments with the French, we did not encourage them to trade more freely with us. As a gesture of peace and goodwill we should remove all duties impeding trade between the two countries in the hope that the French would do the same. 'I do believe that if that were honestly done, done without any diplomatic finesse, and without obstacles being attached to it that would make its acceptance impossible it would bring about a state of things that history would pronounce to be glorious.' Bright's speech inspired Michel Chevalier, the Saint-Simonian, to write to Cobden urging upon him the idea of a commercial treaty. Cobden and Chevalier had been in regular correspondence since 1846, always looking for free trade openings. On a visit to England shortly afterwards Chevalier found that the Cobden family was planning to spend part of the winter in Paris. He then suggested that Cobden should employ his time there in attempting to interest the French Government in the idea of a treaty. Chevalier knew that an approach by Cobden would be both persuasive and entirely free of 'diplomatic finesse', and therefore the more likely to attract Napoleon III and to persuade him that he could overcome the opposition of the powerful French protectionists.

Cobden quickly responded to this proposal. He knew that much would depend upon the attitude of Gladstone, the Chancellor of the Exchequer. He therefore visited the Chancellor at his home at Hawarden in September. Gladstone, the heir of Peel, saw his chance to complete Peel's work of tariff reduction and abolition, and he responded encouragingly to Cobden's suggestion. Gladstone knew that the moment was financially right for Britain because a surplus of £2 m. was in prospect from the expiry of terminable annuities. He also agreed with Cobden that a commercial treaty would reduce tension between the two countries. Tension had recently been encouraged by the press and by Palmerston, who insisted (quite wrongly) that Napoleon, following the example of his uncle, was contemplating an invasion of England. In Gladstone's words, the treaty would be a 'sedative', replacing thoughts of war by thoughts of trade. To Cobden this peace aspect was the essential one. He had not promoted repeal of the Corn Laws for reasons of purely material advantage, and equally he did not regard his 1860 Commercial Treaty in purely commercial terms. He even told Gladstone in November 1859 that he would not step across the street 'to increase our trade for the mere sake of material gain', for we already enjoyed sufficient material property. 'But to improve the moral and political relations of France and England by bringing them into greater intercourse and increased commercial dependence, I would walk barefoot from Calais to Paris.'

Gladstone and Cobden eventually extracted Palmerston's reluctant agreement to an unofficial approach being made to the French by Cobden in Paris. As Cobden remarked to the Chancellor, a majority of the Cabinet was 'not much in love with me or my mission'. But Palmerston could not appear completely negative because of Cobden's reputation in the country and because the Government needed the support of the Manchester School Members of Parliament. Cobden felt that his unofficial status probably helped him at this early point. It emphasised his impartiality, his sincere belief that free trade would benefit both countries equally. On October 27 he secured his first audience with Napoleon. It went well, with Cobden exerting all his great powers of engaging persuasion. Credit, however, must go also to Chevalier, who had already prepared the Emperor's mind. Cobden described to Napoleon the work of Peel as a commercial reformer, stressing the 'great reverence' with which his name was remembered, and encouraging Napoleon in the idea that he might emulate Peel. When Napoleon spoke of the danger of freer trade throwing Frenchmen out of work Cobden replied with his cumulative prosperity argument. At a second meeting just before Christmas Cobden again demonstrated to the Emperor how free trade would bring cumulative benefits, raising demand so much that freer importation of foreign products into France would still leave a market for home productions. Cobden showed how Britain had imported millions of quarters of corn annually since repeal of the Corn Laws, yet British agriculture was more prosperous than ever. 'I told him that his people were badly clothed, that nearly a fourth of his subjects did not wear stockings, and I begged him to remind M. Migne that if a few thousand dozens of hose were admitted into France, they might be consumed by these bare-legged people, without interfering with the demand for native manu-facture.' In this fashion Cobden's down-to-earth logic worked its way to a treaty. Yet he believed that it was the peace aspect of his free trade argument, not the purely material element, which finally decided the Emperor. Napoleon knew the intensity of English mistrust, and sought to allay it. Conscious of the hostility of the other Continental Powers. Napoleon felt that the security of his throne might depend upon good relations with England. His adhesion to Cobdenite ideas of peace and free trade was thus strongly coloured with balance of power overtones, but Cobden was happy to persuade the Emperor into the right course even if he was choosing it for reasons which Cobden did not accept as valid.

When a basis for negotiation had been agreed Cobden was given official status as British plenipotentiary. The Commercial Treaty was finally signed at the end of January. Cobden then withdrew to Cannes until the end of March to protect his throat and chest, which were now seriously affected each winter by the north European climate. The treaty was skilfully designed to encourage international free trade. The French removed all absolute prohibitions upon the import of British goods, and reduced the duties upon a wide range of them. Britain promised not only a reduction in duties on French brandy and wines (which were retained only for revenue purposes), but also a clean sweep of all remaining protective tariffs upon manufactured goods. Cobden enthusiastically summed up the significance of the treaty in a letter to Joseph Parkes:

'We only do what we ought to have done for consistency long ago, whereas the other side enters on a new policy, and is going to do as much in favour of free trade principles in eighteen months as it took Huskisson and Deacon Hume ten years to accomplish. . . . The effect of the treaty will be felt all over the world. It will raise the topic of "international tariffs" into practical importance with all the Governments of Europe . . . French example will do more in two years than ours would have done in twenty. The French Government having made their "concessions" only to us, with the intention of entering into treaty arrangements with other Powers, all the chancelleries of the embassies of Paris will be studying political economy from this moment, which will certainly be an improvement on their old studies. Besides, the French are also busy with the same controversy. For the first time practical questions are the topic of their newspapers. They are a logical people and always move more quickly than others in any direction . . . they will arrive at perfect free trade sooner than a slower people like ourselves.'

In Parliament Cobden left the treaty in the hands of Gladstone, who incorporated its proposals as part of a great free trade Budget. This completed Peel's work of tariff abolition, leaving only a small number of items subject to duties, all of these for purposes of revenue only. Gladstone was forced, however, to defend the treaty and his Budget against both the indifference of many Cabinet colleagues and the attacks of a vociferous group of free trade purists who objected to all commercial treaties as bargains incompatible with complete economic freedom. Opinion in the country was much more clearly favourable to Cobden's work than opinion in Parliament. Bright reported that town councils, chambers of commerce, and public meetings had been almost unanimous in welcoming the treaty and in thanking Cobden. Backed by this outside opinion, Gladstone was eventually able to carry the Commons with him. Bright told Cobden that he had never seen a case 'in which a good cause, backed by public opinion, has made a more striking change in the tone, the speeches and the votes of the House'. Gladstone explained to Members how nothing was given to France which we could have benefited from keeping, while nothing was received from her 'except a measure by which that country conferred a benefit upon itself. At a small loss of revenue we had gained a great extension of trade.'

In negotiating the principle of the treaty Cobden's work was only half done. The treaty itself was little more than a sketch; the details had to be agreed in a supplementary convention. Such work was usually left to officials, but Cobden knew that the tariff details would dictate in total the whole spirit of the arrangement, and he therefore offered to return to Paris as chief negotiator. From April to November 1860 he engaged in exhaustive and exhausting discussion. The whole list of British products and manufactures had to be studied. The French frequently suggested a continuing import duty of 30 per cent upon each item, the maximum allowed under the treaty. But Cobden had told the Emperor that such a figure amounted to virtual prohibition, and he set out in every case to secure a lower figure. Most time was spent in moderating the demands of the French ironmasters, the keenest French protectionists.

Cobden's difficulties during these months were not only with the French. He was compelled to negotiate in Paris against a noisy background of anti-French feeling at home. Fears of a French invasion were widespread. Cobden knew these to be groundless, but he found it impossible in July 1860 to dissuade Palmerston from proposing a large increase in expenditure upon dockyards and arsenals specifically related to the French 'danger'. Palmerston claimed that, although he hoped much from the Commercial Treaty, we could not depend for our security upon treaties alone. When Lord John Russell asked Cobden if he wished to leave the country 'unarmed', Cobden replied by pointing out that nearly £30 m. had already been voted for armaments in the current year even before Palmerston made his new proposals. Again emphasising that he was no pacifist, Cobden declared that he would spend any sum to maintain an 'irresistible superiority' over the French at sea; but we already possessed this, and needed no further defence against what was in any case an imaginary danger.

Cobden was greatly angered by Palmerston's alarmist policy, which, as he remarked to Bright, 'threw ridicule and mockery' over his peace-seeking treaty work. He described the panic as the greatest public delusion since the days of Titus Oates. If forced to choose, Cobden believed that France would prefer war with the whole Continent to war with Britain. 'What a stupid and befooled people you and I have worked for these twenty years past', wrote Bright in July 1860. For the sake of the treaty, however, Cobden refrained from public criticism of Palmerston. He suspected that the Prime Minister would have been glad of an excuse to recall him and to abandon the negotiations. In private Cobden plied Gladstone with exhortations to challenge the alarmists upon the facts, to compare French military expenditure with British, to contrast naval tonnage built and building, and, above all, to recognise the evidence that Napoleon regarded British friendship as vital.

When, despite all impediments, negotiations were completed in November Bright went over to Paris to see Cobden before he withdrew for the winter to Algiers. The pair were received by Napoleon. Characteristically, they used the occasion to advance their cause still further. They argued that a natural corollary of the treaty would be the abolition of passports between England and France. Cobden continued to press this point after Bright's return home, and in December the French agreed. About the same time the French postal authorities approved cheaper rates between the two countries. Thus in one year, wrote Cobden to Bright with satisfaction, tariffs and postal rates had been reduced and passports abolished. 'The question arises naturally, why should not our Foreign Office accomplish some good of this kind?' Cobden believed that more might be done if the will existed in high Governmental places. Bright developed the same theme in his diary. 'Lords and diplomatists, spending £15,000 a year, have been in Paris for half a century past, and have done nothing. Cobden, a simple citizen, unpaid, unofficial—but earnest and disinterested—has done all.'

Bright rejoiced in Cobden's success 'as if some great blessing had happened to myself'. It was a 'crowning reputation' for him. Such, indeed, was the general view. It looked after 1860 as if, gradually, Cobden's vision of international free trade might be realised. 1860 was therefore as important a year in his career as 1846. In the name of the Queen, Palmerston offered him the choice of either a baronetcy or a Privy Councillorship. Predictably, Cobden asked permission to decline both honours. He was proud to remain, as Gladstone had described him in the 1860 Budget debate, 'bearing no mark to distinguish him from the people whom he serves'.

Cobden now became more popular than ever before. In 1846 there had been many hostile protectionists, now there were hardly any. His fiercest opponents in 1860 were free trade zealots who argued that Britain should have removed all duties upon French and other foreign goods without bargaining for French reductions. Even Bright's original proposal in his speech of July 1859 had envisaged simply a gesture by Britain in tariff reduction to which he hoped the French would respond. He did not envisage negotiations to ensure such a response. He cannot therefore be given credit for proposing a treaty, only for setting off the sequence of events out of which a treaty came. As late as October 1859 he was still urging the idea of a unilateral gesture by Britain. 'The thing once done on our side', he wrote to Cobden, 'it would give, as the Irish express it, "much power to his elbow" when the Emperor proposed to do anything in the same direction.' Yet in the Budget debate of February 1860 Bright was to talk as if his July speech had originated the idea of a treaty, and this claim has been generally accepted by historians. In reality, from the British side the conception as well as the negotiation of the treaty was Cobden's, not Bright's. Bright's adjustment of the facts to his own advantage seems once more to have been quite unconscious. He quickly came to believe with complete sincerity that he had proposed a treaty in his July speech. Even in the privacy of his diary, where he can have had no motive for deception, he was assuming this only six months later. Over his connection with Cobden both in initiating the anti-Corn Law agitation and in starting the movement for the 1860 treaty (the two main achievements of Cobden's career), Bright's memory was inaccurate and self-inflating, even though unwittingly so.

Cobden and Gladstone had been told explicitly by Chevalier that the French protectionists would never respond, as Bright envisaged, to mere example, that Napoleon must be assisted to overcome them through a treaty which promised to open British markets only in return for significant French concessions. Cobden and Gladstone were practical politicians as well as free trade theorists, and, after initial hesitation, they accepted the need to play politics in order to apply theory to best advantage. Bright himself soon began to complain of free trade extremists, such as Villiers, who argued 'as if to make a treaty were contrary to free trade'. Such people, remarked Cobden to Bright, seemed to think that free trade could be started in France 'without resorting to stratagem, or anything like an indirect proceeding. They forget the political plots and contrivances, and the fearful adjuncts of starvation, which were necessary for carrying a similar measure in England.' The purists would have had good ground for criticism if Cobden had agreed to restrict British tariff abolitions exclusively to trade with France. But they were to be applied universally. The French, admittedly, made concessions only to us, but there was a clear prospect that they would gradually extend them to other countries through similar treaties. During the next five years France took the treaty as a model for similar trade pacts with Belgium, the German Zollverein, Italy, Scandinavia, Austria and Switzerland. Those countries in turn negotiated further treaties among themselves. So through the operation of 'most favoured nation' clauses, under which a tariff concession given to one state was automatically extended to all others within the group, a general reduction of protection was achieved in Europe during the 1860s. Most countries still retained complex fiscal systems, but absolute prohibition was much diminished. This fell far short of complete European free trade—only the Netherlands, Denmark and Turkey followed Britain's lead in full—but it did represent a tariff transformation which looked as if it might grow into a movement for full free trade. This possibility had been created by the intensity of free trade belief and the assiduity in negotiation of Richard Cobden.[9]

The encouraging progress of Anglo-French trade under Cobden's treaty can be seen from the following table:

|      | Imports | Exports | Re-exports |
|------|---------|---------|------------|
| 1860 | 17·8    | 5·3     | 7·5        |
| 1862 | 21·7    | 9·2     | 12·6       |
| 1866 | 37·0    | 11·7    | 14·9       |
| 1880 | 42·0    | 15·6    | 12·4       |

(all £ m.)

(*Source:* B. R. Mitchell, *Abstract of British Historical Statistics* (1962), 324.)

Cobden hoped that he had begun genuinely to persuade the peoples and Governments of Europe that free trade could be 'not only a law of wealth and prosperity but a law of friendship . . . a web of concord woven between people and people.' But few Europeans appreciated the international peace-keeping aspect of Cobden's free trade policy. The Commercial Treaty was neither generally understood nor generally popular in France. 'The object here', Cobden admitted to Gladstone during the negotiations, 'is of course to *steal* a reform from the majority, and to benefit the public in spite of itself.' At home we have seen how a Palmerstonian war scare could rage alongside negotiations which Cobden regarded as primarily motivated by love of peace. The public did not link the treaty with the promotion of peace, only with the promotion of trade and profit. Cobden was popular in 1860 in commercial circles for the same material reasons as had made him popular in 1846, despite his insistence at both periods upon the greater importance of the moral aspects of his work. This being so, public opinion in Britain in 1860 thought it entirely consistent to praise Cobden for his treaty while continuing to support Palmerstonian diplomacy. In 1862 Palmerston himself corresponded with Cobden about his peace views. It would be delightful, wrote the old Prime Minister, if nations would think of nothing but commerce and peace; but unfortunately man was a fighting animal. Democratic republics, claimed Palmerston, were historically the most warlike of states. British democracy certainly did not assume after 1860 that it could never again fight the French.

Nevertheless, during the 1860s British policy did become less bellicose than it had been in the '50s. Free traders of the time and later claimed credit for this. 'I attribute this remarkable change in the temper of the House since the Crimean War to the enormous amount of material interests at stake', wrote Cobden in 1864.

'We are exporting now at the rate of £160,000,000 a year, threefold our trade twenty years ago. This must have given an immense force to the conservative peace principles of the country . . . I have no doubt the Members hear from all the great seats of our commercial, shipowning, and manufacturing industries that the busy prosperous people there wish to be at peace. This is one of the great effects which we advocates of free trade always predicted and desired as the consequence of extended commercial operations.'

So argued Cobden with satisfaction in the last months of his life. But in reality the main cause of the change in British foreign policy during these years lay not in the influence of free trade, but in military and diplomatic necessities. The Crimean War had shown that Britain could only exert influence in central and eastern Europe at great cost. Thereafter this knowledge checked British Ministers, notwithstanding some blustering, from intervening in the Italian War of Liberation in 1859, in support of the Polish rising against Russia in 1863, and on behalf of Denmark against Prussia and Austria during the Schleswig-Holstein crisis of 1864. Early in the Crimean War Cobden had himself forecast how a new sense of practical realities would ultimately make British policy less interfering, how the Foreign Office would come to realise that it could not dominate events within the great European land mass. As a recent historian of the Liberal Party has pointed out, Liberal Ministers of the '60s came to adopt the principle of non-intervention not under the influence of the Manchester School, but because wars had proved unprofitable, remote, and impossible. 'It was not a conversion, but an adjustment to circumstances.'

The Crimean War was unnecessary, but it was not without results. Russian influence in central Europe was much reduced for the rest of the century, and in this time Germany and Italy were able to achieve nationhood. Russia's defeat also gave Turkey a chance to reform herself. This chance was not taken, but Russian pressure upon Constantinople was not renewed for twenty years. Then in the mid-'70s Britain again rallied to the defence of Turkish territorial integrity, now seen as vital to the safety of the new Suez Canal route to India. Disraeli's Conservative Government and a jingoistic people, ignoring all that Cobden and Bright had taught, made ready to fight a second Crimean War. Bright was forced to repeat his arguments of 1854–5. His oratory, now much diminished in power, made few converts among the general public, but he did find support within the new Gladstonian Liberal Party. Gladstone himself, who had supported the Crimean War, now vigorously opposed the prospect of its repetition. Cobdenite influence within the Liberal ranks lasted well into the twentieth century. Its end was marked by the resignation of John Morley, the biographer of both Cobden and Gladstone, from the Liberal Cabinet in opposition to British intervention in the First World War.

The Gladstonian Liberal Party had only emerged after the death of Cobden, and so Liberals naturally turned to Bright for the transmission of Cobden's ideas upon foreign affairs. Unfortunately, in the process of transmission Bright tended to diminish the breadth of Cobden's vision. Non-intervention had been for Cobden only the beginning of a policy: Bright, both in Cobden's lifetime and after, often gave the impression that it was for him the end. Bright was content to stress 'as little intercourse as possible' between Governments, forgetting that Cobden had placed equal emphasis upon the corollary of 'as much connexion as possible' between nations. Cobden wanted co-operation between people of all nations, but, thanks to Bright, the Cobdenite idea came to be equated within the Liberal Party almost with isolationism. As A. J. P. Taylor has pointed out, we can detect in Bright and his followers 'a high-minded passing-by on the other side'. In 1876, for example, Bright carried non-intervention to the extreme of giving only reluctant support even to Gladstone's campaign against Turkish atrocities in Bulgaria. Bright disliked public feeling being stirred on any foreign policy issue lest this should again lead the country into war. Cobden, if he had been alive in 1876, would not have been so rigid. We have seen how Bright, as an opponent of the Corn Laws, tended to argue too narrowly in terms of his own industry. In advocating non-intervention in foreign affairs he showed a similar tendency to narrowness of mind. Cobden possessed a breadth of view which Bright could never equal.[10]

## 5. RETRENCHMENT AND REFORM

Alongside 'peace' in the cry used by Cobden and Bright in the 1850s and '60s stood 'retrenchment and reform'. The pair laid great stress upon the need to reduce Government expenditure. Cobden even said on one occasion that he regarded the cry for economy as the first of all his demands. Such high priority for this negative demand above all positive reforms seems strange to twentieth-century minds, used to large Government expenditure in peace and war. In the mid-nineteenth century no practical politician thought that Government should exercise a large positive function. 'Whatever is done *for* men or classes', wrote Samuel Smiles on the first page of his immensely popular book, *Self-Help* (1859), 'to a certain extent takes away the stimulus and necessity of doing for themselves; and where men are subjected to over-guidance and over-government, the inevitable tendency is to render them comparatively helpless.' The main function of the British Government was seen as the protection of the British people from internal and external disturbance, and no more. And such protection was itself to be provided as cheaply as possible. 'Cheap Government' was an old slogan, shared by politicians of all shades. They differed only over ways and means. Gladstone, in particular, during his long periods as Chancellor of the Exchequer in the 1850s and '60s made economy the 'great article' of his financial creed. Yet to

Cobden and Bright even Gladstone's policy seemed inadequate. They welcomed his great free trade Budgets of 1853, 1860 and 1861, but they believed his achievement to be seriously marred by the countenance and finance which he found for British involvement in the Crimean War and in the succession of war and rearmament scares of the Palmerston years. Thus Cobden complained strongly to Gladstone of the 'enormous expenditure' upon armaments proposed in the 1860 Budget alongside the peace-seeking proposals for freer trade with France. Later in the year Cobden hoped that Gladstone would resign rather than accept Palmerston's plan for new expenditure upon fortifications. When Gladstone did not resign Cobden and Bright agreed that he was alarmingly inconsistent. Cobden had written of Gladstone in 1857 that he 'sometimes entangles his conscience in his intellect'. Both admired his oratorical power, his high intelligence, and his capacity for hard work, but so long as he remained a main support of Palmerston's 1859 Ministry there could be no general identity of view between them. Cobden told Gladstone in 1862 that their respective approaches were so different that their careers 'must ever be so separate'. Bright detached himself from Gladstone even more definitely than did Cobden. He told his friend in 1858 that although Gladstone could show courage at times, it was spasmodic. 'He dare not accept the lead of a popular party. Oxford and tradition seems to hold him fast.'

Gladstone, for his part, sympathised with much that Cobden and Bright desired, but thought that they often pushed their campaigns to impracticable lengths. He informed Cobden in 1860 that he had chosen the lesser evil of accepting expenditure upon fortifications in order to continue to promote the greater good of national economic progress. He expressly dissociated himself from Cobden, and still more definitely from Bright, because, as he told Palmerston in 1862, 'they seem to contemplate fundamental changes in taxation which I disapprove in principle, and believe also to be unattainable in practice'. Gladstone was quite right in his belief that Cobden and Bright mishandled the cry for retrenchment in these mid-Victorian years. Palmerston was in power, and economy could only be secured with his acquiescence, if not his support. Gladstone did well to stay in Palmerston's Cabinet and to keep the need for economy before his colleagues. Thus in the same letter in which he dissociated himself from Cobden and Bright, he also reminded Palmerston that it would be a 'healthful' day for the country and party 'when the word retrenchment, of course with a due regard to altered circumstances, shall again take its place among their battle cries.'[1]

Cobden had first come forward with his retrenchment ideas in detail at the end of 1848. He then published an elaborate 'National Budget'. Pointing out how annual Government expenditure had risen since 1830 from £18 m. to over £26 m., he proposed to reduce armaments expenditure by £8½ m. and civil expenditure by £1½ m., and also to raise £1½ m. by a probate and legacy duty upon land. The landed interest, argued Cobden, had exempted itself from such a duty for half a century, while compelling merchants and manufacturers to pay over £2 m. per annum in estate duty. Cobden proposed to allocate the £11½ m. thus saved or newly raised to reducing or abolishing the duties upon such necessaries of life as tea, wood, butter, cheese, malt, paper, soap, hops, windows, and advertisements. Cobden explained to Bright how his plan was intended to unite all classes and interests, and to draw both the counties and the towns together in one agitation. The heart of his scheme lay in much diminished arms expenditure. This, of course, linked with his whole free trade peace vision. Under free trade, and following a policy of non-intervention, Britain would not need 'that wasteful expenditure arising from so enormous a display of brute force'.

These words were uttered in a speech at Manchester in January 1849 in which Cobden called upon Mancunians to support a campaign for financial reform. He and Bright joined the National Parliamentary and Financial Reform Association, formed in that same month at a meeting of several hundred reformers in London. This new body was intended to bring middle- and working-class reformers together after the recent collapse of Chartism as a national movement. Like the Anti-Corn Law League, it sought to co-ordinate the work of scattered local reform associations, at least thirty-six of which were in existence by April 1849. Some of these associations were mainly interested in Parliamentary reform, others (mainly middle-class in membership) in financial reform. Foremost among the latter was the Liverpool Financial Reform Association, established in April 1848. Cobden gave most of his attention at this time to the financial side of the movement. He was optimistic that the cry for economy in government would attract both middle- and working-class support, since both classes shared an interest in the question as direct or indirect tax-payers. Cobden wanted all taxation to be made direct, so that every one would realise its extent: 'it is safer to feel the tax when you pay it, than to pay it without feeling it'.

The Parliamentary and Financial Reform Association and its constituent societies were active for some four years after 1849, promoting meetings in the country and motions in Parliament; but the success of the Anti-Corn Law League never looked like being repeated. Wide interest could not be roused, either in Parliamentary or financial reform. By 1853 the Parliamentary and Financial Reform Association had virtually ceased to function, and the Crimean War was about to absorb public interest. By 1856 Cobden was warning George Wilson that it was a delusion to campaign for economy while the country was so keen for an interfering foreign policy. Cobden never again tried to launch a movement specifically for financial reform. He now accepted, what he had earlier denied, that financial reform would only be achieved after Parliament had been reformed. 'I do not believe it is possible', he wrote in 1862, 'with our present Parliamentary system to enforce retrenchment *in the interest of the masses.*' The House of Commons was under the control of the aristocracy and the rich middle classes, who had an interest in extravagant Government expenditure. Parliamentary reform was therefore essential 'to give the masses at least a chance of doing something better for themselves'.[2]

Bright had never shared Cobden's belief that retrenchment should be their next objective after Corn Law repeal. He had always wanted to press for Parliamentary reform, taking over where the Chartists left off. Like the Chartists, he believed that once Parliament had been reformed all other necessary reforms would follow, including economy in Government. We have already seen how as early as 1837 he was expressing disappointment at the working of the 1832 Reform Act. Its franchise had proved too restricted, argued Bright, and its redistribution of seats too limited to produce adequate reform measures. He remarked perceptively in 1864 how it had proved 'not a good bill, though it was a great bill when it passed'. Bright was right in putting Parliamentary reform first, and Cobden was wrong for several years after 1848 in thinking that financial reform might be achieved even

Plate III

© Punch, December 1863

without it. Yet Cobden knew, what Bright refused to admit, that during the 1850s Parliamentary reform was itself unattainable. Because free trade had ended much economic distress, Cobden warned Bright in 1859, people were not interested in Parliamentary reform, even though Bright had recently made 'some of the most eloquent speeches that have ever been delivered' in support of reform. Perhaps, concluded Cobden not seriously, he and Bright should have first campaigned for Parliamentary reform before going for free trade and prosperity. As late as 1865 *Punch* was satirising the dilemma created for Bright by economic prosperity in a colloquy between 'Dr. Bright and his Patient', a working man.

> *Doctor:* 'Do you get good wages?'
> *Patient:* 'Yes.'
> *Doctor:* 'Have you plenty to eat and drink?'
> *Patient:* 'Yes, as far as that goes.'
> *Doctor:* 'Do you do as you like?'
> *Patient:* 'Yes.'
> *Doctor:* 'Do you pay taxes?'
> *Patient:* 'None to hurt me much.'
> *Doctor:* 'Ah! We must change all that. We must go in for reform!'[3]

Bright believed, and many historians have followed him, that after 1848 Cobden not only preferred to press financial rather than Parliamentary reform, but that he was indifferent to, perhaps even actually opposed to, Parliamentary reform. Trevelyan related how in old age Bright liked to tell two stories about himself and Cobden. The one described their Leamington 'compact' against the Corn Laws, the other how after 1846 Bright wanted to make a similar pact in support of Parliamentary reform and how Cobden refused. 'Why, Cobden,' remonstrated Bright, 'you haven't got faith in the working people.' We have already seen how inaccurate was Bright's memory of his Leamington conversation with Cobden. Bright's other memory was still more misleading. We have noted how in old age Bright unconsciously put a self-flattering gloss upon the Leamington meeting. Similarly, he added to his own reputation by misrepresenting Cobden's attitude towards Parliamentary reform after 1846, making Cobden appear much less advanced than himself. In fact, we shall see that the contrary was true, that Cobden was at heart much more democratic than Bright. Bright seems to have persuaded Morley, Cobden's official biographer, to accept his view of Cobden's attitude. Morley did quote passages from letters in which Cobden's democratic sympathies may be detected, but the commentary still inclined to Bright's line. Morley relied too heavily upon one passage in a letter from Cobden to Sturge in 1846. 'Upon the suffrage question, I find that I have gone back, and yet I am something like Peel and free trade. I dare not oppose the principle of giving men control over their own affairs. I must confess, however, that I am less sanguine than I used to be about the effects of a wide extension of the franchise.' Morley forgot that this was written within a few weeks of Corn Law repeal, when Cobden was exhausted by his efforts. We shall see that these half-hearted sentiments did not represent his true feeling.

It is not surprising that in old age Bright misrepresented Cobden's attitude, for he had failed to understand it even in Cobden's own life-time. In 1853 Bright described Cobden in his diary as 'acting as if he were disposed to abdicate as a political leader'. This remark was quoted by Trevelyan in support of the contention that Cobden was tepid on the question of reform of Parliament. Bright played down, and Trevelyan likewise played down, the good reason for Cobden's reluctance to agitate upon the reform question. He was reluctant, not because he dis-liked the cause, but because he rightly saw that sufficient public support would not be forthcoming. 'I have been looking out for signs and omens of the political future,' Cobden told Bright in 1851, 'but cannot say I see any indication of a breeze in the direction of reform. People are too well in the world to agitate for anything.' He assured Bright that he was 'not as you suppose desponding about political progress'. He would be ready when the moment came for reform, but at present there was no spontaneous feeling for it. Two years later he told Bright firmly that he was 'sick of this everlasting attempt out of doors to give the semblance of an agitation which don't exist'. Bright imagined that Manchester could be roused to lead a Parliamentary reform agitation like that against the Corn Laws; but Cobden had realised by the early '50s that Manchester had become too prosperous and conservative for this. 'Do not deceive yourself; the same men will not fight the battle of Parliamentary reform.' At the right time, went on Cobden, the working men would come forward, and in a new place, perhaps London. In this fashion did Cobden foresee the formation of the Reform League of 1865.

Cobden's declining health added to his reluctance to join Bright in an agitation which he believed would fail. But Bright pushed aside both the prospect of failure and the state of Cobden's health. He grew angry at what he regarded as Cobden's temporising, with the result that their differences over the reform question, following their differences over the Manchester candidature in 1846-7, made the period between repeal of the Corn Laws and the Crimean War the coolest in the friendship. Year after year between 1848 and 1853 Bright kept pressing Cobden to launch a 'Commons League' for Parliamentary reform. As yet Bright lacked the confidence to try (and fail) as leader of a reform agitation on his own. This was to come in 1858-9. 'With you', he told Cobden in 1851, 'I shall work with hope, indeed with a certain faith; without you, I should have no spirit.' In the same mood he reminded Cobden in 1853 that he was the 'leader of new principles and a new policy, and without you I should never have made any way in political life.'

> 'Try to shake off your unbelief in political progress', wrote Bright to Cobden in 1851. Trevelyan quoted this sentence as a fair judgement upon Cobden's supposed lack of progressive faith. Yet many times between 1848 and 1864 Cobden made the breadth of his views clear in speeches both inside and outside Parliament. In June 1848 he spoke in the Commons in support of Hume's 'Little Charter' motion, which advocated household suffrage, vote by ballot, triennial Parliaments and a redistribution of seats. Cobden regarded the ballot as an essential corollary of suffrage extension; otherwise workmen would be exposed to the dictation of their employers. He also wanted triennial Parliaments because 'a short lease and frequent reckonings' would best maintain the characters both of representatives and of constituents. In addition, Cobden advocated a redistribution of seats in order to establish a fairer balance between the influence of urban and rural districts in Parliament. He pointed out how Buckinghamshire with a population of one hundred and seventy thousand sent eleven Members to Parliament, whereas Manchester with a population almost half as large again was given only two representatives. Redistribution was thus almost as important in Cobden's view as extension of the franchise.

Cobden spoke in the 1848 debate in support of household suffrage.

He thought that this was probably as much as could be secured in his own lifetime. But he was prepared to go further, if possible. Also in 1848, three days after the last great Chartist failure on Kennington Common, he had explained in a private letter that, like the Chartists, he was ready to support manhood suffrage. Cobden simply added the proviso that this must be linked with a six or twelve months' residence qualification, which would keep off the register 'all the *floating mischief*' in the country. Discussing with Wilson three weeks later the varying views among reformers about the extent of reform, Cobden urged caution, but only from a desire to avoid dissension on the reform side. He told Wilson how he hoped that in the end it would be possible for the old Leaguers to coalesce with the universal suffrage men, 'for they are the most earnest of the movement party'. It is often forgotten that in 1842 Cobden had voted in favour of consideration of the six points of the Charter by the Commons. In 1838 he had remarked that, because he felt 'unbounded faith in the people', he would 'risk universal suffrage tomorrow in preference to the present franchise'. Nineteen years later he was able to claim that he had never voted in Parliament against any suffrage motion 'to whatever extent it went'.

In principle Cobden was thus a democrat without qualification. He was prepared to accept less than universal suffrage only because every step forward was worth taking. In his last public speech at Rochdale in 1864 he reiterated his faith in the working men. Not to enfranchise the workers, he argued, was more dangerous than to give them the vote, for it kept them separated from the classes above them. Cobden refused to believe that if the masses gained the vote they would immediately seek to rush visionary socialist legislation through Parliament. He rightly understood the essential conservatism of the British working class. The workmen would not divide themselves from the other classes, but would range themselves under upper- and middle-class leaders. He noted how the French Assemblies of 1848 and 1849, although elected under universal suffrage to replace the Orleanist Chamber chosen by only a quarter of a million voters, had still returned 'nearly all the eminent men of all parties' and had proved 'eminently conservative'. The people once given power might make mistakes, but, as he told Bright in 1859, 'If the majority in a democracy injure me and themselves at the same time by unsound legislation, I have at least the consolation of knowing that they are honest in their errors, and that a conviction of their mistake will for their own sakes lead to a change. It is far different where you are wronged by a self-interested minority.' In general, Cobden was confident that the people could be trusted to serve both their own best interests and the best interests of the country.[4]

Whilst rightly believing during the 1850s that agitation for Parliamentary reform would be premature, Cobden long remained convinced, too convinced, that Parliament might be silently and substantially reformed through the organised purchase of forty-shilling county freeholds. We have already seen how the Anti-Corn Law League in its last phase had begun to arrange such purchases in the belief that it could thereby gradually win many county seats and force Parliament to concede repeal. For several years after 1848 Cobden again enthusiastically advocated this scheme. 'A county or two quietly rescued from the landlords by this process will, when announced, do more to strike dismay into the camp of feudalism and inspire the people with the assurance of victory, than anything we could do.' So wrote Cobden to Bright in 1851. Cobden believed that the electorate could be doubled in seven years. He liked the scheme the more because it would also encourage thrift and small landownership among the artisans and superior workmen, whom he had particularly in mind as investors of the necessary sum of about £50 per head.

These mixed political and social motives led Cobden to encourage the formation in London in the summer of 1849 of the National Freehold Land Association. The model for this body was the Birmingham Freehold Land Society, formed in 1847. Cobden kept in close touch with the Birmingham society, and became a vice-president of the National Association. The idea was that estates should be bought by gentlemen friendly to the movement and divided into plots of sufficient value to confer voting rights upon all plot purchases. Members could buy such plots at cost price either outright or by subscription. This method was cheaper than buying on the open market, as the Anti-Corn Law League had done. By 1852 a hundred and thirty land societies were in existence with eighty-five thousand members. Nearly twenty thousand allotments of sites worth at least forty shillings a year had been made, and £790,000 had been subscribed. The National Freehold Land Association remained the most important body. Soon, however, its character and that of most other land societies began to change. They came to be regarded not as mainly political instruments but as repositories for working-class savings, deposited without intention of taking pieces of land. The National Association was noting this trend as early as its annual report for 1850. Gradually, the societies were becoming building societies. Today the Abbey National Building Society traces its origins back to the National Association of 1849.

This shift in emphasis underlined how Cobden had been far too optimistic in his political expectations. At the 1852 General Election voting in the county seats of Warwickshire, Lancashire, East Surrey, and Middlesex was said to have been slightly influenced by such created reform freeholds, but this was all. The county representation was not going to be transformed within seven years as Cobden had hoped. Here Bright had been more realistic. He told Cobden in 1849 that the freehold plan would not achieve much if left to stand on its own. It might temporarily win a few county seats, but only temporarily, for the votes of created freeholders were always precariously held because of their relative poverty. The effort necessary to snatch these few seats would only be worth while, contended Bright, if linked with an immediate agitation in the Commons and in the country for real Parliamentary reform. Every extra vote in the Commons would then be valuable.[5]

In the last years of his life Cobden had abandoned hope of achieving reform through indirect means, and he began earnestly to urge the working men to agitate for Parliamentary reform, by themselves if necessary. He had gradually lost patience with the middle classes, who had refused to take up the question. He gave up his belief, firmly held since the days of the Anti-Corn Law League, that working-class advancement could only come with middle-class help. 'We are too apt to forget', he had told Bright in 1851, 'that the mass of the people, however enthusiastic in favour of universal suffrage, have not the power of carrying that or any other measure, excepting with the aid of the middle class.' By 1860 he was still hoping for middle-class participation but he was beginning to think of independent working-class activity. He told a correspondent that 'we must do what we can', taking care, 'not to throw away the support of the majority of the middle class, without whose co-operation no further reform can be affected'. The middle classes might be gradually won over to the side of reform, if the reformers did not frighten them. By 1864, however, Cobden was telling the same correspondent that the longer he lived the more he distrusted the middle class as an instrument for reform. Its members were far too deferential towards the aristocracy. In one of his last letters he remarked that the homage paid to Brahmins in India was no more unreasoning than the deference shown in England towards lords and ladies. 'We have the spirit of feudalism rife and rampant in the midst of the antagonistic development of the age of Watt, Arkwright, and Stephenson.' Cobden had come to the conclusion that the workmen were not so debilitated by this snobbery as the middle class. He told Bright in 1863, with reference to a London trade union meeting in support of the American North, how pleased he was 'to read such straightforward utterances after the namby-pamby middle-class oratory we have been so long used to'. Interestingly, Karl Marx likewise approved of these same speeches for their 'complete absence of bourgeois rhetoric'. Cobden asked Bright if the trade unionists showed any strong feelings upon domestic politics. His hope by this date was that working-class political activity would grow out of social and economic activity. Four months before his death he pointed out how the workmen, 'with that instinct which belongs to multitudes', were making progress through flanking movements such as co-operation, working-men's clubs, and industrial exhibitions. 'Then will come a great crisis, some shock to move the world, and everything will be conceded by our cowardly ruling class to panic fear as has always been the case. I venture the prediction that the next reform will be household suffrage at least, if not manhood.' Cobden had been particularly impressed by the energy of the working men in organising their co-operative movement in his Rochdale constituency. In 1861 he published an approving letter in the *Co-operator*, shrewdly noting the strengths and weaknesses of the movement. He admitted that much enterprise attributed to the operatives really came (as in the case of the mechanics' institutes) from the artisan class above them. There would be many mistakes made by the co-operators, but Cobden concluded that their efforts deserved the support of everyone anxious to see the mass of the people improve their condition.

Yet Cobden was not content to see the workmen devote all their attention to these social movements. He wanted them to organise politically. Had they no Spartacus among them, he asked impatiently in 1861, 'to head a revolt of the slave class against their political tormentors?' Nobody could help the masses until they determined to help themselves. They should be told firmly that the old parties had decided that no further Parliamentary reform was needed, 'that five millions of adult males in the kingdom are politically ignored, or only remembered to be insulted, and that this state of things will endure so long as the five millions eat, drink, smoke, and sleep contentedly under the prescription'. He and Bright were ready to help the masses out of their 'political serfdom' once the people had shown some responsiveness and initiative. They must discriminate between those who would emancipate them and those who would keep them as they were. They must also create 'a bona fide organisation in every large town, composed of their own class, and self-sustained'. Otherwise, it was a waste of Bright's eloquence to attempt to advance their cause in that 'packed assembly', the House of Commons.

By the beginning of 1865 Cobden's sympathy with independent action had become well known among working-class leaders. For long he had been regarded with suspicion as essentially a middle-class figure, certainly not a friend of trade unions. As late as 1856 he was deploring the 'desperate spirit of monopoly and tyranny' underlying the trade union idea. By the 1860s, however, Cobden's hostility to the coercive economic function of the unions was becoming tempered by appreciation of their value as working-class organisations. The workmen, for their part, were coming to understand the strength of Cobden's democratic political feeling. Unfortunately, Cobden's new relationship with the workers and their organisations was to last but briefly, for he died in April 1865. Historians have tended to remember only Bright's prominent part in the reform crisis of 1866–7. Yet at the beginning of 1865 Cobden was encouraging the formation of the Reform League, the main working-class body during the crisis, at a time when Bright, as we shall see, was keeping himself a little apart from the working-class leaders. Bright did not support the League demand for universal manhood suffrage, qualified only by residence and registration. Cobden, by contrast, gladly did so, for this was the ideal to which he had given his support as early as 1848, although always (and still) prepared to accept something less as an instalment of reform. Because his health was finally breaking up, Cobden could not take a personal part during the first weeks of 1865 in helping George Howell, the future League secretary, and other London working men to found the Reform League, but Cobden was active in support by correspondence. He was delighted to find the working men ready at last to organise themselves politically. Discussing the early moves in the formation of the League, he reminded Bright in February 1865 how nothing could be done 'until the excluded classes demand in loud tones their rights'. Howell later recorded how Cobden's 'well-known sympathy was of service in the earlier stages', especially in extracting subscriptions from middle-class sympathisers. 'Had he lived, it is probable that his manly eloquence and his influence would have been used in favour of the Reform League.' At the time of Cobden's death the Leaguers were hoping that he would become their president.[6]

Bright was always much more hesitant and qualified than Cobden in his attitude both towards working-class organisations and towards working-class suffrage. His precise position was never quite clear, even to himself. In 1851 he made a revealingly wavering declaration of Parliamentary reform faith to Joseph Sturge. Bright assured Sturge that 'we all agree' in advocating the ballot, abolition of the property qualification for Members of Parliament, and a redistribution of seats so that no constituency should have less than four or five thousand electors. On the suffrage question Bright began by asserting his belief in 'the widest possible extension'. He admitted that this was not yet practical politics, but he thought the fears of opponents 'very childish'. Nevertheless, he accepted that payment of poor rate (payable six months in advance) plus a year's residence qualification would probably prove to be the most advanced borough franchise that could be secured. Yet in elaborating upon this franchise we find Bright moving away from his opening assertion that his ideal embraced the widest possible suffrage. 'I think it fair that they who never pay poor's rate, and who are in fact virtually receivers if they do not pay their share, should be excluded.' Bright contended that a rating franchise would add six thousand voters to the existing Rochdale electorate of only one thousand, although the requirements of payment in advance and a year's residence qualification would cut the six thousand to five thousand. Bright was prepared to stop at this, claiming that 'substantially it would enfranchise everybody, and give, I believe, a more democratic House than *manhood* without restriction. My restrictions, too, are not directed against any *class*, but operate with a fair quality upon all. I think properly explained to him any intelligent working man would prefer this plan to "universal".' In this fashion did Bright come to the conclusion that a rating franchise would be more democratic than universal manhood suffrage. His drift of thought showed both his surface confusion on the suffrage question, and how at heart he preferred to stop short of that real democracy which Cobden regarded as ideal.

Bright remained uncertain on the surface throughout the mid-Victorian years. It is easy to collect contradictory assertions from his speeches, some apparently indicating his belief in universal suffrage others explicitly denying this and asking for household suffrage or less. A working-class leader of the time remarked how Bright's utterances were too undecided. 'He never seemed to know—certainly no one else ever knew—whether he advocated manhood suffrage or household suffrage, or a suffrage limited to householders who paid a certain amount of rent.' Revealingly, when in 1858 Bright found himself expected by the reformers to draft a Reform Bill, he was quite unprepared for the task and unable to arrange the details himself. He wrote urgently to Cobden for help:

'I am grievously annoyed at being so far away from you at a time when conversation and your advice would perhaps keep me out of, or help me through, some of the difficulties which surround me. This Reform question is not a trifle, and yet I believe we ought to have a Bill prepared in the interest of reformers, and that, under the circumstances in which I was placed, I was not at liberty to refuse the onerous duty which was offered to me. But then comes the question —how is the work to be done? A day's talk with you would help me much.'[7]

Nevertheless, by 1858 Bright was prepared to lead a reform agitation without Cobden, albeit reluctantly. Cobden's contention that sufficient support was lacking no longer checked Bright as it had done five or ten years earlier. From his first address to his new Birmingham constituents in October 1858 Bright set out to work up the reform question. His speeches at a succession of meetings during the winter of 1858–9 secured for Parliamentary reform a volume of publicity such as it had not received since the collapse of Chartism. During the 1850s it had several times been discussed in the House of Commons, but not against a background of widespread interest in the country. It had been mainly an issue around which the political groups manœuvred for office. No measure of comprehensive reform was in view. In 1854 Lord John Russell introduced a bill so feeble that one working-class journal accurately compared it with the old pedlar's razors, made to sell and not to shave.[8] Popular interest was then focused not upon reform but upon the Crimean War. From 1858, however, although he failed to secure any immediate change, Bright succeeded in re-establishing Parliamentary reform as a major question both at Westminster and in the country. It was not yet an urgent question, but it was a question which would one day have to be solved, either because it had finally become urgent or (as reformers often argued during the early '60s) because of a realisation that it had better be solved without waiting for it to become a panic crisis issue.

Bright's speech at Birmingham Town Hall on October 27, 1858 received publicity upon an unprecedented scale. From this period he could be sure that every speech would receive national notice through the newspapers. The removal of the newspaper stamp duty in 1855, in response to an agitation in which Cobden and Bright were prominent, had produced a proliferation of cheap newspapers, and in their columns the words of Bright, as one of the foremost orators of the time, were often reported verbatim. *The Times* reporter visited him before the Birmingham speech to ask when he expected to finish so that the time of a special railway engine could be fixed which was to rush an account of Bright's speech to London. Other politicians, wrote Bright delightedly to his wife, with a show of modesty, 'must be very little, if I am so great'.

Bright opened his Birmingham speech with a personal passage which made a great impression upon his hearers and readers. He remarked how nearly three years had passed since he had been able to address a public meeting. Since then he had been as weak as a little child, unable to read or write or talk for more than a few minutes. Now he had recovered. After a pause he asked, 'In remembrance of all this, is it wrong in me to acknowledge here, in the presence of you all, with reverent and thankful heart, the signal favour which has been extended to me by the great Supreme?' After thanking the Birmingham electors for adopting him, and after reaffirming his belief in the rightness of his stand against the Crimean War, Bright moved into his main theme, the reform of Parliament. A Conservative measure was being prepared by Lord Derby's Cabinet, but Bright warned his audience against another 'country gentlemen's Reform Bill', and asked why the reformers should not introduce their own bill. Would the House of Lords stand in the way? Every peer, noted Bright, whether of good character or bad, could vote against every measure of reform. 'There is another kind of peer which I am afraid to touch upon—that creature of—what shall I say?—of monstrous, nay, even of adulterous birth—a spiritual peer.' Passages like this in Bright's speeches of this period were received with great alarm in influential quarters, helping to give him the reputation of being much more democratic than he really was. Explaining why Bright was not offered office in 1859, Palmerston told Cobden, and Russell told Bright himself, that his exclusion resulted from his attacks upon institutions which were (in Russell's phrase) 'considered essential by the great majority of Englishmen'.

Bright assured his Birmingham audience in October 1858 that the House of Lords would be bound to acquiesce if faced by a 'great national party' demanding a comprehensive Reform Bill. This party must agitate through meetings, petitions, and through votes at elections. Bright declared himself not opposed in principle even to a demand for universal manhood suffrage. But, following a similar drift of argument to that of his 1851 letter to Sturge, he came contentedly down in favour of a borough poor-rate franchise plus a lodger franchise of £10 per annum. Bright's justification was in similar terms to his explanation to Sturge. 'Whatever its omissions, whatever its exclusions, they would not be directed against any particular class.' There would be 'a fair representation of all classes'. In addition, a just redistribution of seats must be arranged. Three hundred and thirty Members of Parliament were at present elected by only a hundred and eighty thousand constituents, whereas another two hundred thousand urban electors were represented by a mere twenty-four members. Bright's peroration, one of his best, reminded the men of Birmingham what their fathers had done in support of the Reform Bill of 1832. 'Do not these eyes look upon the sons of those who, not thirty years ago, shook the fabric of privilege to its base? . . . Shall their sons be less noble than they? Shall the fire they kindled be extinguished with you? I see your answer in every face . . . I speak with diminished fire; I act with lessened force; but as I am, my countrymen and my constituents, I will, if you let me, be found in your ranks in the impending struggle.'

Two days later Bright spoke again at a banquet in Birmingham Town Hall. This time he linked foreign affairs and Parliamentary reform. The people had gained nothing from balance of power foreign policy, and had lost much in taxation and still more in lives. It was time for them to be given a share in controlling their own fortunes. 'Palaces, baronial castles, great halls, stately mansions, do not make a nation. The nation in every country dwells in the cottage.'

A conference held in London on November 5, 1858, attended by many reform Members of Parliament, commissioned Bright to prepare a detailed Reform Bill. On December 10 he told a mass audience in the Manchester Free Trade Hall that a house of hereditary legislators could not be a permanent institution in a free country. On December 15 he spoke at Edinburgh, on the 21st at Glasgow, and on January 17, 1859 at Bradford. The main features of his proposed bill emerged as (1) votes in boroughs for male poor-rate payers and lodgers paying £10 rent per annum, the county franchise to be reduced to £10 rental; (2) vote by ballot; (3) disenfranchisement of eighty-six boroughs and the withdrawal of one representative from a further thirty-four, the seats so released to be distributed according to population, mainly to the large towns. These proposals offered a prospect of much greater power for the urban middle class. In this knowledge they satisfied Bright, but they signally failed to satisfy working-class reformers. Bright's succession of rousing speeches with their strong denunciations of privilege had seemed to promise a democratic measure, but this promise had not been fulfilled. Ernest Jones, the leader of the Chartist rump, scathingly dismissed Bright as 'a halter between many stools', who 'confessedly knows not upon which to sit'.

Bright soon began to qualify his proposals still further. He admitted that he did not mean to establish even a complete poor-rate franchise in the boroughs. Those below a £3 rating should be given the vote only if they personally paid the rate. Since most such small ratepayers compounded for their rates in their rents Bright was in effect excluding them. He stated specifically that he wished to exclude the very poor, 'such as are not likely to have any independence', and also 'such as are utterly careless as to the possessing of a vote'. Here was the idea of what he was to describe in 1867 as the 'residuum', composed of men who could not be trusted with the vote. This idea showed how Bright was not a true democrat.

In February 1859 Disraeli introduced the Conservative Reform Bill. Instead of a broad extension of the franchise, it offered the vote to special categories such as clergymen, schoolmasters, and persons possessing £10 a year in the Funds or £60 in savings banks. Bright dismissed these 'fancy franchises', and urged the Commons to promote a genuine reform. To Bright's satisfaction reformers in the country were quick to share his disgust with Disraeli's measure. Less satisfactory to Bright were the many universal suffrage resolutions passed at meetings supposedly called to demonstrate middle- and working-class unity behind Bright's proposals. Disraeli's bill was defeated at the end of March, but on the very evening when Bright was ready to give notice of his own reform measure the dissolution of Parliament was announced. At the ensuing General Election the Conservatives failed to win an overall majority, and in June 1859 Palmerston became head of a more or less Liberal Ministry, pledged to produce a new Reform Bill.

Bright had been a member of the combination which defeated Disraeli's bill, and in order to keep this grouping together he now accepted from the Palmerston Government in March 1860 a reform scheme which was more limited even than his own proposals. This involved a £6 borough francise. Bright admitted that this would enfranchise only a hundred thousand workmen, but he recommended it as a step forward. Reformers in the country, however, refused to support such an inadequate measure. On the other hand, anti-reformers in Parliament still regarded even this degree of reform as dangerous, and they actively impeded its progress. Many members of the Palmerston Government (including Gladstone) were indifferent or hostile to their own measure, and finally it was withdrawn. Bright protested, but there was logic in abandoning a measure unsatisfactory to reformers and anti-reformers alike. The movement which Bright had launched with stirring language at Birmingham in October 1858 had come to a listless end. Nevertheless, something had been permanently gained. The question of Parliamentary reform had been re-established as a political issue. Friends and opponents of reform both knew that one day it would press forward again, and for this they praised (or blamed) John Bright.[9]

Aspirations and organisations ran through from the agitation of 1858-9 to the victory of the Second Reform Act in 1867. Working-class societies in support of universal manhood suffrage had been formed during 1859 in many parts of the country, and these helped to prepare the way for the National Reform League, founded in 1865. One such body, the Leeds Working Men's Parliamentary Reform Association, was addressed by Bright in December 1860. This seems to have been the first occasion when Bright spoke about reform at a meeting arranged by working men. Like Cobden, he had long been suspicious of trade unions in their economic aspect, but in November 1861 he congratulated the Glasgow Trades Council on its political activity, urging that trade unions everywhere should unite for reform. After this date, however, Bright's interest in the reform question subsided. Not until 1865 did he again become closely involved. In the intervening years he gave his time to business and to the American Civil War. America came so to engross his attention that he told his wife in June 1863 that he could not feel deeply about British or European problems until the war had ended. Cobden was driven to complain in 1864 that Bright's silence on the reform question in the Commons was a 'mistake'.

In May 1864 Gladstone made his famous declaration that every man was 'morally entitled to come within the pale of the constitution'. He added many qualifications, but these were hardly noticed whereas his assertion of a *prima facie* right to the vote was widely publicised. This response made the speech into a landmark in the progress of reform. Bright forecast that it would mark 'a new era in the reform question'. It showed what Gladstone was 'looking towards in the future'. Yet thereafter neither Bright nor Gladstone drove straight towards the Second Reform Act of 1867. Both continued to wait upon events and upon public responses. Thus it was mainly circumstances and public opinion which paired them together as leaders of the reform cause. We have seen how in the early '60s Bright and Gladstone still felt many reservations about each other. Gladstone, in particular, was slow to abandon his doubts. Perhaps he never quite did so, for his appreciation of Bright's virtues seems always to have been closely related to Liberal Party strategy. Before the 1865 General Election, when economy was a main issue, Gladstone first came into close touch with Bright. But Bright was not consulted over the Liberal Bill of 1866, which Gladstone introduced in the Commons. Well into 1867 Gladstone viewed with alarm Bright's ideal of borough household suffrage, which the 1867 Act eventually granted. Only towards the end of the debates, when an election on this unexpectedly broad franchise had become certain, did Gladstone draw Bright into the Liberal Party's ruling circle. ('Bright must be admitted gradually', Russell advised Gladstone.) Three times Gladstone gave Bright a seat in Liberal Cabinets, but on each occasion the needs of the Liberal Party made this desirable. Perhaps the offers would have been made in any event, but from Gladstone's side his attitude towards Bright was never more than one of friendliness, not to be confused with friendship. Bright, by contrast, appears to have developed a real liking for Gladstone from the mid-'60s. Perhaps he was seeking a substitute for Cobden. When Gladstone first retired in 1875, and again when Bright felt bound to resign from his Government in 1882, Bright wrote to him of his great 'pleasure' and benefit from their association. At Birmingham in April 1867 Bright made a warm, indeed an exaggerated eulogy of Gladstone's earnestness upon the reform question. 'Who is there, I ask, in the House of Commons who equals him in knowledge upon all political questions? Who equals him in earnestness? Who equals him in eloquence? Who equals him in the unexampled courage and fidelity of his convictions? If those gentlemen who say we will not have this man to reign over us—if they have his equal, let them show him.'

In this fashion during 1866-7 did Bright build up the reputation of Gladstone as leader of the Liberal Party. This was done almost in spite of Gladstone himself, who withdrew to Italy after the failure of the 1866 Reform Bill and who complained of Bright's autumn speeches as far too advanced. Bright, as much as Gladstone, created the Gladstonian Liberal Party. He drew together Parliamentary Liberals, working-class reformers, and militant middle-class Dissenters in a triple union. He was greatly helped in this role by his own detachment. Although in friendly touch with all three elements, he was not identified with any one of them, and this assisted him in recommending them to each other. He and Cobden had always stood apart from the bulk of the Liberals in Parliament, while Bright's relationship with the working men was friendly but not one of total identification. Finally, Bright was not a mainstream Dissenter. He was always conscious of the under-privileged position of Dissenters, but there was still truth in his claim in 1860 that, as a Quaker, he had 'no particular sympathy' with Wesleyans, Congregationalists or Baptists more than with Anglicans. He refused in 1854 to become leader of the Liberation Society, the militant body formed to press for Church disestablishment. Bright also benefited from his detachment in another way. He knew that the realities of high Parliamentary politics debarred him from aspiring to the Liberal leadership for himself. He could hope for Cabinet office, but no more. Consequently, there was no risk of personal ambition checking his promotion of Gladstone's cause. Gladstone was a high politician in the acceptable mould. Some parallel can be found here between the Bright–Gladstone relationship of 1867 and the Cobden–Peel relationship of 1846. Just as Cobden in the cause of Corn Law repeal had helped to make Peel's reputation, so Bright in the cause of Parliamentary reform helped to make Gladstone's.

Bright's success in 1867, however, was not the outcome of a long, systematic effort as Cobden's success had been. Bright stumbled into his role in the summer of 1866 unexpectedly. A succession of incidents and influences added up until what had been smouldering since 1859 broke again into flame in the summer of 1866. The American Civil War was one contributing influence. Although we shall see that working-class opinion was not at first so markedly favourable to the North as Bright liked to claim, it did become more friendly to the Federal side once slavery abolition had become an open issue between the sides; and the eventual victory of the North in 1865 gave an impetus to democratic ideas in this country. A second such influence was the visit to England in 1864 of Garibaldi. He received an enthusiastic popular reception in London, and the Palmerston Government hurried him out of the country before he could attend what promised to be equally enthusiastic gatherings in the provinces. The National Reform League grew directly out of a body called the London Working Men's Garibaldi Committee. Finally, in October 1865 Palmerston died. In himself he had been the chief obstacle to real progress on Parliamentary reform. He was succeeded as Prime Minister by Russell, whose official career had begun with the First Reform Act and who aspired to end it with a second. In March 1866 Gladstone introduced the Russell Government's Reform Bill in the Commons. It was a cautious measure, proposing to lower the occupation franchise from £10 to £7 in boroughs and from £50 to £14 in counties (with qualifications). Some four hundred thousand voters were expected to be added to the electorate. As with Russell's Bill of 1860, Bright spoke in support only because he thought the measure better than nothing. He regretted the 'remarkable feebleness' of the Government, which left it open to 'great blame' from reformers who had eagerly awaited the bill. These criticisms from Bright made it clear how far apart he and Gladstone still were at this date. Bright's main attack, however, was reserved for two right-wing Liberals, Horsman and Lowe, who from the Government side of the House had fiercely attacked even this cautious measure as dangerously democratic. In what immediately became a famous passage Bright described Horsman as 'the first of a new party who has expressed his great grief, who has retired into what may be called his political cave of Adullam, and he has called about him everyone that was in distress and everyone that was discontented.'* In this manner were the 'Adullamites' given their name. Soon the two had increased to forty, and in June they helped the Conservatives virtually to defeat the Bill. Russell resigned, and Derby formed a Conservative Ministry.

Bright was now deeply dispirited. He confessed to Wilson that he did not know what to do next on the reform question. Only numbers and 'the aspect of force' could influence the Conservative Government, but the working men needed better organisation 'and more life'. Bright did not think that he himself could rouse them. 'We seem to have no definite plan of action. I am not able to suggest one, and I feel too old to go "on the stump" again.' Then events suddenly swept Bright along. The turning point was the trampling down of Hyde Park railings by an angry crowd of London workmen on July 23, 1866. This incident led to the rapid and unforeseen creation of a popular front embracing middle- and working-class reformers.

The Russell–Gladstone Bill had been too timid to attract widespread popular support, but the fact that even such a modest measure could be rejected produced an upsurge of feeling outside Parliament. The Reform League proposed to hold a mass meeting of protest in Hyde Park, but the authorities announced that the park would be closed against such a gathering. This intensified popular indignation still further, since it seemed to underline that, while the privileged few

---

* David in his flight from Saul escaped to the cave of Adullam, 'and every one that was in distress, and every one that was in debt, and every one that was discontented, gathered themselves unto him' (I Samuel, xxii, 1, 2).

could use the park as they chose for walking and riding, the people had no equal right to choose to meet there. Bright was not available to speak at the proposed meeting, but he sent Howell a strong letter in support. 'To meet in the streets is inconvenient, and to meet in the parks is unlawful—this is the theory of the police authorities of the metropolis. . . . If a public meeting in a public park is denied you, and if millions of intelligent and honest men are denied the franchise, on what foundation does our liberty rest?' Only later did Bright remember that the closure policy had originated with Russell's Government. He then tried, too late, to prevent publication of his letter.

On the day appointed for the meeting, July 23, 1866, Edward Beales, the middle-class president of the Reform League, presented himself at the head of an orderly procession at Marble Arch and demanded admission to Hyde Park. The police refused, and Beales and his immediate followers thereupon withdrew. But the less 'respectable' part of the crowd, incensed by what had happened, surged forward and broke down the railings, and for three days and nights inter-mittent skirmishing took place in and about the fenceless park.

This was the 'Sarajevo of reform'. The reform organisations, which up to this time had attracted only limited support, now grew quickly into great movements. The National Reform League remained mainly a working-class body, although with middle-class members, while conversely the National Reform Union, which had been formed in Manchester in April 1864, remained mainly middle-class, though with some working-class adherents. The Reform Union was domin-ated by veterans of the Anti-Corn Law League, notably its chairman, George Wilson. It demanded a vote for all payers of borough poor rate, the ballot, triennial Parliaments, and an equitable redistribution of seats. This compared with the Reform League's bolder demand for 'registered and residential suffrage, protected by the ballot'.

We have seen how Cobden had long preferred this latter pro-gramme, whereas Bright had long favoured the former. While Cobden had warmly encouraged the Reform League in its first days, Bright had been more guarded. At a London conference of middle- and working-class reformers in March 1865 Bright had made it clear that, while he would not oppose the League's demand for manhood suffrage, he would himself advocate only a poor-rate franchise for the boroughs. Howell remembered how Cobden had been much more encouraging than Bright when the League was being formed, although Bright did come later into warmer relations with it. In one of his last letters to Bright, written at the time of the formation of the League in February 1865, Cobden showed concern at Bright's qualified attitude towards the manhood suffrage party. Edward Baines of Leeds had produced a half-measure of reform, promising to enfranchise only some two hundred and forty thousand people. Cobden thought this most inadequate, and was clearly concerned lest Bright should identify himself with it. 'Nothing will be got by cooing', he warned Bright. Cobden wanted a vigorous agitation by the Reform League for manhood suffrage. 'I look upon what is coming from Leeds as little better than child's play. I should be sorry to see you identified with any small and abortive measure.' Clearly, just before his death Cobden realised how Bright was much less democratically inclined than himself.

Unfortunately, because Cobden did not live through the Second Reform Act crisis his identification with the principles of the Reform League has been almost forgotten, while Bright, by contrast, has been well remembered for producing during the second half of 1866 a sequence of stirring speeches which, as in 1859, misleadingly encouraged the idea that he was a truly advanced reformer. The Hyde Park incident had created a crisis, and Bright, who a few weeks earlier had been tired and baffled, seized his chance. His speeches seemed to say more than they really did say, and he now suddenly became a popular hero at the peak of his career. Events and aspirations which he neither entirely controlled nor entirely recommended swept him forward. He did not lead this new movement closely as Cobden had led the Anti-Corn Law League; rather he was placed at its head. Appropriately, Karl Marx complained of 'Father Bright' and of the 'bourgeois infection' which had affected the workers.

Great meetings, at all of which Bright was the central figure, were held at Birmingham in August 1866, at Manchester in September, at Edinburgh, Glasgow and Leeds in October, and in London in December. At each provincial centre the routine was similar. A hundred thousand or more people gathered outside the town upon the largest available open space, while members of local trade unions and trade societies marched past Bright, many with banners bearing the new slogan 'Honour Bright'. Then in the evening Bright spoke in the largest local hall, and on the next morning the whole country read his speech in the newspapers. The cumulative effect of these demonstrations upon opinion inside and outside Parliament was very great. Bright's speeches showed some shift of emphasis from those of 1858–9. He no longer related Parliamentary reform so closely to retrenchment and the checking of aristocratic extravagance. Now he stressed justice more than interest, how the artisans had a moral right to the vote. Less was also heard about the ballot and redistribution, because Bright now felt it prudent to work first for extension of the suffrage.

Bright expected no real widening of the franchise from the Conservatives, now in power. He told the Birmingham meeting on August 27 that the accession to office of Lord Derby was a declaration of war upon the working classes. This striking assertion ran round the country. The people, Bright went on, must rouse themselves; every workshop and factory must become a Reform Association. All shades of reformers should join together. In this spirit Bright asserted that he was 'not afraid of the principles of the Reform League'. He did not mean by this what many of his hearers and readers probably assumed, that he was positively in favour of manhood suffrage. He meant only that he would work with the Reform League to secure that lesser degree of reform which he desired, leaving the League subsequently to press on as best it could to manhood suffrage as a further step. Just before the Leeds demonstration on October 9 the council of the Reform League concernedly discussed Bright's qualified attitude towards itself. On October 16 he spoke at Glasgow. He pointed out how of every hundred men in the United Kingdom eighty-four had no votes. The implication for the unsophisticated was that Bright wanted to give votes to all these eighty-four, although this was not really his aim. There was no country so pleasant as this for the rich, exclaimed Bright, but the rich had not overcome the poverty and misery of the poor. 'The class which has hitherto ruled in this country has failed miserably. . . . If a class has failed, let us try the nation.' Here was another sentence which electrified working men throughout the country, who forgot that in terms of votes Bright's 'nation' was much less than all adult males.

On November 20, 1866 Bright attended a conference called by the Reform Union in Manchester, speaking that evening at a banquet. The middle-class character of his listeners led him to emphasise the importance of Parliamentary reform for them. It was a fallacy to think

that they now had power. While working men were excluded 'roughly
and insolently', said Bright, the middle classes were excluded more
adroitly through the unequal distribution of seats. On December 3 a
final great reform procession was held in Bright's presence in London,
and on the following evening he spoke at St. James's Hall. He urged
supporters of both the Reform League and the Reform Union to
extend their organisation and to collect funds. 'Do not allow my friend
Mr. Beales—or my ancient friend and political brother, Mr. George
Wilson of Manchester—do not allow them to want the means to carry
on and direct the great societies of which they are the chiefs. And let me
beg of you, more than all else, to have no jealousies amongst each
other.' So Bright sought to bind the movement together, glossing over
differences of social background and political objective. 'Be animated
by a great and noble spirit, for you have set your hands and hearts to a
great and noble work.' Swayed by Bright's stirring phrases, his audiences were generally ready not to look too closely into the precise
extent and detail of his conception of that 'noble work'.

If Bright had been required to produce his own Reform Bill popular
excitement might have been followed by popular disillusionment, as
in 1859. Fortunately for the unity of reformers around Bright the
initiative in detail was left this time with the Queen's Ministers. Bright,
instead of drafting his own bill, corresponded confidentially with
Disraeli, who was preparing the Government measure. 'The oldest
and wisest basis for the borough franchise', wrote Bright, is 'household
suffrage.' The next best would be a rental franchise of £6 or a rating
franchise of £5. After airing several outline schemes, Disraeli finally
introduced his Reform Bill in March 1867. It was nominally based
upon household suffrage, but this principle was so much qualified that
Bright denounced the bill as 'a production not of the friends but of the
enemies of reform'. Gladstone and Bright wanted to oppose the bill
entirely, but they were overruled by their followers. This was fortunate, because in committee Disraeli, anxious to secure the credit for
passing any measure, allowed his bill to be transformed. In the background was the pressure of popular opinion. Many skilled artisans, who
had previously held aloof from the reform movement, had swung
round at the beginning of 1867 after the *Hornby* v. *Close* decision,
which threatened trade union organisation. Trade depression and
unemployment were also renewing the old spur of economic distress

behind political feeling. This feeling erupted notably on May 6, 1867 when the Reform League held another mass meeting in Hyde Park in defiance of a Home Office ban and despite the presence of many police and troops. The League thus openly challenged the Government to suppress the reform movement by force, showing that Ministers dare not do so.

The most important amendment to the Conservative bill was moved by a little-known Liberal member on May 17, and unexpectedly accepted by Disraeli. This amendment, which was a simplification of a suggestion of Bright's, required payers of poor rates to pay them personally. This circumvented the problem of whether and how to enfranchise the many thousands of small ratepayers who had compounded for their rates in their rent. To Bright's satisfaction all payers of poor rate were now given the vote. It was estimated that this amendment quadrupled the number of people newly enfranchised under Disraeli's measure. The Second Reform Act finally passed in August 1867. It almost doubled the million electorate, giving the county vote to nearly all landowners, tenant farmers, middle-class householders and to the better class of village tradesmen, and the borough vote to almost all settled householders. A limited degree of redistribution was attempted, including third seats for the provincial great towns.

We have seen how in 1859 Bright had inclined to exclude from the franchise those poor-rate payers who had compounded for their rates, but now he welcomed their inclusion. Bright had realised that in Birmingham alone this group comprised thirty-six thousand house-householders. After making this adjustment, Bright found that the Second Reform Act gave him precisely what he had always wanted in terms of borough suffrage. 'It is discovered in the year 1867', he exclaimed with satisfaction, 'that my principles all along have been entirely constitutional, and my course perfectly patriotic. The invective and vituperation that have been poured upon me have now been proved to be entirely a mistake.' This was true of the suspicions which anti-reformers had shown of Bright's tendencies, but his satisfaction at a measure which stopped far short of 'one man one vote' emphasised how he was not a complete democrat. He did not want, as did Cobden and the Reform League, to establish manhoood suffrage with the sole reservation that it should be 'registered and resident'.

Bright was content to enfranchise the labour aristocracy in the towns, deliberately excluding those below this level, the people whom he described during the reform debates in March 1867 as the 'residuum'. This revealing episode was ignored by Robertson and Trevelyan, Bright's chief biographers, both anxious to exaggerate his democratic tendencies. Bright began the relevant passage by reasserting his belief in borough household suffrage based upon payment of poor rate. But, Bright went on, there existed 'a small class which it would be much better for themselves if they were not enfranchised, because they have no independence whatsoever, and it would be much better for the constituency also that they should be excluded, and there is no class so much interested in having that small class excluded as the intelligent and honest working men. I call this class the residuum, which there is in almost every constituency of almost hopeless poverty and dependence.' Bright then quoted and reaffirmed what he had said in similar terms, though without using the word 'residuum', during the 1859 reform debates. Revealingly, in this 1859 passage Bright does not seem to have regarded the excludable class as a particularly small one. It numbered, he thought, hundreds in some constituencies and thousands in a few of the largest. In another speech in June 1867 he spoke of the residuum as embracing 'scores of thousands'.

Distrust of the residuum was widely shared among Liberal as well as Conservative politicians of the time. Too many working men at the bottom of the scale were certainly drunken and illiterate. But we have seen how Cobden and the Reform League were prepared to take their chance at least with all workmen who were sufficiently settled to become registered and resident voters. We have seen how Cobden thought that the test of registration and residence would be enough to exclude the real undesirables, the vagrants, the 'floating mischief'. Cobden's 'floating mischief' was much less numerous than Bright's 'residuum'. Exactly contrary to that favourite story of Bright's old age, retailed by Trevelyan, it was Cobden and not Bright who showed trust in the people down to the lowest level.[10]

After 1865, resting content with the new urban franchise, Bright welcomed renewed pressure for the vote by ballot, which was finally secured in 1872. He also encouraged the demand for a rural franchise as wide as that of the towns and for a comprehensive redistribution of seats, both of which were achieved with the Third Reform Act of

1884–5. The 1885 redistribution, by dividing large towns into wards, created purely working-class constituencies for the first time. Cobden had foreseen this development and had welcomed it, believing that it would allow working men a better chance of entering Parliament. Bright, by contrast, was not attracted by the idea of purely working-class representatives in Parliament, on the ground that all Members should represent all classes. This attitude had some plausibility, but Cobden showed a greater responsiveness to working-class aspirations. We have seen how Bright could describe as 'democratic' a franchise which stopped far short of universal suffrage. By 1885 he wanted to go no farther, believing that the still limited franchise was enough to produce 'a democratic and a popular House of Commons'.[11]

If Bright's idea of democracy did not include universal suffrage even for men, still less did it include votes for women. Under the influence of John Stuart Mill, he did vote in 1867 to include women within the Second Reform Act franchise. But at heart Bright was not favourable to female suffrage, and he voted against it in 1876, repudiating his earlier vote on the grounds that women had little to complain of and that they were unduly susceptible to clerical influence. In old age Bright did not like women's rights to be discussed by the females of his family. As his sister explained, 'he could praise women, but not Woman— he could worship what he called charming women, but he could *never* bear women to assert themselves'. Such was John Bright, a democrat only within his own sense of the word. Cobden's idea of democracy required no such qualification.[12]

## 6. EDUCATION

'That question underlies all our social and political problems. Our people have not really been prepared for the part which in an industrial and constitutional country they are called on to perform.' So wrote Cobden to Bright in 1853, emphasising the urgent need to provide a national system of elementary education in England. Cobden was a lifelong enthusiast for educational progress. Like Adam Smith, he wanted a national network of schools to overcome the widespread ignorance among both town and country people. Cobden believed that a nation could never be securely prosperous or happy without a population educated at least in the elements of reading, writing and arithmetic. He remarked in 1851 how in terms of manufacturing progress other countries, notably the United States, were already ahead of us in some fields because of their superior systems of education. This had been evidenced by the high quality of many foreign articles displayed at the Great Exhibition. 'How will you be able to rally, how will you attain to further improvement in arts and manufactures but by improving the education of your people? I don't think we can wait.'

Cobden was also convinced that national education was needed to improve the tone of working-class life. Too many people lived in squalor because of poverty, but their poverty sprang as much from ignorance as from vice. Finally, education was essential to secure national peace and harmony. It could overcome class cleavages and tensions by raising the lower classes nearer to those above them. Once good national schools were established the children of the middle and working classes would begin to be educated together. Education would drive away the risk of revolution. 'Revolution or the schoolhouse', that was the choice. National institutions would only be safe when they had the support of an educated people.

The problem of education in relation to revolution was naturally much in the minds of Lancashire reformers in the 1830s and '40s. Cobden's earliest public work was as an advocate of extended working-class education. He assisted in starting a school near his print works at Sabden, and thereafter his firm refused to accept any young employees who could not read. Cobden's first major public speech was delivered at Manchester in October 1835 in support of a proposal to establish a Manchester Athenaeum. By the end of 1837 we have seen how his reputation as an education speaker led to his first meeting with John Bright.

Cobden linked the extension of education closely with the extension of the suffrage. During the first years of his career he hoped to secure improved popular education before the masses were given the vote. He told the electors of Stockport in 1836 that it was equally the interest and the duty of reformers 'who now desire to exalt the rights of the many above the privileges of the few, to declare war against that ignorance from which all our political and nearly all our physical evils spring'. Education, he wrote three years later, not only taught men to appreciate the rights of free citizens, it qualified men to possess them. By the late 1840s, however, Cobden had changed his position. Distressed by the failure to establish a national system because of religious difficulties, he now contended that such a system could only be secured *after* a wide extension of the suffrage. 'With the progress of democracy', he wrote in 1852, 'I look for increased success in our educational projects, and hence I am in favour of extending the suffrage, acknowledging all one risks in giving power to a badly educated people.' He remarked in 1864 that if the House of Commons represented the people the education problem would soon be solved, since fear of the ignorance of the electorate 'would compel people of property to educate the masses *if they had political power*'. Cobden was here anticipating the cry 'we must educate our masters', which followed the passing of the Second Reform Act.[1]

From the 1840s to the 1860s religious suspicions and rivalries seriously retarded progress towards the establishment of a national system of elementary education in England. The Church of England long expected to dominate any national system, in effect using public money to promote instruction in its tenets. The Dissenters vigorously opposed this prospect, the most militant among them coming to the perverse conclusion that no national system was needed, that contrary to all appearances the voluntary efforts of the Church of England and of the Nonconformist sects were together creating an efficient schools' network. This belief in 'voluntaryism' was first asserted in 1843 in response to a Government scheme for educating the factory children, which certainly did seem likely to favour the Anglicans. Edward Baines of the *Leeds Mercury* and Edward Miall of the *Nonconformist* emerged as leaders of the voluntaryists. They produced a mass of misleading statistics, seeking to demonstrate alleged educational progress under private auspices since the beginning of the century. Both Baines and Miall were prominent free traders, but Cobden opposed them plainly and totally on the voluntaryist issue. He thought that Baines was afflicted by monomania on the education question, seeking through distorted statistics to conceal the fact that we were the most ignorant Protestant nation in the world. Cobden was convinced that while free trade was right for commerce, it was wrong for education. 'Any voluntary system is a chimera.'

In the 1830s Cobden hoped that agreement might be reached to allow instruction in the belief of any Christian sect even within schools provided out of public funds. After seeing the strength of sectarian prejudice, however, by the late '40s he had become an advocate of non-sectarian religious instruction in state schools, regarding this as the only possible compromise. On his return from Europe in 1847 he began to speak regularly in support of a non-sectarian system. 'I am for the education of the people. I believe the great mass of the people take less interest in this sectarian squabbling than many others of us are apt to imagine . . . I say now, emphatically, I vote for education; I'll support education; I'll do the best I can for Dissenters; but I'll never oppose a system of education which promises to give to the mass of the people an opportunity of raising themselves in life.'

Cobden had been much impressed by the education system of New England. He praised it in his 1835 pamphlet, and first-hand observation later in the same year made him still more enthusiastic. He had found the New Englanders as much superior in education and activity to the population of Kent as the latter were to the downtrodden people of Naples. This American system provided schools out of local rates, made attendance compulsory, and provided non-sectarian religious instruction, using the Bible without any denominational bias. Cobden liked the emphasis upon local control, believing that this would ensure the maximum of freedom plus efficiency, which a centralised organisation could not offer.

Throughout Cobden's lifetime Manchester was the national centre of debate upon education questions. In 1847 the Lancashire Public School Association was formed there to promote the New England system. It avowedly modelled itself upon the Anti-Corn Law League as it set out to organise meetings and branches throughout the country. Cobden eventually became a vice-president. In 1850 it changed its name to the National Public School Association, but Manchester remained its centre. In 1852 the Association promoted a Manchester and Salford Education Bill, which sought to establish a non-sectarian system locally, financed through a local rate, as an example to the nation. Cobden was active in support of this bill inside and outside Parliament, but it failed to pass the Commons. Later in the same year he summed up the melancholy position of the education question in a letter to George Combe, who had always encouraged his education efforts:

'It is the old story, Church and Dissent, and rival sects. If you propose to teach religion, they object to anything being taught but their own, or they insist upon none being taught at the public expense. If you propose to leave out religion, they denounce you as an atheist, and then reason and argument might as well be addressed to the clouds. . . . I have been for nearly twenty years looking in all directions for an escape from our educational "fix" and am more bewildered than ever.'

Eighteen years were to pass, and Cobden was to be five years dead, before the Education Act of 1870 finally established a schools system including local rating and non-sectarian instruction, as advocated from 1847 by Cobden and the Public Schools Association.[2]

We have hardly mentioned John Bright in connection with Cobden's educational aspirations. Although in the 1830s Bright was an advocate of improved working-class education, during the 1840s, to Cobden's regret, he allowed himself to be half drawn into voluntaryism. Bright's strong dislike of the Church Establishment and Church privilege predisposed him to this. Education thus became another sphere in which Cobden showed himself more forward-looking than Bright. Bright wrote to Baines, the voluntaryist leader, in 1848: 'The question is between your views and those of the Lancashire association, and were I forced to a decision I should go with you, but I prefer to have more time for examination and reflexion.' Six years later, however, Bright was still reflecting, and Cobden told him sharply to 'take sides on the education question. You can't take a neutral part, or a lukewarm attitude. Is not the time come to declare for the New England system?' Bright at last seems to have responded. A few days later he spoke at an education meeting in Manchester sponsored by Cobden. The strength of Cobden's influence over him was made clear in Bright's diary. 'I have some hesitation about it, but do not like to shrink from any good work in which he is engaged.' Bright noted that he spoke for an hour in showing that the voluntaryist arguments were untenable, 'but giving them high credit for their efforts and labours'.[3]

In 1845 Cobden had failed to prevent Bright from taking an opposite side to himself on what was partly an education question. This was Peel's proposal for an increased state grant to the Roman Catholic seminary at Maynooth in Ireland. This was one of apparently only two occasions when Cobden and Bright voted in opposite lobbies in the Commons. Cobden felt that no new principle of endowment was involved at this time since a grant was already being given to the college. He refused therefore to discuss the abstract point, and dwelt instead upon the value of an increased grant as a gesture of reconciliation towards Ireland and also as a step in the improvement of Irish education. The priests were men of unequalled influence, and the better they were educated the more wisely would they use that influence.

Peel's proposal was virulently opposed by some Englishmen on anti-Catholic grounds, but Bright to his credit did not vote against it in this spirit. He opposed the plan because he objected to all state subsidisation of religion. In other words, he insisted upon looking at the abstract issue which Cobden did not regard as under discussion. Bright told the Commons (and Cobden) that 'he should hold himself to have read, thought, and lived in vain, if he voted for a measure which in the smallest degree should give any further assistance to the principle of endowment'. Cobden's answer was sharp and short: 'I believe if all our discussions had been more logical and less theological we should have made more progress in the business of legislation.'[4]

Religious feeling could thus soon distract Bright from schemes of improvement. It is not therefore surprising to find him, after Cobden's steadying hand had been removed, attacking the vital Education Act of 1870 on religious grounds. The Act provided support for existing denominational schools out of local rates, and envisaged the building of Board Schools only where existing denominational provision was inadequate. Bright and many other Dissenters objected strongly to this aspect of the Act because existing Anglican schools greatly outnumbered existing Nonconformist schools, and they therefore believed that the Government was once again inclining to promote the influence of the Established Church at the expense of Nonconformist taxpayers. Bright did not now dispute the need for a national state-aided schools system, but he wanted the establishment of a universal network of non-sectarian schools, leaving existing denominational schools outside the scheme. No public money would then be expended in support of any particular sect. Bright had been nominally a member of Gladstone's Cabinet which produced the 1870 Act, but he had been ill during the vital months of 1870 when the measure passed through Parliament. His criticisms were not therefore publicly heard until 1873, after he had recovered. He failed to see that the Act had made wise use of existing, even if denominational, facilities, concentrating funds upon building non-sectarian schools where they were most needed. Cobden would have welcomed the practical sense of the 1870 Act. For several years Bright continued to exaggerate the religious danger, and he claimed in 1873 that this would lead to the failure of the Act. Cobden would have been aghast at such a forecast. Fortunately, the new system did not break down, and by 1877 even Bright was urging the working men of Rochdale to support it. He had at last come to see the education question in proportion, forty years after a common interest in education had led to his first meeting with Cobden.[5]

### 7. NEWSPAPERS

Cobden and Bright showed a close interest in the newspaper press throughout their careers. Cobden's first pamphlet of 1835 ran on significantly from a discussion of education to a discussion of newspapers. He was confident that once the masses had been educated they would want to read good newspapers, and that such newspapers would in themselves be instruments of popular education. As he once explained, he thought any publication worth while which made people think, whether a newspaper or a book. On another occasion he even rashly went so far as to imply that one copy of *The Times* contained more useful information than all the works of Thucydides.

Yet despite this potential for good, up to 1855 the newspaper press was heavily taxed. These 'taxes on knowledge', as the reformers had named them in order to underline the link between newspapers and education, made daily newspapers far too dear for working men to buy. After 1836 the newspaper stamp duty stood at 1*d.* a sheet; all advertisements were taxed at 1*s.* 6*d.* each, and the excise on paper was levied at 1½*d.* per pound. These taxes forced the price of newspapers of the early 1850s as high as 5*d.* per copy. No penny dailies could be published, and no provincial dailies at any price, until after the repeal of the newspaper stamp duty in 1855. Cobden and Bright believed that the abolition of taxation, by cutting the price of respectable daily newspapers, would win them a large working-class reading public. They knew that under the taxes on knowledge the workers, if they read newspapers at all, mainly read scurrilous Sunday publications, full of sex and violence.

The restricting influence of the newspaper taxes, added to shrewd management, had built up one newspaper, *The Times*, into a position of almost overwhelming predominance. *The Times* carefully followed the drift of middle- and upper-class opinion, and became the one newspaper of the majority of daily newspaper readers. In the early 1850s it sold approximately sixty thousand copies per day, nearly three times the combined circulations of its five main rival London dailies. After 1846 we have seen how Cobden and Bright found themselves increasingly out of touch with public opinion. This meant that they found themselves increasingly opposed by *The Times*. Bright used to say that if *The Times* attacked him on any issue he was then sure that he was right; if it praised him, he became uneasy. 'What an absurd position we are in,' complained Cobden in 1851, 'so completely dictated to and domineered over by one newspaper.'

To destroy the excessive influence of *The Times*, and to make it possible for the lower classes to enjoy penny daily newspapers, Cobden and Bright played an active part in the early 1850s in the last stages of the agitation for the repeal of the taxes on knowledge, and in particular for abolition of the newspaper stamp. *The Times* advocated continuation of the stamp, for it gave newspapers the right to free postage without further charge, and this enabled *The Times* to circulate widely in the provinces in preference to local newspapers. By removing the stamp Cobden and Bright hoped to encourage the emergence of a cheap provincial daily press, which would compete locally with *The Times* at the same time as new cheap national dailies would compete with it in London. In February 1851 at a meeting of middle- and working-class reformers the pair helped to form the Association for Promoting the Repeal of the Taxes on Knowledge. This body took the place of a Chartist offshoot, the Newspaper Stamp Abolition Committee. Milner Gibson became president, and C. D. Collet secretary, with Cobden and Bright as members of the committee. Gibson was especially prominent in the cause, but Cobden and Bright were not much less active. The stamp, Cobden reminded Bright in 1853, lay at the root of 'the great mound of ignorance and helplessness which bars the path of social and political progress in this country'. Yet the very ignorance of the people made them unaware of their need for a free press. The new association perforce acted more as an education pressure group than as a mass movement, campaigning *for* the people rather than *through* them. If the people had never tasted bread, explained Cobden to Collet, they would have been equally indifferent about the question of a big or a little loaf. 'The case must be brought before Parliament and the country as an *education* question.'

Gradually, success was achieved. A select committee into the working of the newspaper stamp was secured in 1850, with Milner Gibson as chairman and Cobden as a member. Its report was something of a compromise, but Cobden secured insertion of a sentence asserting that news was not 'in itself a desirable subject for taxation'. In the event, it was not news but advertisements which were relieved first. Gladstone, Chancellor of the Exchequer in the Aberdeen Government, proved responsive to the agitation, and abolished the advertisement duty in 1853. Early in 1855 he left office when about to propose removal of the newspaper stamp. Fortunately, his successor followed his lead, and the compulsory newspaper stamp finally disappeared at midsummer. In 1861, with Gladstone again at the Exchequer, the work of freeing the press was completed by repeal of the paper excise after a famous battle with the House of Lords.[1]

Repeal of the newspaper stamp led to a newspaper revolution. *The Times*, although still a great influence, no longer stood almost without competition. Daily newspaper reading now became a middle-class habit as penny dailies sprang up both in London and in the provinces. The most successful of these was the *Daily Telegraph*, started in 1855, which achieved the unprecedented sale of over two hundred thousand copies by the 1860s. In Lancashire both the *Manchester Guardian* and the *Manchester Examiner* became penny dailies. The *Examiner*, the Lancashire organ of Cobden and Bright, did especially well. By 1861 it was selling thirty-nine thousand copies each day. Unfortunately, the London penny daily launched as a Cobdenite mouthpiece, the *Morning Star*, did much less well than its Lancashire counterpart. The *Star* first appeared on March 17, 1856, with the *Evening Star* as its afternoon associate. Joseph Sturge was a prime mover and leading subscriber, along with other members of the peace party. Cobden himself did not invest money in the paper, nor apparently did Bright, although both were thought to have done so at the time. By avoiding a financial connection they hoped to make plain their political independence, even in relation to a newspaper friendly to themselves. But it was inevitable that they should be in close contact with the management and policy of the paper. Cobden was full of characteristically shrewd advice for making it successful and influential. 'Will our friends who are subscribing their money so far temporise as to be willing to see the editor of the paper *postpone* a portion or what can be said in favour of peace until a more convenient season? If they cannot tolerate a little of the "wisdom of the serpent" as means of promoting the "harmlessness of the dove", I don't believe it possible *at present* to establish a daily paper in the interest of peace.' The *Star* attracted several outstanding journalists to its staff. These included Samuel Lucas, Bright's brother-in-law and editor from 1858 to 1865, Justin McCarthy, later leader of the Irish Parliamentary party, who succeeded Lucas, and John Morley, who followed McCarthy as the paper's last editor. Yet despite the work of these able journalists the *Morning Star* never really prospered. It began well enough, reaching a daily sale of thirty thousand by 1856, but ten years later it had dropped back to half this and was losing money. The opinions of the Manchester School were not sufficiently popular to win that volume of steady support necessary to maintain a national daily. The last number of the *Morning Star* appeared on October 13, 1869, after which it merged into the *Daily News*, a more moderate and more successful Liberal organ, which had recently reduced its price to a penny.

Yet even successful penny dailies like the *Daily News* and *Daily Telegraph* still failed to attract many working-class readers. The hopes of Cobden and Bright were disappointed, most mid-Victorian working men still preferring to read only the lurid Sunday newspapers. Although well aware of the need for a national system of education, Cobden had been optimistic that the workers would buy respectable dailies, if the price could be reduced to a penny, even without the benefit of good schooling. He assured Bright in 1852 that a penny newspaper press 'would do more to educate the millions than all the schoolmasters in the land'. The event proved Cobden wrong. It took a generation of national education after 1870 before the appearance of the *Daily Mail* in 1896; and even then the *Mail* appealed mainly to lower middle-class readers. Another half century passed before the *Daily Mirror* made the breakthrough to the real working class, ensuring that for the first time almost every adult in Britain was seeing a daily newspaper.[2]

One of the last political incidents in which the names of Cobden and Bright appeared together before the public was a noisy dispute with their old enemy, *The Times*. On November 24, 1863 Cobden and Bright spoke at Rochdale upon, among other things, the need for land reform. *The Times* unfairly interpreted their words as tantamount to a policy of confiscation of the property of the rich for the sake of the poor. Bright, in particular, was described as favouring this policy. When Cobden read this charge he rushed to the defence of his friend. The misrepresentations of *The Times* released all his feelings of anger against its long hostility towards their work. Cobden believed that deliberate misrepresentation by *The Times* had been a major cause of their failure to convert public opinion to a policy of peace, retrenchment and reform. It had 'successfully played the game', he told Bright, 'of making us appear outside, impracticable politicians.' Cobden was convinced that *The Times* was being paid, directly or indirectly, by Palmerston and others to carry out this work of denigration. He now decided to strike back, explaining to Bright

'If we look back for years, *with all becoming modesty*, remember what we have been doing for the public, and then think of the tone of contemptuous disparagement on every occasion with which the writers in that print have treated us, until it has culminated in this outrageous charge of gigantic agrarian violence, have we not borne it with an excess of meekness? Now there is no doubt that when they put on the livery of Palmerston & Co., and they took their wages, one of the jobs they especially undertook was to knock you and me about on all occasions.'

Cobden sent to Delane, the editor of *The Times*, a letter refuting the assertions in the paper. Its language was very strong, and Delane refused to publish it. Cobden denounced not only a 'foul libel', but also the paper's policy of anonymous journalism which enabled it to indulge in such misrepresentation. 'No gentleman would dream of saying, under the responsibility of his signature, what your writer said of Mr. Bright yesterday.' Cobden then hinted at corruption, remarking how the editor, while always incognito to the public, 'drops the mask with very sufficient reasons in the presence of those powerful classes who are at once the dispensers of social distinction, and (on which I might have something to say) of the patronage of the Government'. An interchange of letters now followed between Cobden and Delane, who was soon forced out of his anonymity as editor. The whole correspondence was published by Cobden in other newspapers, and produced widespread excitement. We must agree with Morley,

Cobden's official biographer, that he went too far in these letters. His charges of misrepresentation on the land question were valid. He was also right in charging *The Times* with pursuing a policy of 'continuous disparagement' against Bright and himself; but he was wrong to accuse *The Times* of deriving 'corrupt advantages' in return for this policy. When Cobden tried to collect evidence to be used in Parliament he could find none of any substance in support of the corruption charge. *The Times* under Delane attacked Cobden and Bright, not because it was paid to do so, but because their views were generally unpopular with its middle- and upper-class readers, and it was traditional *Times* policy to follow its public. Cobden's irritation with *The Times* was understandable, but he allowed its unfairness to provoke him into unfairness in reply. Ill-health had perhaps shortened even his remarkably equable temper. But he had been the victim of persistent disparagement, which followed him even into the grave. *The Times* obituary leader on his death in 1865 was a notable specimen of damning with faint praise:

> 'The English gentleman, such as we fondly imagine him, so circumstanced, would never have dealt so rudely [as Cobden] with the great idols that fell before this ruthless iconoclast . . . when a great error is to be corrected, or the chains of a great tyranny to be thrown off, we must be content to welcome our deliverer from some quarter least expected, it may be least loved; the man from the ranks, the man of a peculiar school, the hermit in thought, the agitator with the faults of the class he comes to rescue. We must not complain that he is not one of us in education and feeling.[3]

## 8. THE LAND

Cobden and Bright advocated free trade in land, but *The Times* misrepresented this as a call for free land, a much more extreme policy. The two Radicals did not originate the cry for free trade in land any more than they had originated the cry for free trade in corn, but they were its most distinguished advocates during the mid-Victorian years. They started from the belief that every Englishman, and especially every agricultural labourer, wanted a plot of his own, and that he was entitled to some reasonable chance of satisfying this wish. Cobden asserted in 1846 that there was 'a taste for land in human kind, and especially is it the desire of Englishmen to possess land'. In the way of this desire stood the peers and other great landlords who about 1870 still owned over 40 per cent of the territory of England and Wales. Small proprietors, by contrast, owned only 12½ per cent. There was no other country, concluded Cobden, in which the peasantry were so divorced from possession of land. On his deathbed he was heard murmuring the rhyme

> 'Great is the crime in man or woman,
> Who steals the goose from off the common,
> But who shall plead the man's excuse,
> Who steals the common from the goose.'

The landownership figures just quoted showed how repeal of the Corn Laws had done nothing to reduce landlord control of the land. It had not been the aim of the Anti-Corn Law League to achieve this. But after 1846 Cobden and Bright talked more than once of starting a new league to demand a fairer distribution of the land. In his last public speech in 1864 Cobden exclaimed that if he had still been a young man 'I would take Adam Smith in hand, and I would have a League for free trade in land just as we had a League for free trade in corn'. The writings of Smith, claimed Cobden, justified a Land League as much as a Corn League. In book three of the *Wealth of Nations* Adam Smith had described primogeniture and entail as absurd because they dictated the present and future at the will of the past. They also perpetuated large estates, whereas Smith believed that small estates produced the most efficient cultivation. At the time of his altercation with *The Times* in 1863 Cobden read to a friend a passage from the *Wealth of Nations* which attacked primogeniture and entail. Cobden laughingly pointed out that if Bright had spoken as plainly as Smith, 'how he would have been branded as an incendiary and Socialist'. Cobden and Bright certainly did not intend confiscation of the land of the rich. In the 1880s Bright specifically repudiated Henry George's plan for land nationalisation. They hoped to encourage the break-up of great estates, not by direct intervention, but by the quiet working of changes in land law. Pointing to American and European examples, they wanted abolition of primogeniture and entail, of discrimination between reality and personalty, and of all other practices restricting the division of large estates. Linked to this, they wanted a simplification of the intricate law of land transfer. These reforms would produce a system under which, as Bright explained, it would be almost as easy to buy and sell land as to buy and sell anything else. 'It means no legal encouragement shall be given to great estates and great farms, and that the natural forces of accumulation and dispersion shall have free play.' It meant, too, that unnecessary and expensive work would not be made for lawyers, which at present amounted to 'an enormous tax' upon all dealings in land. A thorough reform along these lines, concluded Bright in 1873, would continue the work begun by the Anti-Corn Law League. 'It would give an endless renown to the Minister who made it, and would bless to an incalculable extent all classes connected with and dependent on honest industry.'

Cobden and Bright expected much, probably too much, from these reforms. They forecast a gradual revolution in the countryside without need for violence or confiscation. Social justice would be ensured by reducing the excessive national and local power of the feudal aristocracy and squirearchy, and by giving many more people a stake in the land. Cultivation standards would be improved in the careful hands of the many new small proprietors. Naturally, such small cultivators could not be exposed to the damage permitted under the Game Laws for the sake of aristocratic sport. The Game Laws would therefore have to be repealed. We have seen how Bright's first success in Parliament had come in 1845 through discussion of the Game Law question. He failed, however, three years later with a bill for total repeal. Thereafter he never pressed the game question alone, but repeal of the Game Laws remained part of his land programme for the rest of his life.

Bright advocated land reform during more than forty years, Cobden for nearly twenty. Yet the cause made little progress. The industrial classes felt an intense deference towards the aristocratic landlords, which distressed Cobden. 'We are a servile, aristocracy-loving, lord-ridden people, who regard the land with as much reverence as we still do the peerage and baronetage. Not only have not nineteen-twentieths of us any share in the soil, but we have not presumed to think that we are worthy to possess a few acres of mother earth.' In one of his last letters Cobden told the story of the Frenchman who, when asked what he found in England to observe, answered, 'Sunday and primogeniture.' Those who worked upon the land seemed as unwilling as the townspeople to start an agitation against the aristocracy and squirearchy.

Bright complained in 1879 how the tenant farmers had failed to support him against the Game Laws, preferring instead 'farmers' friends' who were really only the friends of the landlords. As for the agricultural labourers, the programme of Cobden and Bright promised to pull them out of their extreme poverty, which was notorious; but this poverty had produced so much ignorance and helplessness that the labourers long seemed to lack the spirit to help themselves. They may have wanted land, as Cobden and Bright claimed, but they were the most inarticulate element among the Victorian working class. 'Their power to deliver themselves,' complained Bright in 1866, 'their power to combine, seems at the lowest ebb.' Bright showed great interest in the briefly successful efforts during the early '70s of Joseph Arch and his Agricultural Labourers' Union. Though remaining suspicious of trade unions in their coercive economic aspect, he hoped that Arch's union might help in gaining the vote for the rural workers. When in 1884 the rural franchise was at last greatly extended Bright exclaimed that the land laws would now be reformed, 'and much of them reformed out of existence'.

Yet this never happened. Change was forced upon the countryside before and after 1884, but not by the land reformers. The agricultural depression of the last quarter of the century produced in eastern and southern England a shift from grain to meat and dairy farming. This shift created many more small farmers, and the heyday of the large-scale corn-growing landlords and farmers, the core of the old landed interest, was already long past by the time of Bright's death in 1889. Then during the next thirty years the impact and prospect of death duties led many landowners to dispose of their property. Smaller holdings and freer trade in land were thus developed even without enactment of the reforms advocated by Cobden and Bright and other land reformers. Primogeniture, entail and the rest were thereby shown to have been (in the phrase of a modern agricultural historian) largely 'paper dragons'. They did not in themselves constitute the main supports of the great local and national power of the mid-Victorian aristocracy and gentry.[1]

### 9. IRELAND

The land question stood at the heart of that most intractable of Victorian political problems, the problem of the past, present and future of Ireland. Cobden and Bright wanted abolition of primogeniture in Ireland as well as in England, but they went far beyond this in recommending a system of Irish tenant right and land purchase. They accepted that the extreme misery of Ireland required extreme remedies. Cobden visited Ireland as early as 1825, and his sensitive nature was immediately disturbed by its 'poverty, ignorance, and misrule'. He saw mud cabins, 'collections of huts called towns', pigs living with families, men and women without shoes and stockings. 'There appears to be no middle class in Ireland: there are the rich, and those who are the object of wretchedness and almost starvation.' Bright first went to Ireland in 1832, and in 1849 and 1852 he returned on fact-finding tours. After the terrible Irish famine of the mid-'40s there was now still more misery and squalor than Cobden had found a quarter of a century earlier: 'enough to horrify the stoutest, and to move the hardest heart. Ruined cottages, uncultivated lands, crowded workhouses, fever, cholera, famine, scores of victims buried in trenches, etc., etc. The story is frightful, and I will not write the details.' In 1866 and 1868, when Bright was at a peak of popularity in Ireland as much as in England, he again crossed the Irish Sea. He told a Dublin audience that if he were an Irishman he would tour the country and rouse the people to 'some great and united action'.

Cobden and Bright readily accepted that the Irish had much cause for bitterness. Bright reminded the Commons in 1866 how after more than half a century of union with Great Britain the condition of Ireland had become worse than ever before. A majority of Irishmen, exclaimed Bright, would gladly unfasten their island from its proximity to England and move it across the Atlantic nearer to the United States, whither many thousands of them had been forced to emigrate. Still more Irish people had flooded into England during the nineteenth century, notably into Bright's native Lancashire, where most of them lived in squalor. Cobden and Bright believed that the Irish had a right to be assisted to live contentedly within their own country. This would require not coercion, of which there had been too much, but statesmanship, of which there had been too little.

Cobden and Bright accepted that Ireland's sufferings stemmed (in the phrase coined by Disraeli) from 'an absentee aristocracy and an alien Church'. The Established Anglican Church in Ireland was supported by only a small minority of the population, and yet it claimed all the privileges of a State Church. Cobden emphasised the injustice of this in his earliest political writings in the 1830s. He recommended legislation 'up to the knowledge of the age, by placing Catholic and Protestant upon an equal footing in secular matters; and for the rest I would leave to an unbiased reason the adjustment of speculative opinions, confident of the ultimate triumph of truth'. Cobden was here hinting that Protestantism would be stronger in Ireland after disestablishment. Bright made the same point thirty years later when he remarked how the Church Establishment encouraged the equation of Catholicism with patriotism. In 1852 Bright came forward with a detailed scheme of Irish Church disestablishment and disendowment. His plan was an elaboration of proposals briefly sketched out by Cobden in his 1835 pamphlet. Bright proposed a Church Property Commission to take over all the tithes and other property of the Established Church. He wanted all shades of religious opinion in Ireland to be placed upon an equality, and to assist and emphasise this he proposed that each sect, including the Episcopalians, should be given a share of the wealth appropriated by the Church Commission. These gifts were to be made entirely without conditions, for the state must not appear still to be interfering in Irish religious life. Bright recommended that the Roman Catholic Church should be given £1 million to strengthen its parish organisation. The greater part of the money in the hands of the Commission, however, which Bright estimated at £5-7 million in total, should be 'directed to the educational and moral improvement of the people, without respect to class or creed. This fund would extend and perfect the educational institutions of the country; it would establish and endow free libraries in all the chief towns of Ireland, and would dispense blessings in many channels for the free and equal enjoyment of the whole population.'

In 1869 Bright was a member of Gladstone's Government which finally secured Irish Church disestablishment. Under the 1869 Act the disendowed Irish Church was left with more money than Bright had expected, and no grant was paid to the Roman Catholic Church; but he accepted the measure as substantially just. Payments under the Act for non-religious purposes followed lines envisaged by Bright. Between 1871 and 1882 £2,300,000 was given for educational purposes, almost as much for distress works, nearly £1 million to cover payments under the Arrears of Rent Act (1882) and £250,000 to sea-fisheries.

The Victorians were much less successful in solving the Irish land problem. Cobden and Bright believed that the great estates owned by absentee landlords must be broken up, both for economic and psychological reasons. In Ireland, apart from Ulster, wrote Cobden in 1848, there was 'no property but the soil, and no labour but upon the land, and you cannot reach the population in their material or moral condition but through the proprietorship of the land'. Therefore, he wanted to make the proprietors of the soil resident, by breaking-up the large estates. 'In other words, I would give Ireland to the Irish.' In England Cobden and Bright were content to wait for the break up of the great estates through the abolition of primogeniture and entail, but they argued that in Ireland the Government must accelerate the process. Legislation must be passed to protect tenants against eviction, and a Land Commission must be created to purchase large estates for re-sale farm by farm to tenants and others at interest over twenty years. 'What you want', exclaimed Bright, 'is to restore a middle-class proprietory to the soil.' Here he was echoing Cobden's lament, already quoted, that Ireland lacked a middle class. Cobden and Bright had great faith that a strong yeomanry would achieve for Ireland's agricultural economy what a strong manufacturing middle class had achieved for England. Bright carefully explained that he did not envisage the Irish poor coming into ownership of the land, 'for the poor man, in the ordinary meaning of the term, cannot be the possessor of land'. There were overtones here of Bright's concept of the 'residuum'. What Bright wanted was that 'farmers and men of moderate means should become possessors of land and of their farms'. This process, however, was not to involve compulsory purchase of the land of absentee landlords. The Land Commission proposed by Bright was to buy on generous terms, perhaps 20 per cent higher than the market price, and Bright was confident that this would draw many estates voluntarily on to the market. He expected that all over Ireland a process of land division and improvement would begin, such as had followed the sale of the Somerset estate of the bankrupt Duke of Buckingham a few years earlier. He described to a Birmingham audience in 1868 how on the old Buckingham lands after their division into small units new houses had replaced tumbledown tenements, 'the red soil appearing under the plough, and cultivation going on with such general activity as had not been witnessed till within these last few years'.

Gladstone's first Irish Land Act of 1870 did not go as far as Bright had recommended, but it did contain clauses, included by Gladstone out of deference to Bright, intended to aid the conversion of tenants into owners. The Treasury was empowered to advance two-thirds of the purchase price on the sale of any holding to its tenant; this money was to be repayable by equal annual instalments, with interest spread over thirty-five years at the rate of £5 for every £100 advanced. The 1870 Land Act also extended the custom of Ulster tenant right to all Ireland. Unfortunately, the Act did not work well. The Bright clauses, for example, were little used, because they expected tenants still to find one-third of the purchase price. Eleven years later Gladstone had recourse to a second Irish Land Act, at a time of increasing tension in Ireland. Parnell and the Land League had embarked upon a course of violence at home and obstruction at Westminster, which Bright, in particular, deplored as disloyal. He told the Irish leaders across the floor of the Commons that if only they had conducted themselves like the Anti-Corn Law Leaguers, keeping to constitutional methods, he would have supported their demand for comprehensive land reform. Privately, he remarked to Gladstone that Parnell seemed to hate England even more than he loved Ireland. Bright felt that no business could be done with such a man, and yet there was no alternative party. 'There is no middle class, as there is in England, to stand forward to sustain the good, and to denounce the evil.' Gladstone's second Land Act of 1881 established the principles of free sale, fixity of tenure, and fair rent. It also went some way farther towards promoting Bright's ideas on land purchase. A Land Commission was constituted with power to advance three-quarters of an estate's purchase price, compared with two-thirds under the earlier Act. Bright thought the 1881 measure over-complicated, but, as with the 1870 scheme, he welcomed it as an important step forward. Unhappily, the revised land purchase clauses were still little used, for few tenants could find even the necessary one-quarter of the purchase price, and they could not borrow it except at usurious interest.

So into the 1880s Gladstone and Bright kept together on Irish questions, with Bright always inclined to be the more radical. Then with the Home Rule crisis of 1885–6 came a dramatic reversal of positions. When Gladstone announced his conversion to Home Rule, Bright reluctantly but firmly opposed him, finally losing thereby the high reputation which he had won in Ireland. At heart, Bright had probably always been opposed to Home Rule, but his position had not always been clear. Here, for example, was how he had dealt with the question in a speech of 1868:

'Force and fraud and corruption of an unparalleled character were the means by which the extinction of the Irish Parliament was brought about—and although I have not a word to say, and I hope I may never have a word, in favour of the separation of the two countries—yet I will not hesitate to assert that the Irish people never consented to that legislative union, and that their right to protest against it, and the right to ask for the restoration of their Parliament —if they think it would be advantageous to them—has not and cannot be destroyed. But, however, the question before us is this, and it is a fair question: can we so deal with Ireland as to make union probable and inevitable through its obvious advantages to both countries? . . . I want to know why we cannot make Ireland content to be a portion of a greater nation.'

In this fashion did Bright veer away from his initial admission of the 'right' of the Irish people to ask for Home Rule, if they wanted it. This drift of thought was somewhat reminiscent of Bright's veering away from an initial assertion in favour of universal suffrage in his 1851 letter to Sturge, quoted earlier. In 1866 he had been decidedly ambiguous on Home Rule in a speech at Dublin:

'If you had a Parliament on College Green, clearly the tenantry of Ireland, with the present feeling in Ireland, would be able to force that Parliament to any measure of justice they named; but as you have to deal with a great Parliament sitting in London, all the clamour you make, or the demands you may urge from this side of the Channel, come with a very feeble effect, especially as it can only be represented by about a hundred Members.'

Twenty years later this passage was reprinted in a leaflet published by the Home Rule Union, attempting to prove Bright's apostasy. As with his reform speeches, Bright's speeches on Ireland contained passages such as the two quoted which encouraged those who held very advanced views to believe that Bright was ready to go along with them. In reality, he was no more in favour of Home Rule than he was in favour of universal suffrage. In a private letter written at the time of his 1866 Dublin speech he described the occasion as the first public meeting held in the city for many years at which 'anyone could have spoken in favour of the Union'. This was how he regarded his speech, notwithstanding the apparent tone of the passage quoted. During the 1870s Bright finally removed all ambiguity from his declared attitude on Home Rule. Hearing in 1872 that he was being named in Ireland as an advocate of separation, he issued, a public denial, asserting that two Parliaments at Dublin and Westminster would be 'an intolerable mischief'. Three years later he published a strong attack upon the federal Home Rule proposals of an Irish clergyman, who wanted to constitute separate Parliaments for England, Scotland, Wales and Ireland. Why, asked Bright, should the people of Great Britain over-turn their institutions 'to allay the discontent of a portion of the people of Ireland'. He remained opposed to such federal solutions to the end of his life, not supporting the 'Home Rule all round' scheme fav-oured by Joseph Chamberlain in answer to Gladstone's 1885 proposals.

Gladstone made great efforts to gain Bright's support during the early months of 1886. In March they held a long conversation on Irish questions. Bright admitted that he would be glad to see the obstructive Irish 'rebels' (as he often called them) removed from Westminster; but his pugnacious spirit would not allow him to appear to be giving way to them. Moreover, he told Gladstone that he was convinced that such men could not be trusted to keep their promises, whatever con-cessions were made to them. He was not prepared to see power given to men who had insulted the Queen, torn down the Union Jack, and made a mockery of Parliamentary government. 'If I could believe them loyal,' he wrote to Gladstone, 'if they were honourable and truthful men, I could yield much, but I suspect that your policy of surrender to them will only place more power in their hands to war with greater effect against the unity of the three Kingdoms with no increase of good to the Irish people.' Bright feared that there might even be a restoration of protection in Ireland. Such an abandonment of free trade would constitute Parnell's ultimate disloyalty.

Bright had been dissatisfied with the quality of most Irish politicians for over forty years. He had always regarded them as unpractical extremists. As early as 1847 he criticised the Irish Members of Parliament for never bringing forward 'any proposition of a practical character'. His own practical solution to the problem of Irish government in 1886 was for a Grand Committee of Irish Members at Westminster, to which all Irish legislation would be referred in place of the normal second reading. Bright outlined this plan in an election speech at Birmingham in July 1886, after Gladstone had dissolved Parliament on the Home Rule issue. Up to this point, out of respect for Gladstone, Bright had refrained from speaking against him inside or outside Parliament. On May 31, however, at a meeting of Liberal Parliamentarians opposed to Gladstone, a letter from Bright to Chamberlain had been read out in which he announced his intention of voting against the second reading of the Home Rule Bill. The Liberal Unionists were at this point much divided among themselves, but Bright's letter helped to pull them firmly together round the simple negative of opposition to Gladstone's bill. This was probably more than Bright intended, for he was himself confused and distressed. But Bright's distress turned to anger when Gladstone forced the Home Rule issue to the point of a dissolution of Parliament, for Bright knew that Gladstone was making the split within the Liberal ranks definitive. He felt that he must now speak out, and in this spirit he made his Birmingham speech which was the last important oration of his career. Gladstone was asking for a revolution in Ireland, declared Bright, at the bidding of only one-twelfth of the population of the United Kingdom. He emphasised his refusal to abandon the Ulster Protestants to the mercies of the southern Catholic 'rebels'. 'I will never surrender to a Parliamentary party from Ireland, one half of whom have the dollars in their pockets subscribed by the enemies of England in the United States.' This strong language contributed to the decisive defeat of the Gladstonian Liberals in the election. In February 1887 Bright met Gladstone by chance in the street, and they shook hands; but they could never hope to resume their former harmony. In June of the same year Bright summed up the differences between them as 'not reconcilable'. Gladstone, said Bright, was 'committed to a Parliament in Dublin, I am utterly opposed to it. He is bound by contract with Parnell, and cannot go back, and Parnell is bound fast by the Irish American conspiracy.'

Bright had opposed Gladstone's Irish Land Bill as well as his Home Rule measure. In 1880 in Cabinet discussions before the second Land

Act Bright had developed his land purchase proposals even to the point of recommending a degree of compulsion. Compulsion, he thought, might be applied in the case of land held by corporations, and of waste lands fit for cultivation but neglected by owners unable or unwilling to farm them. Bright was now aiming at a lower social level than that middle-class proprietary which he had envisaged in the 1860s, even hoping that small farms on waste land might be let at almost nominal rents to small occupiers. Within six years, however, he had abandoned all these bold schemes in disgust at the activities of the Parnellites. By contrast, Gladstone, who had long been less advanced than Bright on the problem of land purchase, had by 1886 adopted Bright's former position. Gladstone now proposed that Irish landlords should be given the option of selling at a price to be fixed by a Land Commission. The Treasury was to advance a maximum of £50 m. in the period to March 1890 for the purchase of such land. Bright, however, now objected to this scheme as 'unnecesssary'. 'The Act of 1881 had done all that was reasonable for the tenants', claimed Bright, '—why adopt the policy of the rebel party, and get rid of landholders, and thus evict the English garrison as the rebels call them?'

What would Cobden have done had he been alive in 1886? Would he, like Bright, have been moved by disgust at the Parnellites into an unyielding attitude? Gladstone thought otherwise. He always held that Cobden would have supported him in 1886. Bright denied this. In his first pamphlet in 1835 Cobden had certainly declared that 'a Parliament in Dublin would not remedy the ills of Ireland', for such a system had been tried and failed. In 1848 he wrote that it was 'not by forms of legislation or the locality of Parliaments, but by a change and improvement of the population, that Ireland is to have a start in the career of civilisation and self-government'. But in the same year Cobden also wrote that he was beginning to regard repeal of the union, 'some kind of arrangement for indulging the craving of race and nationality', as indispensable. It would be 'desirable if possible to give them their local business to attend to, if that would satisfy them'. At this date Cobden was clearly uncertain about Irish government, but his flexible mind had not excluded some form of Home Rule. His amiable nature would not have been so disturbed as was the pugnacious Bright by the activities of the Parnellites. He would have recognised that here at least were Irish politicians with a purpose. Like Bright, he had complained in the 1840s that Irish Members of Parliament included 'hardly a man of business amongst them; and not three who are prepared cordially to co-operate together for any one common object'. The evidence is far from conclusive, for Home Rule was not a serious issue in Cobden's lifetime, but Gladstone was probably right in thinking that Cobden would have supported him in 1886. Bright revealingly told Gladstone in 1880 that he did not expect to learn much that was new about Ireland, 'after thirty years of reading and talking and considering the Irish question'. What brought out the rigidity of Bright's mind would probably have shown the responsiveness of Cobden's.[1]

## 10. EMPIRE

Throughout the Victorian years the establishment of both a formal and an informal British Empire went forward, partly impelled by the need for new markets to absorb the products of expanding British industry. Cobden and Bright were eager advocates of increased world free trade, but the methods of Victorian imperialism attracted their strongest censure. For imperial free trade, as practised by the Victorians, meant not only the peaceful exchange of goods between willing buyers and sellers but also the use of force to open and to retain markets. This meant in turn the maintenance of expensive military, naval, and colonial establishments, officered by the sons of the landed aristocracy. Cobden and Bright therefore opposed mid-Victorian colonial policy as firmly as they opposed contemporary British foreign policy, with which it was often linked. Behind both they detected and deplored the Palmerstonian spirit.

Cobden and Bright refused to accept any sort of control or interference in the affairs of overseas territories as necessary for the promotion of trade. They insisted that free trade was best left to make its way peacefully and naturally without the involvement of governments. In particular, seizure of large areas of land served no useful trading purpose. On the contrary, as Adam Smith and his successors had demonstrated, overseas possessions were always expensive to defend and to govern, costing more than they returned in the profits of trade. Three hundred millions of National Debt had been created, exclaimed Cobden in his first pamphlet, and millions of direct taxation was levied annually, so that we could repeat 'the fatal Spanish proverb—"The sun never sets on the King of England's dominions".'

Colonies not only wasted the resources of the colonising power, they corrupted its people and rulers by encouraging the use of violence and fraud. Cobden and Bright believed such to be the methods of Palmerston, and they were depressed to find the British public applauding them. They opposed in quick succession the Borneo War of 1849, the Kaffir War of 1850, and the Burma War of 1852. 'These horrid wars with less civilised people', complained Cobden, were far too popular. 'The public never hears both sides.' Cobden gave the other side in a pamphlet descriptively entitled *How Wars are got up in India, the Origin of the Burmese War*, published in 1853. The wrongs of Pizarro and Cortes 'were scarcely veiled in a more transparent pretence of right than our own report of the outrage at Rangoon throws about those disgraceful transactions'. Public opinion seemed prepared to accept outrages at a distance for the sake of profit at home, but the supremacy of the moral law would never allow permanent gain to come out of evil. Profit-seeking at the expense of life and morality must be resisted by all free traders. There were 'debts and mortgages and pecuniary interests of all sorts impelling certain parties to incessant activity to get the Government to take Sarawak'. Those who wished 'to avoid a repetition of the wars and crimes of the Cape and of India,' concluded Cobden, 'all free traders who really know what their principles mean', must oppose further annexation.

In 1857 the profit-at-any-price spirit in the East produced the *Arrow* incident, already noticed, over which Cobden defeated the Palmerston Government in the Commons, only to be himself defeated at the subsequent General Election. At this same period came the Indian Mutiny, bringing a crisis in the affairs of the richest of Victorian colonies. The government, commerce, and defence of India was a perpetual Victorian problem, as perpetual as that of Ireland. Bright (more than Cobden) took a close interest in Indian questions, just as he took a close interest in Ireland. The task of governing India wisely, wrote Bright in 1883, might prove an impossible one, but we must do our best 'to compensate for the wrong of the past and the present by conferring on the Indian people whatever good it is in our power to give them'. Fifty years earlier, in one of his earliest public speeches at Rochdale, Bright was already addressing himself to 'that land which our imagination has pictured as ever teeming with wealth. . . . We have seen how that wealth may be rendered available to England, and how the blessings of civilisation and Christianity may be spread abroad in that vast empire. We have also had a clear view of that which to this country is most important of all—the immense field which there exists for the extension of British commerce and for the consumption of British manufactures.' In Bright's early days the trade potential of India clearly predominated in his mind, whereas in his old age the moral responsibilities of government were uppermost. By 1850 he was accepted as a leading authority on Indian questions in the House of Commons. In 1868 Gladstone offered him the Indian Secretaryship, which Bright declined because of its onerous character and because he did not like the structure of Indian government.

Bright was first led into detailed study of Indian problems by a desire to secure increased Indian cotton production. He pointed out during the 1840s the dangers to Lancashire of its heavy dependence upon cotton from the American South, which provided three-quarters of our raw cotton supply. War with the United States had threatened more than once. Moreover, the American planters had become jealous of the high profits of the British cotton industry, and were seeking to secure a share of these through increased raw cotton prices. Some Americans were even talking of expanding their own cotton industry to the point where there would be no cotton for export. Above all, American cotton growing depended upon the insecure foundation of Southern slavery. Bright foresaw in the '40s what eventually occurred in 1861, how American supplies of raw cotton might be cut off through blockade of the cotton ports during a civil war between the American slave states and the rest. British over-dependence upon America was made especially plain in 1846–7 when a crop shortage led to a 35 per cent price rise. In Bright's mind Lancashire's interest in encouraging more Indian cotton cultivation would be balanced by India's gain in producing more. A great expansion of cotton growing was seen by Bright as a means of raising standards of living and working in India, where poverty and squalor were general. During the early '40s the British India Society, which contained a strong Quaker element, had first brought forward the Indian cotton question from this point of view. Both Cobden and Bright were members, and in 1841 a written agreement was signed between the society and the Anti-Corn Law League promising mutual support.

In May 1847 Bright asked the Commons for a select committee of inquiry into Indian cotton production. The Indian Government was reluctant to admit the need for this, but eventually the committee was formed with Bright as chairman. Its report described the lack of roads, railways, and bridges, the oppressiveness of the system of raising revenue, and, above all, the extreme poverty of the people. All this was considered from the point of view of increased cotton cultivation, but the process of inquiry inevitably led Bright to begin to study the Indian problem as a whole. Another bad American cotton crop in 1849 impelled Bright to ask for a Royal Commission, which through on-the-spot investigation in India would broaden the London-based enquiries of his select committee. This time, however, he did not get his wish. Supporters of the Indian authorities were able to point out in the Commons that opinion even in Lancashire was not unanimous in wanting further investigation. The Manchester Chamber of Commerce had consistently supported Bright, but the rival Manchester Commercial Association and the *Manchester Guardian* now opposed him. The *Guardian* argued that 'commissions of another sort' were all that were needed to stimulate Indian production. Offers of credit linked with insistence upon good quality (Indian cotton tended to be coarse) would encourage the Indians to produce more and better cotton without further enquiry. Bright and the Manchester Chamber were driven to sending their own unofficial investigator to India, who, it was expected, would reveal the inadequacy of the efforts of the East India Company to increase cotton production. Cobden, who seconded Bright in all his moves to increase the Indian cotton supply, urged a friend not to be deluded by what the Company claimed about future cotton prospects under its auspices: 'look at what they have done but do not rely on what you hear them say'.

Cobden and Bright believed that intensified Indian cotton production would not only improve the standards of the poor in India, it would also help the negro slaves on the cotton estates of the American South. Indian competition would undermine the position of American slave-owners. 'A supply of cotton from India', claimed Bright in 1853, 'would give the first great blow to slavery in the West, and I believe India could give us cotton if we had a Government willing to develop the resources and to give freedom to the industry of the population.' Four years later, however, we have seen how Manchester repudiated Bright as its Member of Parliament, preferring J. A. Turner, president

of the Manchester Commercial Association. In disgust Bright abandoned his efforts to promote Indian cotton growing, not speaking on
the question again in the Commons until 1863, and then at the instance
not of the Manchester but of the Glasgow cotton manufacturers. By
this date the cotton trade was suffering severely from the 'cotton
famine' caused by the American Civil War. Bright's reaction to the
cotton famine showed his character at its most peevish. He had warned
Manchester of the danger of losing the American cotton supply, but
Manchester had not entirely supported him in his quest for alternative
sources, and had then rejected him because of his opposition to the
Crimean War. Bright was not sorry to find cotton operatives and
employers suffering because of their shortsightedness. In August 1862
Cobden urged Bright to offer his name in support of schemes for the
relief of the unemployed operatives. 'I wish you would take a part in
some of the public proceedings respecting the state and prosperity
of the district to which you belong. Your voice ought to be heard.'
But Bright refused, telling Cobden that he had not spoken about the
famine because he would have been bound to regret that his efforts to
increase Indian supplies had not been better supported. He also persuaded himself, at least at first, that there was no real suffering. Finally
the people had preferred Palmerston to himself. 'I know no reason why
we are to expect that national suffering should not follow national
immoralities and crimes.' Characteristically, Cobden showed much
greater generosity of spirit. He told Bright to act *without the slightest
allusion to the past*, in the interest of the masses in your neighbourhood
who will have a very trying winter. . . . Perhaps I say too much, but I
am always jealous of your position, more so than yourself.' Bright's
firm did contribute generously to assist the distressed, but Bright's
grumbling personal attitude was revealing. At the end of 1862 he did
at last speak, though not in Lancashire but at Birmingham. He admitted
that he had been asked many times why he had not spoken earlier.
'Well, I reply, "I told you something when speaking was of use; all I
can say now is this, or nearly all, that a hundred years of crime against
the Negro in America, and a hundred years of crime against the docile
natives of our Indian empire, are not to be washed away by the peni-
tence and suffering of an hour".'

Cobden was more constructive in facing suffering caused by failure
to encourage Indian cotton growing. Bright, on the other hand, was

much more constructive with respect to reform of Indian government. Bright became a leading member of the India Reform Society, which was active in opposing renewal of the East India Company's charter in 1853. He believed that the Indian authorities spent far too little on roads, irrigation, and education, which would assist cotton growing, and far too much on war-making. Bright and the Reform Society wanted abolition of the system of dual government, shared between the Company and the Board of Control. During the 1853 India debates he delivered one of his most successful speeches. In 1850 Palmerston had compared the British to the Roman Empire, recalling the cry *Civis Roman Sum*. Bright now reminded the Commons that the greatness of the Roman Empire had involved not only privileges for its citizens but also good government for its subject races. Little improvement was secured in 1853, but four years later the Indian Mutiny compelled a complete reform of Indian administration, including the winding up of the East India Company.

Although Bright deplored the atrocities committed by both sides during the Indian Mutiny, he told his Birmingham constituents that it would be a mercy to the Indians themselves to suppress the rising. Victory for the mutineers could lead only to anarchy. A private letter from Bright to Joseph Sturge, the Quaker pacifist, began, however, on a different note. Bright assured Sturge that he only acquiesced in forcible suppression of the mutiny because he knew that, whatever he said, it would be put down. 'I oppose evil when I see prospect of doing any good, and am content to be quiet when it seems right to be quiet.' Bright thought that the mutiny should be followed by a complete decentralisation of Indian government. He welcomed the ending of the old dual control, but disapproved of the new centralised viceregal system. India was 'too vast' to be effectively ruled as one unit. Few viceroys would have the capacity to govern it with moderation and honour; many would have their heads turned by their power, and would lapse into annexation. Bright wanted the Indians themselves to share in government as much as possible, as a matter both of justice and of prudence. Such a policy would begin 'to unite the government with the governed'. Bright's Quaker background had given him a belief in the equality of men which left no room for colour prejudice. He believed that a policy of decentralisation and native participation would begin to prepare India for the inevitable day in the future when the British left the Indians to rule themselves. Then each of the five or more separate presidencies proposed by Bright would be able 'to sustain itself as a compact, as a self-governing community'.

Cobden, like Bright, believed that the Indians should be brought much more into the government of India. He deplored the use of the word 'nigger' to describe the Indians, with its implications of inferiority. In general, however, Cobden found it hard to think constructively about Indian administration. His mind was dominated by the conviction that we had no right to be ruling India and would gain no benefit from it. This feeling came out strongly in his last public speech in 1864. 'The world never saw such a risk as we run, with 130 or 140 millions near the antipodes, ruling them for the sake of their custom, and nothing else. I defy you to show that the nation has any interest whatever in that country, except by the commerce we carry on there. I say that is a perilous adventure, quite unconnected with free trade, wholly out of joint with the recent tendency of things, which is in favour of nationality and not of domination.' Cobden noted in 1857 that some Lancashire men were claiming that if we had not occupied India there could have been no trade with her, or that another power would have monopolised it, 'forgetting that this is the old protectionist theory which they used formerly to ridicule'. It was doubtful, argued Cobden, if the British occupation had added anything to Indian trade, and certain that such trade would have been larger if coercion and occupation had not been employed; wherever, as in India, the elements of self-government had been destroyed, international commerce ultimately suffered. Like Bright, Cobden was certain that one day we would abandon India. The climate alone ensured this, for white men could not settle in tropical climates. We held power only 'by a constant succession of adult visitors which is the most unnatural and worst of all governing powers, and the more widely it is set up the greater will be its fall'.

Cobden was well aware how greatly his approach to the Indian question differed from that of Bright. He wrote to him in 1850:

'I am quite incapable of working myself into a sufficiently sanguine state of mind to be able to make an effort for the improvement of the Indian administration. The world never yet beheld such a compound of jobbing, swindling, hypocrisy, and slaughter, as goes to make up the gigantic scheme of villainy called the "British rule in India". I have a presentment . . . that God's chastisement upon us as a nation will come from Hindostan. . . . Your energies could not be more worthily employed than in trying to avert from us this judgement, by endeavouring to do justice to the Indian population.'

Cobden thus seems to have felt able to take a despairingly detached attitude upon Indian questions because he knew that Bright was addressing himself to them with characteristic vigour. In this field the partnership left Cobden largely as a sleeping partner. Bright shared Cobden's regrets that we had undertaken to rule India in the past, but for the present he felt it our duty to govern the country as well as we could. 'I accept the possession as a fact. There we are; we do not know how to leave it, and therefore let us see if we know how to govern it.' Even Cobden did not directly advocate immediate withdrawal from India. His first anxiety was that we should not repeat our Indian involvement elsewhere, notably in China or Japan. He recommended the establishment in the Far East of trading enclaves on the model of the Hanse enclave in medieval London, where foreign merchants were allowed to live under their own jurisdiction on condition that they confined their activities to trade. 'This is the only way in which col-lisions can be avoided, and in which trade can be carried on with these Eastern people with profit to the English people.'

Cobden and Bright were sure that all our dependencies, white and coloured, would eventually detach themselves. This would be to the good of both sides, as the American example had shown. Despite American independence, the economic inter-relationship between Britain and the United States had become vital to both countries. *The Times* pointed out in 1851 that 'for all practical purposes' the United States were 'far more closely united with this kingdom than any one of our colonies'. America, exclaimed Cobden in 1849, was 'a colony emancipated; and we may thank our stars it has broken loose; it would never have been such a customer if the aristocracy of England had held that field of patronage for their younger sons'. When, as in the case of Canada after 1859, the colonies began to adopt protection in defiance of Britain's free trade example, the pointlessness of the imperial connection seemed to Cobden and Bright to have been finally under-lined. They argued that this link certainly did not benefit the mother country. During the American Civil War Britain was forced to send troops and spend money to shield the Canadian protectionists against possible attack from the United States. Cobden pointed out to Gladstone in 1862 how the French tariff on British manufacturers was now lower than the Canadian. 'Surely there would be as much sense and justice in our finding a garrison for Lille as for Montreal.' In addition, Cobden contended that geography made it impossible for us to defend Canada against the United States. The sooner we severed the political thread the better, leaving 'individuals on both sides to cultivate the relations of commerce and friendly intercourse as with other nations'. Cobden supported the plan for Canadian confederation, eventually formed in 1867, because he saw it as 'a step in the direction of an amicable separation'. Bright, speaking on the question in 1867, was not quite so decided, leaving to the Canadians the choice between independence, union with the United States, or continued association with this country.

In Africa and elsewhere during Bright's last years British Governments found themselves drawn into extensive formal annexation for the sake of imperial consolidation and defence. Rival French, Russian, Portuguese and even American colonial empires were developing, based upon protection. The free trade era was passing outside Europe as well as inside it. Trade without rule was becoming increasingly difficult, and the new cry was 'trade follows the flag'. During his 1880–5 Ministry Gladstone hoped to follow a policy of Cobdenite detachment in relation to Egypt, but he soon found himself accepting increasing British involvement to protect the Suez Canal route to India and to defend British interests against French encroachments and Egyptian incompetence. When in 1882 the Gladstone Cabinet countenanced the bombardment of Alexandria Bright regretfully resigned. The bombardment, he told Gladstone, contradicted all that he had advocated in foreign and colonial policy for forty years. Bright's colonial policy now seemed outdated. It was symptomatic that from 1876 his colleague in the representation of Birmingham in Parliament was Joseph Chamberlain. By 1882 Bright was complaining of a speech of Chamberlain's against the 'ignoble doctrine of non-intervention' as, in Bright's words, 'exactly of the stuff on which the foreign policy of Lord Palmerston, and I may almost say of Lord Beaconsfield, was defended. I can have no part in it.' After Bright's resignation Chamberlain kept from the

Birmingham Liberal Party a letter addressed to it by Bright, which Chamberlain described as 'boiling over with moral indignation'. In the mid-twentieth century, however, it is Chamberlain's grandiose imperial ideas which seem outdated, not those of Cobden and Bright. In his very last public speech we have seen how Cobden had foretold that 'nationality' would one day prove stronger than 'domination'. The Indian people, he had forecast in 1857, would 'prefer to be ruled badly, *according to our notions*, by its own color, faith, and kin, than to submit to the humiliation of being better governed by a succession of transient intruders'. Cobdenite principles of respect for colonial peoples, of commerce and contact without rule, are now seen as the enduring ones. 'If you want to benefit the races who properly belong to such regions as Borneo, India, or Africa, send your missionaries, both religious and secular, teach them what you know, and try to inspire them with the ideas of a better social and political status, and the desire for a better government. But don't attempt to govern them or to exert your influence through the Government. Do, in fact, as St. Paul did!'[1]

## II. ECONOMICS

Cobden and Bright believed that in advanced Western economies private enterprise could normally be left to flourish unaided under the operation of the laws of supply and demand, but that in backward countries the Government must give a lead. They therefore wanted Government intervention to encourage the growth of cotton in India. The rules of economic orthodoxy, declared Bright plainly in 1853, could not be applied in such a society. Here was one important sphere where Cobden and Bright did not seek to enforce the doctrine of *laissez-faire*. Even at home they were never total advocates of unqualified economic freedom. The impression that they, or any other leading figures in early-Victorian politics, believed in a total economic free-for-all was a myth encouraged by a few later historians. Cobden had carefully read the political economists, and he knew that Adam Smith and his successors had accepted the need for important qualifications in the application of *laissez-faire*. We have seen how Cobden was a strong advocate of state intervention in education, how he himself negotiated the 1860 treaty regulating trade with France, and how (with the cry 'no free trade in cutting throats') he opposed on moral grounds the floating of the Austrian and Russian loans of 1849–50. 'I take my stand on one of the strongest grounds in stating that Adam Smith and other great authorities on political economy are opposed to the very principle of such loans.'

Cobden often cited Adam Smith. Bright had also read the political economists and accepted their guidance, but it was probably significant that his reprinted speeches never once quoted or cited Smith. Bright's mind was not, like Cobden's, eager and able to master intricate economic arguments. His speeches, as he himself said, ran from headland to headland of argument. He accepted the conclusions of the economists without following all their detailed reasoning. Moreover, Bright's economic and social attitudes were shaped at least as much by his Quaker background as by political economy. The Quakers had traditionally opposed state interference with business, even while encouraging benevolence as employers. This was how Bright thought, both as a master cotton spinner and as a politician. State interference as a normal procedure within an advanced economy offended his Quaker ideas of equality and freedom. Capitalists should be free to employ their resources as they chose, and workmen should be free to offer their labour as they chose. Bright took pride in the achievement of his family in creating a large business out of small beginnings. Others could do the same. Moreover, in reaching prosperity his firm had given work to thousands of operatives, whom it had always treated well. This proved to Bright that masters and men had a common interest in economic freedom.

Against this background must be set Bright's opposition to the Ten Hours factory movement of the 1840s, the campaign in Parliament and in the country for limitation of working hours for women and adolescents in textile factories. In response to the persistent pressure of the factory reformers the Ten Hours Act was finally passed in 1847. The reformers anticipated that a ten hour day for women and young persons would encourage a similar limitation of hours for men, since factory labour was interdependent. Bright was a firm, often fierce, opponent of the Ten Hours Act. He did not regard this opposition as inconsistent with his emphasis upon the common economic interest of masters and men. On the contrary, he believed that he was taking a stand on behalf of the true interests of workers as well as of employers. He admitted that 'serious evils' existed in the cotton towns, but he claimed that they were caused, not by the factory system, but by the urban environment. Even so, conditions were not as bad by the 1840s, argued Bright, as they had been in earlier years, and very much better than claimed by the factory reformers.

> 'The people ask for freedom for their industry, for the removal of the shackles on their trade; you deny it to them, and then forbid them to labour, as if working less would give them more food, whilst your monopoly laws make food scarce and dear. Give them liberty to work, give them the market of the world for their produce, give them the power to live comfortably, and increasing means and increasing intelligence will speedily render them independent enough and wise enough to bring the duration of labour to that point at which life shall be passed with less of irksome toil.'

If all employers had been as benevolent as Bright's own firm a ten-hour day by agreement might have been possible. But they were not. As even Trevelyan admitted in his official biography, Bright assumed too readily that all cotton masters shared his own good intentions.

The factory question came to a crisis soon after Bright entered the Commons in 1843. At this early period his Parliamentary manner was at its sharpest, and the language with which he opposed the Ten Hours advocates aroused great hostility towards him both inside and outside Parliament. He quickly came to be regarded as an enemy of the working classes, his good (albeit misguided) intentions being concealed by his over-strong presentation of his case. One of his major speeches on the factory question in 1844 was described by the factory reformers as in 'a style perhaps the most vindictive towards the working classes ever made in the British Parliament'. In this speech Bright made an attack upon the personal integrity of Lord Ashley, the Parliamentary leader of the movement, for which he was afterwards required to apologise. 'I know I am of a warm temperament', admitted Bright, 'but I mean no personal insult.' Writing some years later, Ashley described Bright as 'ever my most malignant opponent'. Bright, for his part, remembered Ashley as 'the calumniator of the factory population . . . in many things a mischievous character'. He was made especially angry in 1844 because Ashley was still at this date a supporter of the Corn Laws, and Bright believed that he was promoting factory legislation only in order to embarrass the manufacturers who were demanding Corn Law repeal. Bright contended that conditions were worse upon the estates of the Conservative agricultural landlords than in the cotton factories. 'The noble lord and hon. gentlemen opposite, when they view from their distant eminence the state of the manufacuring districts, look through the right end of the telescope; what they see is thus brought near to them, and is greatly magnified. But when they are asked to look at the rural districts, they reverse the telescope and then everything is thrown to the greatest possible distance, and is diminished as much as possible.' There was some truth in this charge, but (as Trevelyan admitted) Bright's attempts to dismiss the factory question as no question at all for Parliament led him into inconsistencies. The *Ten Hours Advocate* quoted one passage in which Bright argued that a Ten Hours Act would destroy a large part of the cotton trade; it compared this with another passage in which Bright agreed that he would support a ten-hour day if voluntarily negotiated. Why, asked the *Advocate* tellingly, would a ten-hour day ruin the cotton trade if fixed by legislation, but not ruin it if negotiated voluntarily?

To the end of his life Bright remained opposed to legislation restricting adult hours of factory work. In 1875 he opposed W. E. Forster as a candidate for the Liberal leadership because Forster was 'very unsound . . . fond of Factory Bills, and the rotten legislation which has come too much into favor of late years'. As late as 1884 Bright was still asserting that limitation of factory hours was 'unwise, and in many cases oppressive'.

The attitude of Cobden upon the factory question cannot be so certainly fixed as that of Bright. There are some grounds for thinking that he was not so rigid as his friend. In 1836 he first outlined his views for the Stockport electors. He was sure at this time that adult workers did not need protection. 'Am I told that the industrious classes in Lancashire are incapable of protecting themselves from oppression unless by the shield of the legislature? . . . Mine is that masculine species of charity which would lead me to inculcate in the minds of the labouring classes the love of independence, the privilege of self-respect, the disdain of being patronised or petted, the desire to accumulate, and the ambition to rise.' In the last resort emigration offered an escape from the factory system. £20 would take a working man to America. Cobden was firm, however, in opposing any employment of children aged thirteen or under in textile mills. He accepted that the harmfulness of child labour had been proved from medical evidence. 'I will not argue the matter for a moment with political economy; it is a question for the medical and not the economical profession.' In thus opposing all child labour in textile factories Cobden was ahead of contemporary legislation. Even for adolescents he thought that hours should be 'moderate and the labour light'. Medical arguments seem also to have inclined Cobden to accept some regulation of hours for women. Thus in 1842 he was won over to support of Ashley's Mines Act, which prohibited the employment of women and girls underground. Cobden told Ashley, 'I don't think I have ever been put into such a frame of mind in the whole course of my life as I have been by your speech.' Three years later, after securing modifications, Cobden also supported Ashley's Calico Print Works Act, which prohibited night work for women and children. Looking back upon these years, Ashley himself differentiated Cobden from Bright. 'Cobden, though bitterly hostile, was better than Bright.' Cobden objected to the Ten Hours Act of 1847 because it implied a restriction of hours for men. He was abroad when it passed, but thereafter he seems to have approved of women and children working in relays so enabling men to labour for longer than ten hours. This loophole was closed by an amending Act of 1850. Thereafter our knowledge of Cobden's attitude becomes uncertain. In the early '60s several notable *laissez-faire* opponents of factory legislation, Roebuck, Graham and Gladstone among them, admitted the error of their earlier opposition. Hutchins and Harrison in their standard *History of Factory Legislation* add Cobden to this number, remarking that the cause of this changed attitude was probably the evidence in the reports of the factory inspectors showing that production had not been reduced or costs increased by limitation of hours. No evidence has been found in Hansard, however, or in Cobden's correspondence to confirm that before his death in 1865 he had become a total convert. Yet it seems possible. His attitude in the 1840s had not been so uniformly hostile as that of Bright, and his mind was always the more flexible. One thing is certain, that he abandoned his early advocacy of emigration as a means of protecting factory workers against exploitation. In 1857 he dismissed proposals for mass emigration to relieve pressure upon the labour market as 'downright quackery'.

On the trade union question Cobden's attitude seems to have

remained steady throughout his career. The classical political economists did not like trade unions because they aspired to interfere with the
free working of the market, and Cobden shared this dislike. He felt that
the unions aimed at terrorising both workers and employers. There was
'a desperate spirit of monopoly and tyranny' about them, seeking to
regulate the numbers of workers, seeking to force employers to raise
wages, regardless of the state of trade. 'They might as well attempt to
regulate the tides by force, or change the course of the seasons, or
subvert any of the other laws of nature, for the wages of labour depend
upon laws as unerring.' This hostility towards trade unions was stimulated by the sometimes violent methods of the mid-Victorian unionists.
But, as Morley admitted in his official life, it was illogical of Cobden to
ask working men to assert their independence (as he did in his 1836
Stockport declaration upon factory legislation), and yet to object to
them asserting and strengthening that independence through trade
combinations. Cobden can be given credit for his anxiety to protect the
personal liberty of every workman and employer. He remarked in
1853 'how abjectly subservient the working classes are to the dictation
of a trades union junta. I think we shall not get right till there is a revolt
against all such organisations, whether on one side or another, in the
interest of liberty, Personal Liberty.' But the fact that trade unions
were sometimes misguided did not deprive them, as Cobden seemed to
assume, of all potential value. Indeed, Cobden himself in his last years
was coming to hope much from them as centres of popular political
opinion.

Bright too in the 1860s encouraged the trade unions as political units,
even while remaining suspicious of their economic role. In a public
letter in 1860 he argued that it was the working men's lack of the vote
which had encouraged them in the false belief that their interests were
automatically opposed to those of employers. Trade unions assumed
permanent conflict between capital and labour, which Bright, as we
have noted, thought quite contrary to the natural economic state. 'If
the wall of partition between classes were broken down by the admission of the great "Labour interest" into the rights of citizenship'
then their common problems and aspirations would necessarily bring
employers and employed together. In such circumstances trade unions
would tend to wither away as superfluous.*

Bright spoke confidently about trade unions, but on financial matters he was much more hesitant. Finance was an aspect of economics which could not be reduced to simple rules. During the financial crisis of 1857 he confessed to Cobden that he did not understand the Bank of England question, 'and I know nobody who does so as to convince me that he is right, so I never speak upon it'. Cobden was more confident. He welcomed Peel's Bank Charter Act of 1844, which gave the Bank of England a quasi-monopoly. Here was another area where he was not a supporter of *laissez-faire*. He was a firm opponent of paper currency. To abandon the gold standard, he wrote in 1847, would produce a social revolution and 'more confusion, demoralization and misery than if we were conquered by another Napoleon'. Fortunately, noted Cobden, Manchester had always been strong against paper currency.

Bright's attitude to the drink question showed *laissez-faire* in its best light. Bright believed strongly in temperance, but he could never be induced to support a Permissive Drink Bill. He refused to accept that Parliament had any right to decide what people should drink, or that restrictions upon drinking would make men sober. '*Law* must be founded on broad and general principles, such as are consistent with political economy, but individuals may use their own discretion as to what they abstain from.' Bright felt that the right approach was for private temperance propaganda to influence this individual discretion. In a similar spirit Bright would not support legislation seeking to prevent juveniles from smoking. 'We have rather too many laws already.' Parental supervision and improved education should be left to deal with the problem.

Less attractive to twentieth-century minds were the attempts of Bright to follow a *laissez-faire* line in relation to public health regulation, the great urban need of the mid-Victorian period. Cobden and Bright, although not opposed to all public health provision, disliked the strong centralising tendencies of Chadwick's 1848 Public Health Act. Bright was characteristically vigorous in criticism and

---

\* Bright's attitude echoed that of Francis Place forty years earlier. Place had successfully campaigned against the Combination Laws, which had made trade unions illegal. After his victory he prophesied that 'combinations will soon cease to exist. Men have been kept together for long periods only by the oppression of the laws; these being repealed, combinations will lose the matter which cements them into masses, and they will fall to pieces. All will be as orderly as even a Quaker could desire.'

opposition. In the Commons in 1851 he alleged that the Act was discreditable, that Chadwick was a wirepuller with Lord Shaftesbury (formerly Ashley) as his puppet, and that Chadwick was becoming 'the arbitrary dispenser of more patronage than was in the gift of officers filling the highest stations in the Government'. Chadwick composed at this time an unpublished fragment replying to the repeated attacks of Bright:

'Those popular politicians, who deem every measure for the relief of human pain visionary, and the promoters of them impracticable who deem those sanitary measures which are beyond the power of individuals and are not within the capacity of any local administrations, to be beyond the province of Government or legislation:— whose notion of duty in respect to Governments is that it is an object of paralysis to make them impotent, and making them impotent see no need of special qualifications for administration, and with whom every salary is money paid for no work and all appointments patronage and mere waste—

"The Member for Manchester
A man who gave to misery all he had to give
A sneer—" '

Whereas Bright characteristically allowed his dislike of Chadwick's centralized system to colour his whole attitude, Cobden retained some sense of proportion. He told Chadwick plainly in a letter in 1848 that he would prefer a locally controlled public health organisation, but he was keen for legislation of some sort: 'I have always felt satisfied that you were doing good service to the public by your labors.' Unfortunately, Cobden was much less prominent than Bright in discussion of public health arrangements.

It must be admitted that Cobden and Bright were not far-seeing on economic and social questions. In this sphere they were only men of their time, their class and their industry. Moreover, they expected that free trade would bring general prosperity without need for much positive social and economic legislation. Free trade did help to produce working-class improvement in the mid-Victorian years, but many people remained near the poverty borderline. At Christmas 1875 the *Manchester Guardian* remarked how it was 'not only a season of

festivity but of charity. Bumble himself would not grudge the paupers
their Christmas dinner. . . . In the battle of life it is necessary that now
and then there should be a truce in which the wounded may be suc-
coured.' This mid-Victorian system, with charity treated as an essential
function, was willingly accepted by Cobden and Bright. Cobden's
London was also Mayhew's London where poverty was widespread
and obvious. Cobden reminded Bright in 1855 how political economy
possessed 'a heart as well as a head'; it did not say 'that no half-pence
shall be given to Italian organists in the London streets'. But after the
Victorian masses had begun to be given the vote they started to demand
a juster system than this. They began to expect that the state would
protect them when they could not protect themselves. By Christmas
1895 the *Manchester Guardian* was writing in a very different tone from
twenty years earlier. 'That the world must be made a better place for
the unprivileged many is a conviction that has come home to us, however little of Socialists we may be, and the old easy contentment with a
social system largely unjust but tempered by "charity" and Christmas
effusion has passed away, never to return. We are on the threshold of a
much more difficult, anxious, and arduous time.' For such a time the
social and economic attitudes of Cobden and Bright had little to offer.
'Socialism' to them had been an incendiary word. Their view was the
*Guardian*'s of 1875, not of 1895. 'Cobden would hardly recognise the
world', exclaimed an *Economist* article of 1894 on 'The Advance
towards State Socialism'. Cobden and Bright had not foreseen the
need for intensified state action, how the negative protection of individual liberty would come to seem less important than the positive
promotion of mass well-being. 'There are some further things which a
wise legislature may do for them', Bright told the working men of
Rochdale in 1877, 'but the main thing to be done for them must be
done for themselves.' Matthew Arnold in *Culture and Anarchy* (1869)
launched a notable attack upon Bright for his inadequate response to
'pauperism and ignorance, and all the questions which are called social'.
Admitting to the workmen of Edinburgh in 1868 'the vast weight of
poverty and ignorance that exists at the bottom of the social scale'
even under free trade, Bright could offer only indirect remedies:

'If Government were just, if taxes were moderate and equitably
imposed, if land were free, if schools were as prominent institutions

in our landscapes and in our great towns as prisons and workhouses now are, I suspect that we should find people gradually gaining more self-respect; that they would have much more hope of improvement for themselves and their families, that they would rise above, in thousands of cases, all temptations to intemperance, and that they would become generally—I say almost universally—more virtuous and more like what the subjects of a free state ought to be.'

This cannot be called a positive programme. The great emphasis laid by Cobden and Bright upon retrenchment in Government expenditure precluded such an approach. 'Our children must carry on the work', exhorted Cobden eighteen months before his death. 'There is still the question of direct and indirect taxation; there is still the question of large reduction in expenditure in the Government.' As Trevelyan admitted fifty years later, Cobden and Bright entirely failed to foresee how the enfranchisement of working men would lead not to a decrease but to a great increase in Government expenditure. The workers did not give first priority to reducing the number of aristocratic office-holders; they indulged instead in 'tax-eating' on their own account, through state insurance, state education, and the rest. 'Reform' and 'Retrenchment' proved to be incompatible cries. The success of the first meant the undoing of the second.[1]

### 12. THE AMERICAN CIVIL WAR

The American Civil War of 1861-5 exhibited Cobden and Bright in a much more progressive light than did economic questions. Their great admiration for the American experiment had already won them the description of 'the two Members for the United States'. Yet posterity has tended to underrate the extent of Cobden's liberalism in the process of emphasising that of Bright. Three misrepresentations have become current in the history books. Firstly, that Cobden was hesitant initially in opposing the slave-owning Confederate South. Secondly, that Bright soon persuaded him to join in support of the North. And thirdly, that Bright also quickly persuaded the bulk of the English workmen to do likewise. On all three points the truth was never so clear-cut as this.

In 1859 Cobden had paid his second visit to the United States, a visit which confirmed him in his long-standing enthusiasm for American society and institutions. The first purpose of his visit had been to see the Illinois railway in which he had unwisely made such heavy invest- ments; but he saw much more than this during nearly four months of intensive travel, reaching as far west as the Mississippi and finishing in Canada. Writing home to Bright, Cobden exclaimed how American progress since his 1835 visit 'in material and moral prosperity realizes all that I had expected to see'. In particular, Cobden noted how work- ing-class living standards were much higher than in England. His only complaint was that American women tended to be over-assertive, a complaint to be set alongside that of his first visit about their deficiency in bust and bustle.

The intensity of Cobden's admiration for the United States meant, as Bright remembered years later, that Cobden was 'more broken down in heart and feeling' by the outbreak of the civil war than any- one else known to Bright. In his biography of Cobden, Morley told how the two men discussed the war together many times during its first months. In June 1861 Cobden was to address his Rochdale con- stituents. It was at this point, claimed Morley, that Bright converted him to his own strong support for the North. ' "Now", said Mr. Bright, with a final push of insistence, "this is the moment for you to speak with a clear voice".' The evidence for this story, retailed by Morley and repeated by Trevelyan, seems to have come only from Bright himself. Unfortunately, it has gained general acceptance. Once again, as with his retrospective account of the first meeting and of the 1841 Leamington conversation, Bright was presenting himself to posterity in a self-flattering light, reducing the stature of Cobden in the process. In reality, Cobden was not persuaded by Bright in 1861 to share his views upon the war. Cobden followed a course of his own, different from but just as liberal as that of Bright. When Cobden spoke at Rochdale in June 1861 he devoted only one paragraph to America. He emphasised how Bright and himself shared an admiration for American policies of non-intervention and economy in govern- ment, but he did not say that he and Bright were in agreement about the war. 'I will not allude to the lamentable strife in America, further than to say that I hope the principle of non-intervention will still be practised.' Six months later he sent a letter to a Rochdale banquet held in Bright's honour. This would have been an excellent opportunity to express total agreement with Bright on American questions, but he did not do so. He stressed only the need for British non-intervention, for restraint in handling the *Trent* affair (an American warship had stopped the British mail packet *Trent* and seized two Confederate commissioners travelling to Europe), and for reform of maritime law in the interests of neutrals and of trade.

Morley himself quoted a letter of Cobden's in January 1862, long after his supposed conversion, which showed how Cobden was well aware that he was taking different ground from Bright. 'I can't see my way through the American business. I don't believe the North and South can ever lie in the same bed again. Nor do I see how the military operations can be carried into the South, so as to inflict a crushing defeat. . . . But our friend Bright will not hear of anything against the claims of the North. I admire his pluck, for when he goes with a side it is always to win. I tell him that it is possible to wish well to a cause without being sure that it will be successful.' A month later Cobden remarked in a letter to Charles Sumner, an American Senator and friend of both Bright and himself, that he knew hardly anyone 'except our courageous friend Bright, who rather likes to fight a battle with the long odds against him, that thinks you can put down the rebellion'. In October 1862 Cobden was still writing in the same vein about a speech which he was to deliver at Rochdale. 'I shall avoid as much as possible all allusion to American affairs except to deprecate intervention. It is a horrible business which it is useless to discuss . . . I cannot see my way out of it. And I ought to know the country as well as most people.' It was in a letter of December 1861 to a mutual friend about the American war that Cobden made the revealing remark which we have already highlighted. 'Our friend Bright is so abused by other people that I never find it in my heart to tell him even when I differ from him.'

All this did not mean that Cobden ever wanted the South and slavery to win. He urged Bright before the Rochdale banquet in December 1861 'to remind the ignorant people who seem to be inclined to side with the South that the future of America is with the North, that slavery can have no future if Christianity is to endure', and that people now living would one day see 'a hundred millions of free men' in the anti-slavery states. Cobden merely doubted if the North possessed the strength and the organisation to crush the South, knowing that a stale-mate would be enough to ensure Southern survival. The reasonableness

of Cobden's doubts was proved by the four years of war needed before
the final Northern triumph. Cobden's one certainty was that Britain
should not become involved. She should neither let herself be embroiled,
nor should she deliberately intervene, notwithstanding the suffering
caused in Lancashire by the loss of Southern cotton supplies. Cobden
long feared that the Palmerston Government might risk war with the
North through a meddlesome offer of mediation tantamount to recognition of the South, or through an attempt to break the blockade.
Cobden wanted no repetition of the unnecessary Crimean War. He
deplored all war, 'this vulgar and unscientific and endless butchery'.
He knew also that war would divert attention from much needed
reform at home. He told a friend in 1863 that the friend 'and perhaps
even Bright, have been occupied for the last year more on American
than British politics. Yet how much there is to do at home! In fact
there is everything to do for our political serfs.' In discussing Parliamentary reform we have seen how Cobden was complaining by 1863
of Bright's over-concentration upon the American question. Bright's
daughter later remembered the intense atmosphere at One Ash in these
years, how the family used to live for the latest news brought twice a
week by the transatlantic steamers. 'America and its history, past and
in the making, was the breath of our nostrils.' Had war broken out over
the *Trent* crisis in December 1861 Bright might well have abandoned
politics. He told Cobden that he would not kill himself 'proving it
wicked', as he had nearly done during the Crimean War.

By the end of 1862 events, rather than Bright's persuasion, had
begun to convince Cobden that the North really could win the war.
A year later this conviction came out strongly in a speech at Rochdale
in which he linked his new confidence in a Northern victory with the
reminder that he had always believed that the North deserved to win.
The war was 'an aristocratic rebellion against a democratic government', and, asserted Cobden, history showed that democracy always
eventually won. Cobden declared himself not 'indifferent to the process
of misery and destitution'; but the South had fired the first shot. 'I
take, probably, a stronger view than most people in this country, and
certainly a stronger view than anybody in America, of the vast sacrifices of life, and of economical comfort and resources, which must
follow to the North from this struggle. . . . But that being so, makes me
still more indignant and intolerant of the cause; but of the result, I

have no more doubt than I have on any subject that lies in the future.'

The Northern cause had by now clearly become the anti-slavery cause. Initially, Lincoln had not made it so. His first proclamation liberating the slaves was published only in September 1862. For some weeks Cobden was not sure how to respond, for Lincoln's move meant the risk of a slave rising in the South and great bloodshed. Much as Cobden hated slavery, he hated violence more. When, however, no sanguinary slave insurrection took place Cobden came to accept Lincoln's move. He admitted to Sumner that if in 1861 he had been arbiter of the fate of the negroes he would have refused them freedom 'at the cost of so much white men's blood and women's tears'. But he did not blame the North. On the South 'righteously falls the male-diction that "they who take the sword shall perish by the sword".'

Cobden and Bright were able to exert a significant influence upon Lincoln during the war. From their unofficial position they were able to ease tensions and resolve misunderstandings in a manner not open to Palmerston or Russell as Prime Minister and Foreign Secretary. Both Cobden and Bright were in regular correspondence with Charles Sumner, Chairman of the Senate Foreign Relations Committee, and Sumner often passed their letters to Lincoln. When, for example, in December 1861 the *Trent* affair threatened war between the two countries Cobden and Bright used this channel to explain the British attitude and to urge moderation upon the Americans. The American Government accepted that Cobden and Bright were interested only in international peace, standing above national prejudices, and this gave their advice great weight. 'We are, I think,' Cobden wrote to Sumner during the *Trent* crisis, 'both more of Christians and Cosmopolitans than British or Yankees.' Cobden strongly advised the Americans in their own interests to give way regardless of rights and wrongs in terms of international law. 'Formerly England feared a war with the United States as much from the dependence on your cotton as from dread of your power. *Now* the popular opinion (however erroneous) is that a war would give us cotton. And we, of course, consider your power weakened by your Civil War. I speak as a friend of peace and not as a partisan of my own country in wishing you to bear this in mind.' Bright wrote in a similar vein. 'You know that I write to you with as much earnest wish for your national welfare as if I were a native and citizen of your country. . . . At all hazards you must not let this matter grow to a war with England, even if you are right and we are wrong. War will be fatal to your idea of restoring the Union.' On Christmas morning 1861 Sumner attended a meeting of the American Cabinet and read out these letters. After two days' discussion the American Government agreed to release the Confederate commissioners, and so peace was preserved. Perhaps it would have been saved even without the efforts of Cobden and Bright, but the balance was a fine one, and their advice may therefore have been crucial.

When in July 1862 the British-built and largely British-manned *Alabama* was allowed to sail from the Mersey to begin a long career as a destroyer of Northern merchant ships, Cobden and Bright again played an important part. They explained that the ship had sailed against the intentions of the British Government, which had acted too slowly. This explanation was believed when it came from Cobden and Bright at a time when explanations by British Ministers might have been disbelieved. Cobden reported that Russell, 'whatever may be the tone of his ill-mannered despatches', was against the use of British harbours to prepare Confederate commerce destroyers. 'He was bona fide in his desire to prevent the *Alabama* from leaving, but he was tricked, and was angry at the escape of that vessel. . . . If Lord Russell's despatches to Mr. Adams are not very civil, he may console himself with the knowledge that the Confederates are still worse treated.'

In the interest of peace Cobden, but not Bright, was also urging Lincoln's Government during 1862 to raise its blockade of Southern ports in order to avert all risk of intervention by Britain or France. Cobden advised the North to lift the blockade, 'take high ground with Europe for a complete sweep of the old maritime code, and then take your own time to deal with the slave states, either by fighting them at your leisure or by leaving the West to outgrow them or slavery to undo them'. With characteristic pugnacity, Bright did not agree with Cobden on this issue. Believing the war to be just, he wanted it pursued by the North with all possible rigour. 'War is barbarous, and this is but an act of war.'

Cobden and Bright possessed greater influence at this time over the American Government than over the Government of their own country. Most credit for exercising a quiet but significant influence upon British Ministers on behalf of the North must apparently go to W. E. Forster. Towards the end of the war the American Minister in

London noted in his diary that, on the whole, Forster had been the North's 'firmest and most judicious friend. We owe to his tact and talent even more than we do to the more showy interference of Messrs. Cobden and Bright.'

The cotton blockade and the *Alabama* and *Trent* affairs drew attention to international maritime law relating to the rights of neutrals and belligerents in time of war. Cobden was deeply interested in this legal aspect, for he was anxious to encourage as much trade and intercourse as possible even in wartime. He elaborated his views in *A Letter to Henry Ashworth*, published in April 1862. Cobden contended that all private property, of enemies as well as neutrals, ought to be exempt from right of search or seizure, and, most important of all, the ports of an enemy ought to be free from blockade. As a great commercial nation dependent upon overseas supplies of food and upon large exports of manufactures, explained Cobden, Britain had more interest than any other power in maritime freedom in time of war. 'Free trade, in the widest definition of the term', argued Cobden, 'means only the division of labour, by which the productive powers of the whole earth are brought into mutual co-operation. If this scheme of universal dependence is to be liable to sudden dislocation, whenever two government choose to go to war, it converts a manufacturing industry, such as ours, into a lottery, in which the lives and fortunes of multitudes of men are at stake.' Cobden summarised his proposals under three heads:

(1) The exemption of private property from capture at sea during war.

(2) Blockades to be restricted to naval arsenals, or to towns besieged by land, with the exception of contraband articles of war.

(3) Neutral ships to be free from interference by ships of belligerent powers.

Cobden regarded these changes as necessary corollaries of repeal of the Navigation Acts and of the Corn Laws, and of the abandonment of colonial protection. If the interests of trade failed to stop war, then at least, in Cobden's view, the interests of war must not be allowed to stop trade. 'Hurrah for anything that tends to make war a mere duel between professionals, for it will make the calling less profitable and therefore less popular.'

Cobden found, however, that British Governments refused to

abandon the right to use the blockade weapon in some future war. He deplored their assumption that Britain would one day again be engaged in major hostilities. By adopting free trade, he claimed in 1862, Britain had made itself 'the great neutral power of the world'. But Palmerston and Russell would not accept this. 'The battle for the freedom of the seas in time of war,' Cobden therefore concluded, 'as was the case for freedom of trade in time of peace, will have to be fought with our feudal governing class.'

Unlike Cobden, Bright believed that the preservation of the American union was even more important than the preservation of peace. Bright's opposition to secession by the South foreshadowed his opposition twenty-five years later to Irish Home Rule. 'When the people of Ireland asked that they should be allowed to secede, was it proposed in London that they should be allowed to secede peaceably? Nothing of the kind. . . . No man is more in favour of peace than I am; no man has denounced war more than I have. . . . But I cannot for the life of me see upon any of those principles upon which states are governed now—I say nothing of the literal word of the New Testament—I cannot see how the state of affairs in America with regard to the United States Government, could have been different from what it is at this moment.' After the Southern victory at Bull Run in July 1861 even Bright briefly shared Cobden's doubts about the practicability of a total Northern victory; but these doubts evaporated within a few weeks. His certainty in a Northern triumph was basically determined by his conviction that the Northern cause was just. Because it was just, Bright soon persuaded himself that it must prevail. It was the cause of freedom for white and black, of equality for all, the anti-aristocratic cause. 'Privilege has shuddered at what might happen to old Europe if this grand experiment should succeed.' Bright reminded his audience at the Rochdale banquet in December 1861 how within a few years the population of the United States would exceed that of Great Britain. 'When that time comes, I pray that it may not be said amongst them, that, in the darkest hour of their country's trials, England, the land of their fathers, looked on with icy coldness and saw unmoved the perils and calamities of their children.' Bright summed up the American example as 'a free Church, a free school, free land, a free vote, and a free career for the child of the humblest born in the land. My countrymen who work for your living, remember this: there will be one wild shriek of freedom to startle all mankind if that American Republic should be overthrown.'

The one blot upon American society was the institution of slavery, and from the outset, long before Lincoln's proclamations, Bright equated the Northern cause with its destruction. He told his wife in July 1862 that the continuance of the war was necessary 'to bring the slavery question into its due prominence . . . I believe the deliverance of the black Negro race may come from this terrible strife, and that twenty years hence men will wonder at the changes wrought out of the hurricane of passion which is now sweeping over the North American continent.' Bright advocated abolition of slavery on Christian grounds, but he was not surprised to find practical advantage stemming from this good cause. He was sure that the South would grow more cotton for Lancashire with free labour. 'I am glad when matters of business go straight with matters of high sentiment and morality.' True, the South supported free trade, whereas the North did not; but (Bright told Cobden) 'freedom of individual industry' was 'the basis of all freedom'. Cobden accepted this unreservedly. He had never inclined, as Morley suggested, to support the South because of its free trade leanings. Cobden simply regretted that the North would not accept free trade: 'they are unsound and ignorant on economical questions which *we* at least know to be of vital importance in the affairs of nations.'

In October 1862 Gladstone, Chancellor of the Exchequer in Palmerston's Government, publicly announced his personal belief that the North would have to admit failure. The South, said Gladstone, had made an army, was making a navy, and, more important than either, had made a nation. Bright reminded Cobden that Gladstone came from a Jamaican slave-owning family, 'and I suppose the taint is ineradicable'. Gladstone had not said that he positively supported the South, merely that he thought it could not be defeated. But much upper-class opinion in England did markedly favour the South, especially before Lincoln had clearly identified the North with the abolition of slavery. The Southern plantocracy was favourably regarded by the British aristocracy as the transatlantic equivalent of itself. The courteous manners of the Southerners were contrasted with the brashness of the Northern Yankees. Most London newspapers, headed by *The Times*, supported the South. Bright was already disliked by *The Times* and its readers for his advocacy of 'democracy' at home, and his persistence in holding

up Northern democracy as an example to England made him still
more disliked. One peer declared that he would like to 'blow President
Lincoln from a mortar with a bombshell, and if there weren't wadding
enough, I'd ram John Bright down in after him'.

What of working-class attitudes? Bright set out to persuade the
working men that the Northern cause was their cause; but not until
1863 did he begin to draw a wide response. It is no longer accepted, as
Trevelyan claimed in his Bright biography, that the restraint of the
Lancashire cotton operatives during the cotton famine sprang from an
acceptance of the justice of the Northern cause, and that the operatives
consciously and nobly preferred to sacrifice their livelihoods rather
than support intervention against the North to break its blockade of
the Southern cotton ports. *The Times* and the *Manchester Guardian*
contended that the restraint of the cotton operatives did not indicate
any strong working-class feeling against slavery and in favour of
Northern democracy, but simply reflected a realisation that the British
Government was not responsible for the loss of cotton supplies. In this
spirit the *Oldham Standard* dismissed as 'ridiculous' Bright's attempts to
identify the workers with support for the North, claiming that they
understood how this was a subject which 'they were not called upon to
discuss'. The *Weekly Budget*, which claimed a large circulation among
the factory workers, positively called for recognition of the South,
exclaiming that it had 'no desire to see the government of this country
Bright-ridden'. Bright tried to gloss over this opposition, but Cobden
was well aware of it. Bright assured Sumner in November 1861 that
the sympathies of 'the great body of the people' were 'quite right,
although some papers supposed to be read by them are wrong'. But
Cobden was probably nearer the truth in telling Sumner a fortnight
later that the English people felt 'no sympathy with you on either side'.
They found on the one hand protectionists, on the other slave-owners.
'The protectionists say they do not seek to put down slavery. The slave-
owners say they want free trade. Need you wonder at the confusion in
John Bull's poor head? He gives it up! Leaves it to the Government.'
As late as December 1862 Cobden still thought it necessary to urge
that 'more should be done to elicit the sympathy of the masses for the
North'. Clearly, Cobden did not think that up to this time Bright had
succeeded in converting them. The man who in large measure succeeded in doing this was not Bright, but Lincoln. Once he had clearly

identified the North with the abolition of slavery popular opinion began to swing round. From the beginning of 1863 a sudden succession of well attended working-class meetings in support of the North began to be reported from all parts of the country. In the spring of that year increased supplies of raw cotton reached Lancashire from India, breaking the cotton famine and making it easier for the cotton operatives to favour the North despite its cotton blockade. Bright's speeches in support of the North now began to make a significant impact; but only because Lincoln had opened the way. On March 26, 1863 Bright spoke at a notable meeting of trade unionists in St. James's Hall, London. His speech closely linked victory for the North with hopes for future progress at home. Millions of Northerners were emigrants from this country. Two and a half millions had crossed the Atlantic in the last fifteen years. 'You wish the freedom of your country. You wish it for yourselves. You strive for it in many ways. Do not then give the hand of fellowship to the worst foes of freedom that the world has ever seen.' After Bright's speech the trade unionists unanimously agreed to send an address of support to Lincoln.

From about this time Lincoln began to emerge as a hero in the eyes of ever wider sections of British opinion. At the start of the war even Cobden and Bright had felt reservations about him. They thought him well-meaning but lacking in depth. Cobden remarked to Bright in October 1862 that Lincoln possessed 'a certain moral dignity, but is intellectually inferior'. As a result, Cobden believed that Lincoln had chosen poor advisers and generals, thereby endangering the Northern cause. As Bright later admitted, Lincoln's simplicity 'for a time did much to hide his greatness'. By 1864, however, Cobden and Bright had come to appreciate his high quality, and they were keen for his re-election. Cobden now dwelt upon Lincoln's honesty, self-control, and common sense. 'It is the fashion to underrate Lincoln intellectually in part because he illustrates his arguments with amusing anecdotes. In the autumn of 1864 Cobden was so anxious to hear news of Lincoln's election campaign that, as he told Bright, he sometimes found himself walking half-way to Midhurst to meet the newspaper boy.

Lincoln, and Northerners generally, came to hold Cobden and Bright in high regard. Bright, in particular, became almost a national hero because of his speeches in support of the North. Northern audiences burst into applause whenever his name was mentioned.

American writers sent copies of their books to him with flattering tributes. And when the young brother of one of his Birmingham constituents was imprisoned in California for assisting the South, he was freed at Bright's intercession by special order of Lincoln out of respect for Bright's character and friendship. Curiously, Bright never visited the United States, declining many official and unofficial invitations. He was not a good sailor, and by middle age he felt little enthusiasm for foreign travel, even to view the great American experiment.

Lincoln was assassinated in April 1865, less than a fortnight after Cobden's death. Bright was much distressed at this fresh blow, but he took comfort in the knowledge that the North had now virtually won the war. Opinion in England among all classes showed remarkable unanimity and intensity in mourning Lincoln. *The Times* and *Punch*, which had long been hostile to him, quickly reversed their attitudes. Those who had doubted Lincoln's greatness in times of Northern adversity now admitted it after the total victory of the North. 'From that time', noted Bright three months after Lincoln's death, 'there has been a rapid change of opinion and of feeling here on all American questions.' Under Lincoln's leadership, and with the cancer of slavery removed, the United States was seen to have become more united and powerful than ever before. The era of contemptuous British conde-scension towards Americans, which Cobden had deplored throughout his career, was passing away rapidly by the time of his death. The power of America, which he had often forecast for the future, was becoming a present reality. In November 1864 he described the 'fabulous *increase* of every kind of production in the Northern States during the last three years of war. It is quite clear that America stands on a different footing from the old world, and that its powers, whether in peace or war, are to be measured by a different standard.' Here was a portentous truth, which was at last beginning to be understood by the British people, a truth which Cobden had taught in speech and writing for thirty years and which Bright had presented in some of his most powerful orations during the years of the American Civil War.[1]

# IV

# *Conclusion*

## 1. DEATHBEDS

RICHARD COBDEN died on Sunday, April 2, 1865, the very day on which Northern troops entered Richmond, the Confederate capital. His health had never been robust, and he had often reminded his friends that the Cobdens were not a long-living family. We have seen how as early as 1825 he was promising his father that he would succeed in Manchester if only his health allowed it. The strain of leading the anti-Corn Law movement left him exhausted by the summer of 1846, but his long Continental tour seems to have restored him. During the 1850s, however, Cobden began to find the cold, damp English winters too harsh for his weak chest. He was increasingly forced either to winter by the Mediterranean or to shut himself up at Dunford, leaving his house only in mild weather or in the middle of the day. During the last winters of his life he was able to intervene in politics only through the written word, giving up speaking at meetings and finally abandoning attendance in the Commons during the early part of each session. Unfortunately, in 1864 Cobden delayed his withdrawal to Dunford too long. He travelled north to speak to his Rochdale constituents as late as November 23, and from the effects of this exposure and effort he never fully recovered. He afterwards wrote to his wife from Rochdale that he would never again address a meeting later than September. 'I have been much affected in my breathing, and have a cold. This climate of Lancashire is enough to kill anybody, except those who have native constitutions.' During the winter of 1864–5 Cobden was continuously in the grip of, or threat of, what his doctor called 'nervous asthma', which often so obstructed his breathing that he hardly dared to move. In addition, he was afflicted by chronic bronchitis, which threatened to extend to his lungs, and as a final burden his stomach was disordered. By the beginning of March, however, he had made a slow but decided improvement. Bright came to visit him, and they took short walks together. Then a few days after Bright had left Dunford Cobden made what proved to be the fatal mistake of deciding to visit London to speak in a Commons debate on Canadian fortifications. He travelled in bitter weather on March 21, and the effort proved too great. By the time he reached London he was prostrated by asthma, soon joined by severe bronchitis. By April 1 it was clear that he would not recover. Early the next morning Bright was called to the bedside of his sinking friend. Bright and another old friend joined the family in watching out Cobden's last hours. In Victorian fashion Bright detailed this notable deathbed scene in his diary:

'There was no apparent pain. Not a limb stirred. He lay breathing out his precious life, and for three and a quarter hours I watched my greatest friend of more than twenty years as his life ebbed away. At quarter past eleven o'clock the breathing ceased. There was a moment of suspense: a pallor spread over the face, and the manly and gentle spirit of one of the noblest of men passed away to the rewards which surely wait upon a life passed in works of good to mankind, a life of unselfish benevolence, and of unspotted honour.

'And what a scene as the spirit passed! The wife on one side, the daughter on the other—kissing the pale face as it grew every moment more pale, with plaintive exclamations, "Darling, my own darling!" and "Oh, Papa, why do you go away?" It was a scene never to be forgotten. . . . I pressed his hand for the last time, and kissed his forehead, and left him with a sense of the loss I have suffered.'

Some years earlier Cobden had made it clear that he did not want the inappropriate pomp of a Westminster Abbey funeral. He was buried on April 7 by the side of his son in the small local churchyard at Lavington. Bright, Gladstone, Villiers and Gibson were among the pallbearers. As Cobden's body was placed in the vault Bright broke down in tears. In the Commons on the day after Cobden's death he had been able to say only a few sentences of tribute. 'I shall leave to some calmer moment when I may have an opportunity of speaking before some portion of my countrymen the lesson which I think may be learned from the life and character of my friend. I have only to say that after twenty years of most intimate and almost brotherly friendship,

I little knew how much I loved him until I had lost him.' 'I will thank God', exclaimed Bright in his diary, 'that I have had such a friend, and that I have been permitted to be the friend of such a man.'

It was unlucky that the two friends were not together during Cobden's last public political appearance at Rochdale in November 1864. Bright was unable to attend because of the recent death of his son. Instead, he had withdrawn to Leamington with his wife. From a house in the same square where Cobden had consoled him after the death of his first wife in 1841, Bright regretted to Cobden his absence from the Rochdale meeting. 'I always like to be by your side, where I have been now for more than twenty years.' Leamington thus figured almost at the beginning and almost at the end of the partnership, giving it an unexpected and poignant symmetry.[1]

Bright survived for twenty-four years, during which he never ceased to regret the loss of Cobden's guidance. In his old age he once told a friend that every night he was consoled in his dreams by the spirits of the two men who had most shaped his life, his father and his friend. But Cobden was no longer present to help with specific problems. 'My dear friend Cobden,' Bright exclaimed in his diary on the day in 1882 when he decided to resign from Gladstone's Government; 'how often have I wished him here for his counsel and help.' By this date, although Bright's interest in politics remained strong, his powers were gradually declining, notably his power as a speaker. Beatrice Webb was disappointed when she heard him address a Birmingham demonstration in 1884. His speeches now dwelt more and more upon the past. 'Still, there was something nobly pathetic in the old old story of Tory sinfulness told by the stern-looking old man, who seemed gradually to lose consciousness of the crowd beneath him, and see himself confronted with the forces of the past.' Bright's final illness began at Rochdale in May 1888, and lasted, with periods of temporary improvement, for some ten months. This final battle of his life was fought amidst national concern. As he grew weaker he faced the inevitable with Quaker calmness, sending farewell messages to his private and political friends, including Gladstone. After some hours of unconsciousness Bright finally died on the morning of Wednesday, March 27, 1889, surrounded by his family. His daughter described how his workpeople came to pay their last respects to their old master in his coffin. 'They came from the mill in their working clothes—the women with their shawls over their heads, and many brought their children . . . a constant stream, walking gently in single file round the coffin and out again, in perfect silence, many quietly weeping, especially the older people who had been at the mill all their lives.' On the Saturday he was buried, as he had wished, according to the simple Quaker rites in the graveyard of Rochdale meeting house. Thousands came to Rochdale to line the funeral route, but all was order and silence in the town. The strife of Bright's earlier career was long forgotten, and he went to his grave universally acknowledged as an eminent Victorian.[2]

## 2. COBDEN AND BRIGHT IN HISTORY

Late-Victorian public opinion accepted an uncritical, flattering picture of John Bright, and of his relationship with Richard Cobden, which the present study has tried to correct. We have seen how in his reminiscent old age Bright, unconsciously but none the less effectively, encouraged the idea that his partnership with Cobden was from the first an alliance of equals, equals moreover who were in complete agreement except over Parliamentary reform and initially over the American Civil War, on which questions Cobden was supposed to have been less progressive than his friend. We have noted the inaccuracy of this picture drawn by Bright and usually accepted in the history books, including even Morley's official life of Cobden. We have seen how Bright gave misleading, self-complimenting accounts of his first meeting with Cobden in 1837 and of their Leamington anti-Corn Law 'compact' in 1841. We have seen how Bright was definitely Cobden's junior throughout the whole anti-Corn Law campaign, and how his free trade views at this time, and to a lesser extent throughout his life, were narrower than Cobden's. Cobden's strong desire to unite classes at home and nations all over the world through free trade was adopted by Bright only slowly and partially. We have seen how Cobden, far from feeling less democratic than Bright over Parliamentary reform in the 1850s and '60s, was ahead of his friend. Cobden sincerely believed in 'one man one vote', whereas Bright was content with the limited urban franchise of 1867. We have noticed the skill and persistence of Cobden as negotiator of the 1860 Commercial Treaty with France. Cobden must share credit for its inspiration with Chevalier, but not with Bright, who had envisaged only unilateral action by Britain. We have seen, finally, that although Bright played a vigorous and liberal part in supporting and publicising the Northern cause during the American Civil War, he did not, as he afterwards claimed, convert Cobden to his views. Cobden followed a liberal line of his own, deploring the use of force even to suppress slavery, and anxious to ensure that Britain was not drawn into the war.

In general terms we can say that Bright was a reformer on many issues, but that Cobden was always abreast of him and on some important questions ahead of him. Bright's character, unlike Cobden's, contained within it an element of conservatism which set a limit to his reform aspirations. In 1876 Walter Bagehot published an article actually entitled 'The Conservative Vein in Mr. Bright'. Bagehot noted how Bright was marking time politically, how his reform sympathies were confined to causes which he had adopted in his youth, notably free trade, peace, economy, the ballot, and 'a popular franchise of the old kind'. 'The creed of the Mr. Bright of 1876 is probably far less altered from the creed of the Mr. Bright of 1840 than is the creed of the Duke of Richmond of 1876 from the creed of the same peer in 1840. The Duke of Richmond has reluctantly abandoned many articles of his old creed—Mr. Bright has abandoned none.' The Reform Act of 1867, The Irish Church Act of 1869, and the Irish Land Act of 1870 marked the limit for Bright. He still pressed for disestablishment and land reform in England, for extension of the 1867 urban franchise to the countryside, and for what he described as a 'free breakfast table', otherwise abolition of the revenue duties upon tea sugar, and coffee; but these proposals represented only a further application of his old ideas.

Revealingly, after 1867 middle- and upper-class opinion, which had previously distrusted Bright as a threat to established institutions, came to accept him as not so dangerous after all. The very strength of earlier distrust may have helped to produce an equally strong reaction in his favour once it began to be realised that at least he was not a revolutionary. Bright's increasingly patriarchal appearance encouraged this new attitude. 'Bright spoke grandly,' noted Lady Frederick Cavendish in her diary in 1869, 'rather like Isaiah! His voice is painfully hoarse, and he is astonishingly aged, but it doesn't mar the effect much.' Thus Bright became widely accepted as a respectable elder statesman, a role which he played with satisfaction for the rest of his life. Trevelyan wrote of the 'odour of sanctity' surrounding him in old age. The changed attitude of *Punch* was symptomatic. In the 1850s and early '60s it had attacked him fiercely, portraying him as an arrogant Quaker, and as late as 1865 numbering him among its April fools. During the 1870s and '80s, by contrast, it treated Bright with great deference. By the end of 1870 Bagehot was remarking how even anti-reformers were coming to accept him. 'We have often been amused to see how much, in the depths of Tory districts where "John Bright" was bitterly execrated, the regular residents were puzzled because their own M.P.'s and the most conservative people who went to London always mentioned him with geniality and toleration, and if young, would say, in the modern dialect—"Well, after all, he is a great *institution*".'

Bright's strong, publicly expressed support for the monarchy showed how little of an ultra-Radical he was, and this helped to secure his acceptance by 'respectable' late-Victorian opinion. In the 1830s he had proposed and carried a motion at the Rochdale Literary and Philosophical Society 'that a limited monarchy is best suited for this country at the present time'. This remained his lifelong view, as he explained forty years later to an enquirer who asked whether he would accept the presidency of the English republic if offered it. Both Cobden and Bright felt that the practical success of the British monarchy rendered discussion of the theoretical merits of republicanism super-fluous. After joining Gladstone's Government in 1868 Bright quickly became a personal favourite with Queen Victoria, who, like many of her subjects at about this time, was pleased to find him less dangerous than she had once feared. Out of respect for his Quaker views she allowed Bright to dispense with wearing full court dress. When illness forced his resignation in 1870 she was genuinely sorry. Cobden never went to court, and never came much into contact with the Queen; but by the 1860s he too was describing himself as 'the most disinterested of courtiers'. He was impressed by the Queen's conscientiousness after the death of the Prince Consort in visiting hospitals and poorhouses, 'offering sympathy to individual suffering and rebuking evil amuse-ments, whilst all the while she is unequal to the pageantries of her office, which a less earnest nature would, under the plea of duty, have flown to for distraction'. Cobden thus gave Queen Victoria positive credit for abandoning her ceremonial duties at a time when critics were using this very fact as an argument in favour of a republic.[1]

Cobden was well aware of the inherent conservatism in Bright's character. He knew, even if history has usually forgotten, that he, and not Bright, was the more democratic by inclination. We have clear evidence about this from Justin McCarthy, whose work for the *Morning Star* brought him into close contact with both Cobden and Bright during the 1860s. In his widely-read *History of Our Own Times*, first published in 1879, McCarthy wrote:

'There was, in Mr. Bright's nature, a certain element of Conservatism which showed itself clearly enough the moment the particular reforms which he thought necessary were carried; Mr. Cobden would have gone on advancing in the direction of reform as long as he lived. It was Mr. Cobden's conciliatory manner, and an easy genuine *bonhomie*, worthy of Palmerston himself, that made the difference between the two men in popular estimation. Not much difference, to be sure, was ever to be noticed between them in public affairs. . . . But where there was any difference, even of speculative opinion, Mr. Cobden went further than Mr. Bright along the path of Radicalism.'

Here was a plain statement of the true relationship of Cobden and Bright to each other and to political progress, the more valuable because it was made long before the Home Rule crisis emphasised the limits of Bright's range. Even then, however, many late-Victorians declined to draw from his opposition to Home Rule any general conclusions about Bright as a reformer. Though no longer anywhere regarded as a potential revolutionary, he was still widely accepted as very advanced. When Bright died in 1889 G. J. Holyoake, a veteran working-class Radical who had known him for many years, and who knew that he had never been a genuine democrat, was forced to publish this view under the revealing title of 'Quite a New View of John Bright'. 'Mr. Bright was no friend of democracy . . . the reader will ask, "How is it that he was so widely mistaken for an aggressive and uncompromising Liberal?" Most men think that because a man goes down the same street with them he is going to the same place.'

Justin McCarthy made a more extended comparison between Cobden and Bright in his *Reminiscences*, published in 1899. This source would have been suspect if McCarthy had not given the substance of his views twenty years earlier, for in the 1880s Bright and McCarthy ceased to be on speaking terms. In 1879 McCarthy had entered Parliament as an Irish Member, becoming a close friend and follower of Parnell. This made him in Bright's eyes one of the chief Irish 'rebels'. In his reminiscences McCarthy nevertheless still wrote of Bright in a friendly spirit, although taking care not to do so at the expense of Cobden, for whom clearly he felt the greater regard.

'Cobden passed with many men, and indeed with the public in general, for being a much less extreme Radical and Democrat than Bright. Bright had all the passion of the orator, and he fought his political battles with something of the spirit of the gladiator. . . . The natural sweetness of Cobden's disposition inclined him rather to quiet argument leading to persuasion and conviction; he felt little or nothing of that joy of the strife which was one of Bright's inspiring characteristics. . . . Therefore the natural inclination of men was to regard him as more moderate in his views and more ready to accept a compromise than his combative friend and political associate. But in truth Cobden was far more of a Democrat than Bright. I have heard him often compare their political views in his usual tone of sweet good temper. He used to declare that he was himself a convinced Democrat: that is, a believer in the right of the majority to have the final settlement of all political questions. Bright, he used to say, was not in that sense a Democrat at all; Bright was convinced of the necessity of certain great constitutional and political changes; on these he had set his heart, and to the accomplishment of these he devoted his intellect and his eloquence. Let these once be carried, and Bright, he continued, would be quite content if the democratic principle were pushed no further in his time. . . . Of course Cobden never talked in this way with the faintest thought of disparaging Bright. . . . It was only his good-humoured way of trying to persuade people that Bright was not by any means the sort of iconoclast in politics that most of his opponents supposed him to be: and of showing that in point of fact Bright could be more easily satisfied than he (Cobden) could profess to be.'[2]

We have noticed how Bright never came to advocate free trade in the same positive international spirit as Cobden. In the days of the Anti-Corn Law League Bright tended to dwell upon the purely material benefits of trade freedom. He could not have spoken in 1846 as Cobden did:

'I believe that the physical gain will be the smallest gain to humanity from the success of this principle. I look farther; I see in the free-trade principle that which shall act on the moral world as the principle of gravitation in the universe—drawing men together, thrusting aside the antagonism of race, and creed, and language, and uniting us in the bonds of eternal peace. I have looked even farther. I have speculated, and probably dreamt, in the dim future—ay, a thousand years hence—I have speculated on what the effect of this principle may be. I believe that the effect will be to change the face of the world, so as to introduce a system of government entirely distinct from that which now prevails. I believe that the desire and the motive for large and mighty empires, for gigantic armies and navies, for those materials which are used for the destruction of life and the desolation of the rewards of labour, will die away. . . . I believe that the speculative philosopher of a thousand years hence will date the greatest revolution that ever happened from the triumph of the principle which we have met here to advocate.'

We have seen Cobden working until the end of his life to convert this vision into reality. At his death in 1865 success still seemed possible. Distant as the day might be, declared the *Manchester Guardian* in an obituary leading article, 'when the several members of the human family will practically regard themselves as constituting a great federation with common interests, it is towards that point that we all believe ourselves to be going'. The *Guardian* remained optimistic about the free trade millennium into the '70s, claiming in 1878, for example, that there was no government in Europe, except the Russian, 'whose members are not for the most part convinced of the benefits of free trade'. By 1890, however, the *Guardian* was admitting that the trend towards free trade had been reversed into a trend towards protection, militarism and antagonism. The paper was driven to hoping rather desperately that a reaction would set in: 'Give it rope enough.' Britain was still the world's leading trading nation, and one day foreigners would realise that this was the consequence of free trade. But by 1901, looking back over the reign of Queen Victoria, the

*Guardian* had ceased to expect that free trade would produce Cobden's united world. 'The men of the great free trade epoch believed that neither commercially, intellectually, or morally is one nation's gain another's loss, and they looked forward to a growing commercial intercourse not merely for its material benefits but for the sake of the links they believed it would forge between nation and nation. They did not then imagine that within half a century the Great Powers of the world would be standing like vultures over the spoils of the world's peoples, only deterred from tearing them to pieces by dread of one another.'

What went wrong? International free trade failed because of an upsurge of economic nationalism in the years after Cobden's death. In his last speech in 1864 Cobden had himself welcomed 'the recent tendency of things' in favour of nationality. But he was thinking only of political nationality. He assumed that all nationalities, and especially business middle-class nationality, would appreciate the wisdom of free trade. But in the event the business middle classes of the world never did accept that they shared a common interest in free trade. Instead, in order to encourage industrial growth, which was regarded as essential to national independence, most countries followed increasingly protectionist policies during the last quarter of the nineteenth century. Such countries were able to point out that even John Stuart Mill had accepted the need for nation states to shelter their infant industries. Bright deplored this passage, complaining that it had outweighed all the good done by Mill's other writings. In the end Germany, the United States, France and other states (new and old) went much farther than ever Mill had contemplated. The freer trade system created round Cobden's 1860 treaty gradually collapsed. Cobden came to be increasingly regarded on the Continent and in the United States not as a disinterested internationalist, but as a British economic nationalist anxious to perpetuate through free trade a world economic system in which his own country was the predominant manufacturing power, expecting other states to accept subordinate roles as mere producers of food and raw materials. *The Times* noted in 1866 how a prominent American had declared that 'free trade was a system devised by England to enable her to plunder the world'. Foreign writers as different as Engels, the communist, and List, the nationalist, shared this view. List's *National System of Political Economy* (1841) became the textbook of late nineteenth-century protectionists. List had visited England in the year of Corn Law repeal, meeting Cobden but returning home to Germany still more certain that Britain was seeking to maintain world economic hegemony through free trade. Disraeli's description of Britain as 'the workshop of the world', so pleasing to Victorians, was an increasing source of irritation to foreigners. List did not oppose Cobden's ideal of international harmony within a free trade world, but he believed that the way to it must be through bargaining between strong and equal nation states, which had first built up their strength under protection. 'All examples which history can show are those in which the political union has led the way, and the commercial union has followed. Not a single instance can be adduced in which the latter has taken the lead, and the former has grown up from it . . . under the existing conditions of the world the result of general free trade would not be a universal republic, but, on the contrary, a universal subjection of the less advanced nations to the supremacy of the predominant manufacturing, commercial, and naval power.' That List's ultimate goal was the same as Cobden's was largely forgotten after his death, but his advocacy of economic nationalism became increasingly influential.

Economic nationalism was encouraged from the 1870s by trade depression, which reached troughs in 1873, 1882, and 1890. Such depression was now the more damaging because industrial output was growing rapidly. At this same time European agriculture was facing increasing competition from American and Australian wheat. Finally, in the case of France, defeat by Prussia in 1870 produced an intense desire to reassert her national identity. Economic protection seemed to be the answer to all these problems. Indeed, to the sorrow of Cobden and Bright, the United States had established a high tariff as early as 1861. Austria, Germany, Italy, France and Russia each resorted to a succession of tariff increases between the late '70s and the early '90s. Further increases took place early in the twentieth century and only the Netherlands, Denmark, Finland, Turkey and Great Britain retained general free trade.

Cobden's treaty with France was renewed, after some uncertainty, in 1873, but it lapsed in 1882. The French were no longer interested in the treaty as a step towards international free trade. They now wanted only to make specific bargains, and in this spirit they simply signed a declaration in 1882 whereby the two countries granted each other most favoured nation treatment for ten years.

By 1880 List was beginning to attract a following even in England, and his *National System* was first translated into English in 1885. Britain was no longer unchallenged economically. In 1840 she had controlled nearly one-third of the world's trade: by 1880 she controlled less than one-quarter. Depression was affecting British industry severely at intervals, while British agriculture was being submerged beneath an influx of cheap American corn. Some businessmen, economists and politicians began to ask if free trade still paid. Ought we, in the face of growing economic nationalism elsewhere, to adopt policies of economic nationalism ourselves? The Cobden Club, formed in 1866 as a convivial commemorative body, found itself within a few years perforce transformed into a fighting instrument. The arguments which it had to counter were conveniently listed in Buxton's *Handbook to Political Questions of the Day* (1880). The usual case for a change in policy did not demand complete protection, only reciprocity, 'fair trade', the abandonment by Britain of free trade with countries which refused free trade with her. The fair traders argued variously, (1) that free trade required a free interchange of goods throughout the world, and since this had not been achieved free trade could not be said to exist; (2) that while universal free trade would benefit the world, partial free trade only injured the country which adopted it; (3) that the universal adoption of free trade would be more probable if Britain retained the power of forcing other nations to adopt it by mutual adjustment of tariffs; (4) that the increase of British wealth since the 1840s had been produced not by free trade, but chiefly by improvements in machinery, the use of railways, and the like; (5) that our free trade policy tended to alienate the affections of our colonies, which, to prevent themselves being undersold, were obliged to impose heavy protective duties; (6) that Britain alone among major powers had adopted free trade, 'and it would be presumptuous to say that we were in the right and all other nations in the wrong'. Free traders of the 1880s replied (1) that a policy of tariff retaliation would not work, since import duties on our raw materials would injure our manufacturers; (2) that we did not import enough manufactured goods, in proportion to the amount exported, to make it profitable for any nation to come to terms with us; (3) that the fewer the obstacles in the way of trade the better it flourished, since unimpeded capital always found the most profitable investment; (4) that but for free trade, and subsequent low prices, distress would have been more prevalent in Britain; and (5) that depression in trade was not confined to Britain but was more severe in protectionist countries.

A significant feature of this free trade defence was its material emphasis. By the '80s even total free traders were retreating from Cobden's high line that free trade would soon bring the world to peace and union. They were compelled to concentrate upon the argument that free trade benefited Britain materially even in a protectionist world. One Cobden Club pamphleteer even went so far in 1887 as to suggest that universal free trade would be positively disadvantageous, since Britain would then lose 'the one enormous advantage which we now possess; that none of our products are loaded with duties on the raw material thereof, as those of our competitors are'. Under universal free trade articles would be manufactured where they could be most cheaply produced. 'If so, we have to ask ourselves, is Great Britain the cheapest place for the production of iron, and steel, or of ships, or of cotton goods, or of woollen goods, or of machinery?' Eleven years later a leading academic, the author of *The Free Trade Movement and its Results*, while avowing himself in favour of free trade for economic reasons, explicitly repudiated Cobden's high moral expectations. Cobden, he wrote, 'had exaggerated notions of the effects of commerce in producing universal peace'. In a spirit which would have appalled Cobden this late-Victorian author contrived to reconcile free trade with large armaments. 'In his continual attacks on the expense of the army and navy he [Cobden] seemed to forget that it was "the strong man armed that keepeth his goods in safety". He was unconsciously influenced by the prejudices of his class and occupation, and though his patriotism was sincere, it was perhaps not sufficiently comprehensive to embrace all the important factors of national greatness.'

With the free trade case shorn of its high moral aspect even by free traders, it is less surprising that from about 1880 until 1914 free trade was always under attack in Britain, especially in times of trade depression. 1881 saw the formation of the Fair Trade League, which conducted a persistent campaign during the 1880s led by a group of prominent provincial businessmen and Conservative Members of Parliament. Its influence was considerable for a time, and threatened to become even greater. The majority report of the Royal Commission on the Depression of Trade and Industry (1885–6) still supported free trade, but a minority report advocated fair trade. Although the Fair Trade League wilted with trade revival in 1887, public discussion for and against free trade was not submerged for long, even though no new agitation was mounted during the '90s. The erosion of British confidence during the Boer War encouraged further questioning of established policies. Was Britain falling into a dangerous decline, militarily and economically? If so, could she reverse this trend? Finally, in 1903 Joseph Chamberlain came forward with a gloomy analysis of British economic weakness, present and prospective, and a bold solution for it. He described his new policy as 'tariff reform'.

Tariff reform promised both a stronger Britain in the world as leader of a more united empire, and a stronger Britain at home through more assured economic prosperity. Free trade had never succeeded in totally establishing itself even within the British Empire. As early as 1859 with defiant explicitness Canada had affirmed her determination to protect her young national industry against Britain's established manufacturing power, and thereafter the other self-governing colonies had gradually followed suit. In 1897 protectionist Canada initiated a new system of imperial preference, and began to press for Britain to show her special relationship by adopting preference in return. In 1897 Chamberlain, as Colonial Secretary, was not yet ready to respond, pointing out that British trade with Germany and Belgium alone was larger than with all the colonies combined. By 1903, however, he had decided that we needed the moral and material support of a united empire in a hostile world. Our major industries, claimed Chamberlain, were all suffering severely, or likely to suffer severely, from foreign competition protected by high tariff barriers. 'Agriculture, the greatest of all trades and industries, has been practically destroyed. . . . Sugar has gone, silk has gone, iron is threatened, wool is threatened; the turn of cotton will come. . . . At the present moment these industries and the working men who depend on them are like sheep in the field.' Chamberlain therefore proposed that the colonies should reduce their tariffs upon British manufactures while retaining them on foreign goods, in return for which Britain would impose duties upon foreign goods but would admit those from the colonies duty free. Here would be the beginnings of an imperial customs union, bringing the benefits of freer trade within the empire as a substitute for the failure of world free trade.

Chamberlain never converted the self-governing colonies to acceptance of full empire free trade. The spirit of List was as influential in Ottawa and Melbourne as in Berlin. The colonists were eager for imperial preference, but they would never have exposed their infant industries to a full system of imperial free trade. In the event, the colonials were never put to this test for Chamberlain failed to convert the British public even to his more modest initial proposals. He promised that his new tariffs would increase empire trade by £26 m. per annum, giving work to one hundred and sixty-six thousand workers. He promised also that the revenue collected from tariffs would finance old age pensions and other social reforms. But these promises counted for nothing against the fear, carefully exploited by the free traders, that tariff reform would bring dearer food. Chamberlain admitted that the cost of bread might rise, but he proposed to balance this by reducing the existing revenue duties upon tea, coffee and cocoa. This promise, however, could not overcome the fear that tariff reform meant the 'little loaf'. Chamberlain wanted to go back, said the free traders, to the 'hungry forties'. This last phrase seems to have been coined in 1903 by Cobden's daughter, Jane Cobden Unwin, whose husband published under this title a widely-read collection of memories of life before 1846. In the same year he had issued a cheap edition of Morley's life of Cobden, almost a thousand pages for only two shillings and sixpence. The 'little loaf' argument was especially effective in areas where local industry seemed generally prosperous under free trade. Where trade was depressed Chamberlain found more response, notably in the Birmingham and Sheffield metal trades. He attracted less support from the woollen districts, and very little from the cotton and coal mining areas. On the whole, Chamberlain could not prove that free trade had failed. Although Britain no longer held its mid-Victorian position of predominance, the British public could not see the need for a reversal of traditional policies. Facts and figures exchanged by both sides probably went over the heads of most electors, but most of them did not feel the shoe pinching as much as Chamberlain claimed, especially during 1905 when trade improved in all industries. At the 1906 general election the free trade Liberals won an overwhelming victory, and only just over a hundred Chamberlain supporters were elected.

1906 was a victory year for free trade, but only on material grounds. The British public was not now endorsing Cobden's international free trade vision. This vision was kept alive, however, by middle-class intellectuals within the Liberal Party and by working-class intellectuals within the new Labour movement. Such men had led the opposition to the Boer War in a spirit consciously similar to that of Cobden and Bright against the Crimean War. J. A. Hobson's widely-read analysis of *Imperialism*, published in 1902, was heavily influenced by Cobden. But few electors who voted for free trade in 1906 did so under the influence of Hobson. In the 1900 'khaki' election many of the same electors had voted the other way, all against Cobden's peace ideals. A few years later, with revealing forgetfulness, even Manchester was to erect a Boer War memorial at the opposite end of the square in which stood its commemorative statue of Cobden.

Arguments and prospects fluctuated up to 1914, but it was fortunate for Edwardian England that she did not abandon free trade. Economic circumstances were very different from Cobden's day, but even so British free trade still greatly benefited both the United Kingdom and the world. Britain now stood at the centre of a developing multi-lateral system of international payments. This system, by allowing other industrial powers to obtain food and raw materials from primary producing countries without necessarily exporting manufactured goods directly in return, relieved British exports of much competition in certain non-European primary producing areas which provided vital markets for British manufacturers. In addition, the multilateral international market meant that Britain's loss of markets for manufactures in Europe and America did not involve payments difficulties for her with those areas. If Britain had attempted to raise tariff barriers against foreign manufacturers and to extend colonial preference, both industrial Europe and the United States would have been forced either substantially to adjust their internal economies and to seek new sources of supply by developing their colonies and spheres of influence, or to intensify world competition in manufactured goods. As it was, in the words of a modern economic historian which Cobden would have delighted to read, 'the whole world was bound together in an economic unit by a network of commercial and financial transactions, as never before; and that achievement, involving a great expansion of activity, was secured with relatively little friction'. This world economic system depended upon John Bull's commitment to free trade, and, paradoxically, free trade protected British industry against foreign competition in important markets outside Europe and North America. Even though most of the world persisted with protection, Cobden would have been well pleased to find Britain's free trade policy so notably promoting the prosperity of the world.

The outbreak of the First World War changed everything. The McKenna duties introduced in 1915 upon imports of cars, cycles, clocks, watches, films and musical instruments were not repealed after the war. In 1921 the Safeguarding of Industries Act was passed to protect certain industries which had been launched during the war to produce goods previously imported from Germany. In theory the country remained committed to free trade, and as late as the 1923 General Election Baldwin was defeated when he asked the country for a mandate in favour of protection. But the underlying trend was now all against free trade. Even in Manchester cotton merchants, watching the increasing output of cheap Indian and Japanese textiles, began to press for a protective tariff. The world slump beginning in 1929 led to the final abandonment of British free trade. The catastrophic decline in demand for British goods convinced the business world and the Government that at least the home market must be preserved for British producers. Temporary measures taken in 1931 were followed in 1932 by the Import Duties Act, introduced by Neville Chamberlain, which levied a general 10 per cent duty upon most manufactured imports. Preferential rates were soon arranged for empire products, while the general duty was subsequently raised to a top limit of $33\frac{1}{3}$ per cent.

All this seemed inevitable in the desperate economic climate of the 1930s. The economic confidence which had first produced free trade seemed far away. The British public quickly forgot that it had ever believed in free trade, becoming (as Sir Charles Petrie remarked in 1938) 'uncertain whether Cobden was a man or a horse'. A shift in emphasis took place in the minds even of those who continued to call themselves free traders. We have noticed that many late-Victorian free traders had stressed the material benefits of free trade, even to the exclusion of its international peace-building function. By the 1930s, however, free traders had perforce given up claiming that free trade was the best way to prosperity, and were emphasising instead the necessity of establishing international harmony and peace. They rightly explained that this was Cobden's highest aim, and that even he regarded economic policy only as a means towards it. 'When I advocated free trade', Cobden had declared at a peace meeting in 1850, 'do you suppose that I did not see its relation to the present question, or that I advocated free trade merely because it would give us a little more occupation in this or that pursuit? No; I believed free trade would have the tendency to unite mankind in the bonds of peace, and it was that, more than any pecuniary consideration, which sustained and actuated me.' In this spirit free trade meant much more than the abolition of tariffs. Starting from this point, Sir John Clapham, the economic historian, who had been brought up as a late-Victorian free trader, was still able in 1945 to describe himself as a free trader, even while admitting that in the world of the 1940s he would not be 'too fastidious about tariff or no tariff'. Clapham argued that free traders could support 'any economic policy or act directed to the encouragement of the view that as the economic world is one, the nations in it must co-operate'.

We have seen, however, why Cobden had placed little faith in formal world government, a League of Nations or a United Nations Organisation. He doubted the constructive potential of government in any form. Certainly, the history of the League of Nations and of the United Nations cannot be said to have proved him wrong. Cobden believed that an international spirit would be best encouraged by a non-institutional influence like free trade, that individual pursuit of self-interest under free trade would draw mankind together. Free trade acting alone has long since shown itself unable to do this; but Cobden was right to look outside mere formal organisation in his search for world peace and prosperity. An external force has now kept the world free from major war for over twenty years. This force is the fear of nuclear destruction. The motive of self-interest has operated in the light of mankind's knowledge not (as Cobden hoped) of economic science, but of physical science.

Under cover of the nuclear balance of power Europe has moved towards internal free trade within the European Economic Community. The spirit of E.E.C. is exclusive, as Britain has found, rather than world-inclusive as Cobden would have wished. General de Gaulle is much more a pupil of List than of Cobden. But Cobden would probably have recommended the Community, as he recommended his own 1860 treaty with an earlier French nationalist freer trade auto-crat, as at least a step in the right direction. Cobden would probably have wanted Britain to join E.E.C., not simply for possible material advantages, but also in the hope of displacing the influence within the Community of Listian free trade by a more generous outward-looking spirit.

Modern science may shape and pacify the world not only through fear of the hydrogen bomb, but also by finding the means to produce such abundance as will remove all differences and tensions between rich and poor nations. In his last days Cobden himself foresaw that science might transform world society, exercising an influence greater than that of Christianity or of free trade. Writing in 1863 to thank Samuel Smiles for a copy of his *Industrial Biography*, he wondered if 'the world will be indebted for its civilisation, and for the amelioration of its international relations, less to those precepts of religion which every nation disregards when convenient, than to the progress of physical science, whose laws will bind all countries in equal and inevit-able subjection.' In another letter at this time Cobden regretted that there seemed to be no hope of the international relations of mankind being established on New Testament principles. 'Must we turn our hopes', he asked, 'to physical science?'

Here was Cobden looking far ahead of his time. When he died in 1865 the *Leeds Mercury* praised him as 'the man of the moment, perhaps of the future, not yet merely of the past'. We may compare the same newspaper's remarks on Bright's death twenty-four years later, when it observed how Bright had 'scarcely advanced beyond his first principles'. Bright remained essentially an early-Victorian reformer with the limitations of his time and background. We quoted at the beginning of this study the remark of J. L. Hammond that there was as much difference between Cobden and Bright as between Cobden and Palmerston. 'In comparison with Gladstone, Palmerston was an insular Englishman with the high spirit of a schoolboy; in comparison with Cobden, Bright was an insular Englishman with the stern con-science of a Quaker.' Hammond, who was himself a late-Victorian free trader, has been one of the few historians to compare Cobden accurately with Bright. Hammond briefly remarked, and we have tried to demonstrate in detail, how Cobden's image in history has suffered from the custom of linking his name with that of Bright. We must not undervalue what Bright achieved. He was a notable Victorian. But Cobden, whom Bishop Wilberforce fittingly described as 'the international man', was more than simply a notable Victorian. He was an internationalist and a democrat who has stood out as an inspiration not only for his own time but for future time, including our own. The era of high protection, extreme nationalism and rampant militarism, which began after his death, and which culminated in two global wars, is now seen as a disastrous interlude. In an important sense the world of the 1960s is continuing from the point where Cobden hopefully left the world of the 1860s a century ago.*3

---

* See, for example, the broadcast talk by Professor Harry Johnson, 'After the Kennedy Round' (*The Listener*, August 24, 1967), urging the United States 'to move unilaterally towards freer trade, or even free trade. This would be a policy that Britain would be wise to emulate (or try to persuade her Common Market partners to emulate). For there is no reason to believe that the tariff structures that have emerged from past legislation and negotiation serve any useful national purpose in a more economically sophisticated modern world and a more closely integrated world economy.'

# References

(British Museum Additional Manuscripts are cited simply as 'Add. MSS.')

## INTRODUCTION

page

viii 1 G. M. Trevelyan, *An Autobiography* (1949), 34; J. H. Plumb, *Men and Books* (1963), 238; *Proceedings of the British Academy*, XLIX (1963), 380–1.

viii 2 *The Great Victorians* (ed. H. J. and H. Massingham, 1932), 144–5.

ix 3 Cobden to Paulton, Dec. 27, 1861 (Add. MSS., 43, 662); R. Cobden, *Speeches on Questions of Public Policy* (1870), II, 74; J. Bright, *Public Addresses* (1879), 356; J. Morley, *Life of Richard Cobden* (1903 ed.), 648–9.

## CHAPTER I: COBDEN

### 1 Background

1 1 Cobden to Bright, Sept. 2, 1851 (Add. MSS., 43, 649).

1 2 Priscilla Cobden to Richard Cobden, June 20, 1833 (West Sussex Record Office, Cobden Papers, no. 19).

2 3 Cobden to Mr. and Mrs. Cole, Sept. 24, 1815; Cobden to W. Cobden, March 25, 1818 (W.S.R.O., Add. MSS., 6,009); Emma Jane Cobden, Draft History of the Cobden Family (Cobden Papers, no. 302); Cobden to Parkes, May 30, 1856 (Add. MSS., 43, 664); P. Collins, *Dickens and Education* (1963), 105, 108.

4 4 *Blackwood's Magazine*, XXXIII (1833), 423; Cobden to Bright, Nov. 5, 1855 (Add. MSS., 43, 650); List of Books in Richard Cobden's Library (Cobden Papers, no. 506); Morley, *Cobden*, 920; D. H. MacGregor, *Economic Thought and Policy* (1949), ch. 3; L. Robbins, *The Theory of Economic Policy in English Classical Political Economy* (1952), esp. 34–46; R. K. Webb, *The British Working Class Reader, 1790–1848* (1955), 98–102; R. K. Webb, *Harriet Martineau* (1960), 101–7.

5 5 Cobden to Cole, April 24, 1835 (Cobden Papers, no. 19); Cobden Papers nos. 321–2; C. Gibbon, *Life of George Combe* (1878), I, 314–15; Morley, *Cobden*, 120–1.

5 6 Cobden to W. Cobden, Aug. 21, 1825 (Cobden Papers, no. 19).

6 7 Cobden to F. Cobden, Aug. 26, 1825 (Cobden Papers, no. 19);

# References

*page*

C. Dickens, *The Old Curiosity Shop*, ch. XLV; *Political Writings of Richard Cobden* (1866), I, 194.

6  8  Morley, *Cobden*, 15–16.

6  9  Cobden to F. Cobden, Jan. 6, 30, 1832 (W.S.R.O., Add. MSS., 2, 762); Morley, *Cobden*, 19–21, 117–18.

7  10  J. D. Chambers, *Workshop of the World* (1964), 16–24; Phyllis Deane, *The First Industrial Revolution* (1965), ch. 6.

8  11  J. G. Kohl, *Ireland, Scotland, and England* (1844), pt. 3, 106–7; B. Disraeli, *Coningsby*, bk. IV, ch. I; T. Carlyle, *Chartism* (1839), ch. VIII; *Manchester Guardian*, Sept. 10, 1953.

9  12  *Manchester Times*, Dec. 16, 1837; Cobden to Villiers, Feb. 17, 1838 (Add. MSS., 43, 662); *Postage Sel. Comm. Mins. of Evid., P.P. 1837–8* (709), Q. 6, 703.

9  13  *Mary Barton*, ch. VI.

10  14  D. Read, *Peterloo* (1958); A. Briggs, 'The Background of the Parliamentary Reform Movement in Three English Cities (1830–2)', *Cambridge Historical Journal*, X (1952); A. Briggs, *Victorian Cities* (1963), chs. I, III; D. Read, 'Chartism in Manchester' in A. Briggs (ed.), *Chartist Studies* (1959).

10  15  S. Smiles, *Autobiography* (1905), 112.

11  16  Cobden to F. Cobden, June 4, 1844 (Add. MSS., 50, 750); E. Chadwick, *Report on the Sanitary Condition of the Labouring Population* (ed. M. W. Flinn, 1965), 243–4; F. Engels, *Condition of the Working Class in England* (trans. W. O. Henderson and W. H. Chaloner, 1958), 53–6; Briggs, *Victorian Cities*, 103.

12  17  Morley, *Cobden*, 27–8.

13  18  Elizabeth H. Cawley (ed.), *The American Diaries of Richard Cobden* (1952); F. Thistlethwaite, *America and the Atlantic Community* (1963), esp. 165–72; K. Fielden, Richard Cobden and America (Ph. D. thesis, Cambridge Univ., 1966).

13  19  Cobden, *Political Writings*, I, 1–153.

14  20  Ibid., I, 155–354.

15  21  Ibid., I, 160; S. J. Reid, *Life and Letters of the First Earl of Durham* (1906), II, 92–4.

15  22  *Manchester Times*, May 9, 1835, July 9, 1836; A. Prentice, *History of the Anti-Corn-Law League* (1853), I, 46–8; *Absalom Watkin, Extracts from his Journal* (1920), 191–2; D. Read, *Press and People, 1790–1850* (1961), 162–3.

17  23  Cobden to Tait, Oct. 3, 1836 (Add. MSS., 43, 665); *Manchester Times*, Dec. 17, 1836, May 13, 20, 27, July 1, 29, Aug. 5, 1837; Morley, *Cobden*, 113, 116, 951–5; Reid, *Durham*, II, 93.

18  24  Morley, *Cobden*, 123–5; W. E. A. Axon, *Cobden as a Citizen* (1907); Shena D. Simon, *A Century of City Government* (1938), ch. III; A. Redford, *History of Local Government in Manchester* (1939–40), ch. XV.

18  25  Axon, *Cobden*, 31–2.

# References

19 26   *Postage Sel. Comm. Third Rep. Mins. of Evid.*, P.P. *1837–8*, xx, pt.
II, 708, 46–63; Cobden to Hill, May 12, 1838 (Add. MSS., 31, 978);
Cobden to Paulton, March 8, 1865 (ibid., 43, 662); R. and G. B. Hill,
*Life of Sir Rowland Hill* (1880), I, 276, 382, 477–8, II, 31; A Redford,
*Manchester Merchants and Foreign Trade, 1794–1858* (1934), 192–3;
H. D. Jordan, 'Richard Cobden and Penny Postage', *Victorian Studies*,
VIII (1965).

## 2 Industry and Agriculture

21 1   *Nottingham Gazette*, May 27, 1814; *Manchester Mercury*, Oct. 8, 1816;
A. Prentice, *Historical Sketches and Personal Recollections of Manchester*
(2nd ed., 1851), ch. V; J. A. Langford, *A Century of Birmingham Life*
(1868), II, 333; D. G. Barnes, *History of the English Corn Laws* (1930);
D. Fraser, Newspapers and Opinion in Three Midland Cities, 1800–
1850 (M.A. thesis, Leeds Univ., 1962), 214–16; Chambers, *Workshop
of the World*, ch. 3; Deane, *First Industrial Revolution*, ch. 12; J. D.
Chambers and G. E. Mingay, *The Agricultural Revolution, 1750–1880*
(1966), chs. 5, 6.

21 2   Redford, *Manchester Merchants*, chs. X, XI.

21 3   Prentice, *Anti-Corn-Law League*, I, 194; Cobden, *Political Writings*,
I, 149; ibid. (1886 ed.), 1–2.

22 4   *16th Annual Report of the Directors of the Manchester Chamber of Commerce*, 14; *Manchester Times*, June 17, 1837.

22 5   Redford, *Manchester Merchants*, 153–4.

23 6   Cobden to F. Cobden, July 6, 1846 (Add. MSS., 50, 751); Prentice,
*Anti-Corn-Law League*, I, chs. V, VII; Cobden, *Political Writings*, I,
31–2; Morley, *Cobden*, chs. V, VI; N. McCord, *The Anti-Corn Law
League, 1838–1846* (1958), ch. 1.

## 3 Leader of the Anti-Corn Law League

26 1   Cobden to his wife, Aug. 15, 1843 (Add. MSS., 50, 748); Cobden to
Smith, May 23, 1845 (Smith Papers, Manchester Reference Library);
Harriet B. Stowe, *Sunny Memories of Foreign Lands* (1854), 307;
W. Bagehot, *Biographical Studies* (1902), 362–3; Lady Dorothy
Nevill, *Reminiscences* (1906), 190; Morley, *Cobden*, 184–5.

26 2   Cobden to Gladstone, Jan. 1, 1864 (Add. MSS., 44, 136); Cobden,
*Speeches*, II, 541–2; Morley, *Cobden*, 694, 941; J. McCarthy, *Reminiscences* (1899), I, 57; *Leaves from the Note-Books of Lady Dorothy Nevill*
(1907), 67; F. W. Hirst, *In the Golden Days* (1947), 51.

28 3   Cobden to Combe, April 30, 1844 (Add. MSS., 43, 660); Cobden to
his wife, Jan. 16, 1845 (ibid., 50, 748); Cobden to Prentice, Oct. 12
(?1847), Cobden Papers, no. 21; *Annual Register, 1865*, 189; Cobden,
*Speeches*, I, 202, II, 374; Bright, *Public Addresses*, 359; Morley, *Cobden*,
41, 193–9, 207–8, 317–18, 388; B. Disraeli, *Endymion* (1880), ch. LXII;
A. Bisset, *Notes on the Anti-Corn Law Struggle* (1884), 15; *Lord Beaconsfield's Correspondence with his Sister, 1832–1852* (1886), 11; L. Stephen,

*Henry Fawcett* (1886), 358; Sir E. W. Watkin, *Alderman Cobden of Manchester* (1891), 117–18; J. McCarthy, *Portraits of the Sixties* (1903), 97–8; J. A. Hobson, *Richard Cobden, the International Man* (1918), 231.

29  4  J. Parkes to F. Place, Dec. 14, 1838 (Add. MSS., 35, 151, ff. 114–15); Cobden to Ashworth, April 7, 1842 (ibid., 43, 653); Cobden to Parkes, July 18, 1846 (ibid., 43, 664); A. Poulett Scrope, *Memoir of the Life of the Right Honourable Charles Lord Sydenham* (1843), 90; W. O. Henderson, 'Charles Pelham Villiers', *History*, XXXVII (1952).

29  5  Cobden to Ashworth, Sept. 14, 1851 (Add. MSS., 43, 653); Bisset, *Anti-Corn Law Struggle*, 8.

29  6  Cobden to Villiers, c. Feb. 28, 1841 (Add. MSS., 43, 662).

30  7  Cobden to Sturge, Nov. 27, 1841 (Add. MSS., 50, 131); Cobden to Smith, Dec. 4, 1841 (Smith Papers); Cobden to Villiers, Jan. 19, 1842 Add. MSS., 43, 662); Watkin, *Cobden*, 89–90, 94; Smiles, *Autobiography*, 118; Trevelyan, *Bright*, 66–7; M. Hovell, *The Chartist Movement* (2nd ed., 1950), 240–50; Briggs, *Chartist Studies*, 364–5; McCord, *Anti-Corn Law League*, 111–16, 131–2.

31  8  Cobden to Gladstone, Jan. 22, 1841 (Add. MSS., 44, 135); Brief Notes by Mrs. C. A. Cobden on Richard Cobden's Religious Views, Cobden Papers, no. 309; Cobden to Bright, April 10, 1858 (Add. MSS., 43, 650); Gibson, *Combe*, II, 217–20; Morley, *Cobden*, 126, 199–202, 295–6, 506; W. Robertson, *Life and Times of the Right Hon. John Bright* (1883), III, 18–19; *Diaries of John Bright* (1930), 471.

32  9  Cobden to Villiers, June 6, 1841 (Add. MSS., 43, 662); Cobden to Sturge (? 11 Dec.), 1841 (ibid., 50, 131); Prentice, *Anti-Corn-Law League*, I, ch. XVI; R. G. Cowherd, *The Politics of English Dissent* (1959), ch. 10; McCord, *Anti-Corn-Law League*, 104–7.

33  10  Prentice, *Anti-Corn Law League*, II, 269; Edith H. Fowler, *Life of Henry Hartley Fowler* (1912), 70.

34  11  J. Morley, *Life of William Ewart Gladstone* (1905 ed.), I, 249.

35  12  Cobden to Sturge, Nov. 2, 1841 (Add. MSS., 50, 131); *Manchester Times, Manchester & Salford Advertiser*, March 20, 1841; Prentice, *Anti-Corn-Law League*, I, 319–24, II, 51–3; Cobden, *Speeches*, I, 15, 28.

36  13  Morley, *Cobden*, 248–9.

37  14  Cobden to Sturge, July 25, 1842 (Add. MSS., 50, 131); Morley, *Cobden*, 248–9; Lucy Brown, 'The Chartists and the Anti-Corn Law League' in Briggs (ed.), *Chartist Studies*.

38  15  *Northern Star*, Feb. 3–March 24, Aug. 10, 1844; *The League*, Aug. 10, 1844; Prentice, *Anti-Corn-Law League*, II, 228–35; R. G. Gammage, *History of the Chartist Movement* (2nd ed., 1894), 253–5.

39  16  Bright to Cobden, May 10, 1841 (Add. MSS., 43, 383); Cobden, *Speeches*, I, 201–2; Morley, *Cobden*, 134–5.

39  17  Cobden to Sturge, June 10, July 16, 1846 (Add. MSS., 50, 131);

Accounts of the Richard Cobden Tribute Fund (W.S.R.O., Add. MSS., 5,547); H. Ashworth, *Recollections of Richard Cobden* (2nd ed., 1877), 221–4; Morley, *Cobden*, 158–60, 411–14.

39 18  Cobden, *Speeches*, I, 440–1; Morley, *Cobden*, 466–70.

40 19  Morley, *Cobden*, 684–8, 749–50; Watkin, *Cobden*, 190; Cobden, *American Diaries*, 41–58; Fielden, Cobden and America, 173–84.

41 20  Cobden to his wife, Jan. 7, 1842, Jan. 11, 1843, Jan. 26, May 2, 1846 (Add. MSS., 50, 748); Bright to his wife, April 10, 1851 (Bright MSS., University College, London).

41 21  Cobden to Parkes, April 13, May 30, 1856 (Add. MSS., 43, 664); Cobden to F. Cobden [June 10, 1856], (ibid., 50, 751); Cobden to Sturge, June 12, 1856 (ibid., 43, 661); Cobden to Sturge, Aug. 31, 1857 (ibid., 43, 722); Morley, *Cobden*, 160–1, ch. XXV; Nevill, *Reminiscences*, 186–7; Fielden, Cobden and America, 182, 217 n., 240.

41 22  Morley, *Cobden*, 467–70; Nevill, *Reminiscences*, 185, 188.

### 4 The Progress of the Anti-Corn Law League

42  1  Prentice, *Anti-Corn-Law League*, I, ch. VII.

42  2  A. D. Gayer et al., *The Growth and Fluctuation of the British Economy, 1790–1850* (1953), I, 276.

44  3  Parkes to Cobden, Jan. 31, 1839 (Wilson Papers, Manchester Reference Library); Cobden to Smith, Feb. 3, 1839 (Smith Papers); Prentice, *Anti-Corn-Law* League, I, ch. VIII; McCord, *Anti-Corn Law League*, ch. 1.

44  4  Prentice, *Anti-Corn-Law League*, I, 124–5; McCord, *Anti-Corn Law League*, 53–4.

45  5  Cobden to Wilson, undated (Wilson Papers); Cobden to W. Lyons, June 14, 1840 (ibid.); Prentice, *Anti-Corn-Law League*, I, 141–2, II, ch. I; McCord, *Anti-Corn Law League*, ch. II.

45  6  Cobden to Smith, June 1, 1840 (Smith Papers).

46  7  Prentice, *Anti-Corn-Law League*, I, 175–83; McCord, *Anti-Corn Law League*, 83–90; Read, *Press and People*, 148–50.

46  8  Cobden to Place, Oct. 5, 1840 (Add. MSS., 35, 151, f. 284); Prentice, *Anti-Corn-Law League*, I, 196, 226–7; Cobden, *Speeches*, II, 76; Watkin, *Cobden*, 200–2; Redford, *Manchester*, II, 29.

47  9  Cobden to Wilson, June 14, 1840 (Wilson Papers); Cobden, *Speeches*, I, 1–14; Morley, *Cobden*, 174–8, 242–3.

48  10  Cobden to Wilson, Oct. 6, 9, 12, 1841 (Wilson Papers); Cobden to Baines, Oct. 12, 1841 (Baines Collection, Leeds Reference Library).

49  11  Cobden to Wilson, Feb. 27, March 17, 1842 (Wilson Papers); Cobden to Bright, March 4, 12, May 10, June 21, 1842 (Add. MSS., 43, 649); Bright to Cobden, March 9, 16, May 9, June 24, 1842 (ibid., 43, 283); Morley, *Cobden*, 220–9, 240–1; Trevelyan, *Bright*, 73–9; McCord, *Anti-Corn Law League*, 121–5; Chambers and Mingay, *Agricultural Revolution*, 150.

page

49  12  T. E. Ashworth, *An Account of the Todmorden Poor Law Riots and the Plug Plot* (1901), 19; *Manchester Guardian*, Jan. 21, 1843; Gayer, *Growth and Fluctuation of the British Economy*, 276–303; R. C. O. Matthews, *A Study in Trade-Cycle History* (1954), 137–48; Chambers, *Workshop of the World*, 159–60.

51  13  Bright to Wilson, Aug. 12, 14, 1842 (Wilson Papers); Cobden to F. Cobden, Aug. 15, 16, 1842 (Add. MSS., 50, 750); Prentice, *Anti-Corn-Law League*, I, ch. XXIV; J. B. Mackie, *Life and Work of Duncan McLaren* (1888), I, 252–3; Trevelyan, *Bright*, 79–83; G. Kitson Clark, 'Hunger and Politics in 1842', *Journal of Modern History*, XXV (1953); A. G. Rose, 'The Plug Riots of 1842 in Lancashire and Cheshire', *Trans. Lancs. and Ches. Antiq. Soc.*, LXVII (1957); McCord, *Anti-Corn Law League*, 125–31; F. C. Mather, *Public Order in the Age of the Chartists* (1959), 22.

55  14  Cobden to Smith, Dec. 5, 1842 (Smith Papers); *The Times*, Nov. 18, 1843; Kohl, *Ireland, Scotland, and England*, pt. 3, 143–4; Prentice, *Anti-Corn-Law League*, II, chs. I–III, 118–20; H. Jephson, *The Platform* (1892), II, 316–17; McCord, *Anti-Corn Law League*, chs. VI, VII.

56  15  Cobden to Wilson, April 2, 1844 (Wilson Papers); Prentice, *Anti-Corn-Law League*, II, ch. VI; Watkin, *Cobden*, 67–97; Smiles, *Autobiography*, 111–13; McCord, *Anti-Corn Law League*, 96–103; Briggs, *Chartist Studies*, 342–71.

56  16  Cobden to Smith, March 18, 1846 (Smith Papers); Cobden to Hargreaves, Nov. 16, 1861 (Add. MSS., 43, 655); Prentice, *Anti-Corn-Law League*, II, 252–5, 261; Cobden, *Speeches*, I, 209–12, 237–44, 255–8, 316–19, 333–4, 375–6; Morley, *Cobden*, 304–7; H. D. Jordan, 'The Political Methods of the Anti-Corn Law League', *Political Science Quarterly*, XLII (1927), 71–5; F. M. L. Thompson, 'Whigs and Liberals in the West Riding, 1830–1860', *English Historical Review*, LXXIV (1959), 226–8.

57  17  *Manchester Guardian*, Oct. 5, 16, 1844, Aug. 9, Dec., 17, 1845; *Preston Chronicle*, Nov. 29, Dec. 6, 13, 1845; Cobden, *Speeches*, I, 198–200; Morley, *Cobden*, 342; Briggs, *Chartist Studies*, 369–70.

59  18  *Speeches of the Late Right Honourable Sir Robert Peel* (1853), IV, 582–604; D. C. Moore, 'The Corn Laws and High Farming', *Economic History Review*, second series, XVIII (1965); S. Fairlie, 'The Nineteenth-Century Corn Law Reconsidered', ibid.

60  19  *Parliamentary Debates*, third series, LXXVIII (1845), 785–810; Cobden, *Speeches*, I, 52, 69–88, 99–104, 114–15, 133–71, 191–6, 220–3, 230-2, 259–83; Morley, *Cobden*, 293–4, 317–22.

61  20  Cobden to his wife, Jan. 23, 28, 1846 (Add. MSS., 50, 748); Cobden to Wilson, Jan. 29, March 4, 1846 (Wilson Papers); Cobden to Sturge, Feb. 2, 1846 (Add. MSS., 43, 656); Prentice to Wilson, Feb. 12, 1846 (Wilson Papers); Morley, *Cobden*, 374–6; McCord, *Anti-Corn Law League*, 200–3.

# References

62 21 Morley, *Cobden*, 388–9.

62 22 *Parliamentary Debates*, second series, IV (1821), 1003–4; third series LVIII (1841), 817.

62 23 Cobden to Parkes, May 26, 1856 (Add. MSS., 43, 664).

64 24 Cobden to Villiers, Sept. 13, 1841 (Add. MSS., 43, 662); Cobden to Smith, May 27, 1845 (Smith Papers); Harriet Martineau to Peel, Feb. 22, 24, 1846, and Peel to Harriet Martineau, Feb. 23, 1846 (Add. MSS., 40, 585); Harriet Martineau, *Autobiography* (1877), II, 259–64; Morley, *Cobden*, 256–61, 352–3, 398.

64 25 Prentice, *Anti-Corn-Law League*, II, 159–60; Cobden, *Speeches*, I, 77–9; McCord, *Anti-Corn Law League*, 30–1, 194–6.

64 26 *Lord Melbourne's Papers* (ed. L. C. Sanders, 1890), 389; G. Kitson Clark, 'The Repeal of the Corn Laws and the Politics of the Forties', *Economic History Review*, second series, IV (1951); McCord, *Anti-Corn Law League*, 203–4; Betty Kemp, 'Reflections on the Repeal of the Corn Laws', *Victorian Studies*, V (1961–2), 200–4.

65 27 Cobden, *Speeches*, I, 391–2; Morley, *Cobden*, 387.

66 28 Cobden to Wilson, Aug. 11, 1852 (Wilson Papers); Cobden to Ashworth, Oct. 16, 1852 (Add. MSS., 43, 653); A. H. Imlah, *Economic Elements in the Pax Britannica* (1958), esp. chs. V, VI; J. R. T. Hughes, *Fluctuations in Trade, Industry and Finance, A Study of British Economic Development, 1850–1860* (1960).

68 29 Cobden to Ashworth, Oct. 16, 1852 (Add. MSS., 43, 653); Peel, *Speeches*, IV, esp. 604, 696, 717; H. Dunckley, *The Charter of the Nations* (1894), 27–8; Cobden, *Speeches*, I, 295–7; G. Wallas, *The Life of Francis Place* (4th ed., 1951), 396; Kemp, 'Reflections on the Repeal of the Corn Laws'; Chambers & Mingay, *Agricultural Revolution*, 158–9.

68 30 Cobden to Wilson, March 4, 1846; Morley, *Cobden*, 545.

CHAPTER II: BRIGHT

## 1 Background

70 1 On Rochdale see E. Baines, *History, Directory and Gazeteer of the County Palatine of Lancaster* (1825), II, 523–35. On Bright's family and early days see Robertson, *Bright*, vol. I; *Fortunes Made in Business* (1884), by various writers, II, 181–230; Bright's 'Memoir' in his *Diaries*; and J. Travis Mills, *John Bright and the Quakers* (1935).

70 2 Cobden to Jacob Bright, Oct., 1837 (Add. MSS., 43, 667, ff. 4–5).

71 3 R. W. Dale, 'Mr. Bright', *Contemporary Review*, LV (1889), 639–41; Trevelyan, *Bright*, 103–4, 107, 173, 424; *Diary of Lady Frederick Cavendish* (1927), II, 229; E. Halévy, *Victorian Years* (1951), 382–3.

72 4 Cobden to Combe, Nov. 4, 1856 (Add. MSS., 43, 661); Bright to his wife, May 2, 1860, May 11, 1867 (Bright MSS.); Bright to Cobden, July 3, 1860 (Add. MSS., 43, 384); Dale, 'Bright', 650–1; Bright,

*Diaries*, 219–20, 227; J. Vincent, *The Formation of the Liberal Party, 1857–1868* (1966), 164.

73  5   Trevelyan, *Bright*, 23–4; Mills, *Bright*, II, 6; Halévy, *Victorian Years*, 383.

73  6   Bright to Sturge, May 5, 1858 (Add. MSS., 43, 723); Morley, *Cobden*, 523–5; Trevelyan, *Bright*, 25; Mills, *Bright*, II, 24–7, 71–80.

74  7   Robertson, *Bright*, I, 70–4; Trevelyan, *Bright*, 24.

74  8   Bright, *Diaries*, 13–14, ch. II.

75  9   *Manchester Guardian*, April 12, 19, 1837.

77  10  Cobden to Bright, Dec. 14, 1837 (Add. MSS., 43, 649); *Manchester Times*, Dec. 23, 1837; Bright, *Public Addresses*, 355–66; Morley, *Cobden*, 189–90; Robertson, *Bright*, III, 181; C. S. Miall, *Henry Richard* (1889), 129–30; Trevelyan, *Bright*, 29–30.

80  11  Cobden to Bright, May 5, June 2, 1841 (Add. MSS., 43, 649); Bright to Cobden, June 5, Sept. 10, 12, Oct. 9, 23, 1841 (ibid., 43, 383); Prentice, *Anti-Corn-Law League*, I, 112–13; Bright, *Public Addresses*, 355–66; Morley, *Cobden*, 190–1; Robertson, *Bright*, VI, 352–3; Trevelyan, *Bright*, 42–4; Bright, *Diaries*, 52, 54–5; McCord, *Anti-Corn Law League*, 112–13.

81  12  Cobden to Bright, Feb. 6, 1839 (Add. MSS., 43, 649).

82  13  J. Bright, *Speeches on Questions of Public Policy* (1869), 538–46; Robertson, *Bright*, ch. IX; Trevelyan, *Bright*, 35–41, 193; Mills, *Bright*, II, 82–94.

82  14  Trevelyan, *Bright*, 43.

83  15  Morley, *Cobden*, 647; Trevelyan, *Bright*, 334–6.

83  16  Trevelyan, *Bright*, 423.

84  17  Bright to his wife, Feb. 18, 1854 (Bright MSS.); Cobden to Bright, March 1, 17, 1856 (Add. MSS., 43, 650); Cobden to Parkes, Nov. 11, 1856 (ibid., 43, 664); Morley, *Cobden*, 648–9; Trevelyan, *Bright*, 254–7.

## 2 Cobden's Lieutenant

86  1   Cobden to Combe, Dec. 9, 1854 (Add. MSS., 43, 661); Cobden to Bright, April 8, Dec. 3, 1855 (ibid., 43, 650), Feb. 19, 1861 (ibid., 43, 651); Cobden to Wilson, Oct. 30, 1857 (Wilson Papers); Cobden to Paulton, Dec. 27, 1861 (Add. MSS., 43, 662); Bright to Smith, Oct. 28, 1865 (Smith Papers); *Memories of Old Friends, being Extracts from the Journals and Letters of Caroline Fox* (3rd ed., 1882), II, 280; Robertson, *Bright*, I, 135; E. Hodder, *Life and Work of the Seventh Earl of Shaftesbury* (1887), III, 187; Dale, 'Bright', 637–8; G. W. Smalley, *London Letters* (1890), I, 133–5; G. J. Holyoake, *Sixty Years of an Agitator's Life* (1892), II, 283–4; Morley, *Gladstone*, I, 257; Lady St. Helier, *Memories of Fifty Years* (1909), 246; Hobson, *Cobden*, 109, 115; Cavendish, *Diary*, II, 9, 229; Bright, *Diaries*, 154, 184, 223; *The Amberley Papers* (ed. B. and Pamela Russell, 1937), I, 471; D. Southgate, *The Most English Minister* (1966), xxv–xxvi.

91  2  Bright's Notes for Speeches (Add. MSS., 43, 392, esp. ff. 146–9; Bright to his wife, July 21, 1855 (Bright MSS.); Bright, *Speeches*, ix–x, 175, and *passim*; *Edinburgh Review*, CXXIX (1869), 274–5; G. Barnett Smith, *Life and Speeches of the Right Hon. John Bright* (1881), II, 193–4, 606; Robertson, *Bright*, I, 183–4, IV, 369, 379, VI, ch. LI; Dale, 'Bright', 652–7; Holyoake, *Sixty Years*, ch. CVIII; C. A. Vince, *John Bright* (1898), ch. IX; Trevelyan, *Bright*, 97–9, 276–8, 383–6; G. W. E. Russell, *Fifteen Chapters of Autobiography* (n.d.), 290–2; Sir A. Chamberlain, *Down the Years* (1935), 259–61; *Amberley Papers*, II, 34.

92  3  Cobden to Sturge, Jan. 5, 1853 (Add. MSS., 50, 131); Bright, *Speeches*, 536–7; Morley, *Cobden*, 199–200, 814–15; Mills, *Bright*, ch. XIV; McCord, *Anti-Corn Law League*, 30–1; Vincent, *Liberal Party*, xxix, 163.

92  4  Bright to Cobden, Oct. 7, 1842, Sept. 20, 1845 (Add. MSS., 43, 383), July 25, Nov. 10, 1860 (ibid., 43, 384); Cobden to Bright, Feb. 19, 1861 (ibid., 43, 651); Morley, *Cobden*, 334–6.

93  5  Cobden to Bright, May 12, 1842 (Add. MSS., 43, 383); Trevelyan, *Bright*, 108.

93  6  *Public Letters of the Right Hon. John Bright* (1885), 331–40; Trevelyan, *Bright*, 80–3.

94  7  Prentice, *Anti-Corn-Law League*, II, 108–10; Trevelyan, *Bright*, 110–15; D. Large, 'The Election of John Bright as Member for Durham City in 1843', *Durham University Journal*, Dec. 1954; McCord, *Anti-Corn Law League*, 158–9.

94  8  Cobden to his wife, Aug. 15, 1843 (Add. MSS., 50, 748); *Parliamentary Debates*, third series, LXXI (1843), 338–42, 661–8; Bright, *Speeches*, 437–44; Cobden, *Speeches*, I, 286; Morley, *Cobden*, 316; Robertson, *Bright*, II, 226–33, 254–7; Trevelyan, *Bright*, 115–18; C. Kirby, 'The Attack on the English Game Laws in the Forties', *Journal of Modern History*, IV (1932); Mills, *Bright*, II, 156–60.

95  9  Bright, *Speeches*, 415; Morley, *Cobden*, 342; Robertson, *Bright*, II, 280; Trevelyan, *Bright*, 136–7, 139.

96  10  Bright to Wilson, June 26, 1846 (Wilson Papers); Cobden to Coppock, July 17, 1846 (Cobden Papers, no. 41); *The League*, July 4, 1846; G. B. Hertz, *The Manchester Politician, 1750–1912* (1912), 51–3.

97  11  Robertson, *Bright*, II, 349–50.

CHAPTER III: COBDEN AND BRIGHT

1 The Partnership after 1846

99  1  Cobden to Parkes, Nov. 11, 1856 (Add. MSS., 43, 664); Morley, *Cobden*, 648–9.

102  2  Cobden to Coppock, July 17, Aug. 4, 1846 (Cobden Papers, no. 41);

Bright to Cobden, July 29, Nov. 29, 1846 (Add. MSS., 43, 383); Cobden to Bright, July 30, 1846, Jan. 18, 1847 (ibid., 43, 649); Bright to Wilson, July 31, Aug. 2, 18, Nov. 26, 1846, Jan. 24, 1847 (Wilson Papers); Cobden to Wilson, Aug. 3, Dec. 29, 1846 (ibid.); Cobden to Potter, Sept. 17, 1846 (W.S.R.O., Add. MSS., 2, 760); *Manchester Guardian*, Dec. 2, 16, 1846; J. A. Williams, Manchester and the Manchester School (M.A. thesis, Leeds Univ., 1966), ch. VIII.

102   3   Morley, *Cobden*, 465–6; Robertson, *Bright*, II, 360–6; Trevelyan, *Bright*, 180; Thompson, 'Whigs and Liberals in the West Riding', 228–31.

102   4   Bright to Cobden, Aug. 29, 1851 (Add. MSS., 43, 383); Cobden to Sturge, Aug. 26, 1852 (ibid., 43, 656).

## 2 The Manchester School

104   1   Cobden to Bright, Feb. 7, 16, 1864 (Add. MSS., 43, 652); Robertson, *Bright*, III, 10; A. D. Elliot, *Viscount Goschen* (1911), I, 75–6; T. S. Ashton, 'The Origin of "The Manchester School"', *Manchester School of Economic and Social Studies*, II (1931); W. D. Grampp, *The Manchester School of Economics* (1960), 4, and *passim*; Vincent, *Liberal Party*, xxxiv.

105   2   Cobden to Smith, Dec. 28, 1852 (Smith Papers); Cobden to Bright, Jan. 17, 1853, Jan. 5, 1855 (Add. MSS., 43, 650); Cobden to Parkes, Feb. 11, 1860 (ibid., 43, 664); Cobden, *Speeches*, II, 540–2; Morley, *Cobden*, 343–5, 403–4, ch. XXVIII, 814; *Letters of Queen Victoria* (1908), II, 130–2; F. W. Hirst, *Early Life and Letters of John Morley* (1927), II, 92; *Amberley Papers*, I, 522.

106   3   Bright to his wife, Dec. 20, 1852, July 22, 1855, May 1, 1858 (Bright MSS.); Cobden to Sturge, Jan. 5, 1853 (Add. MSS., 50, 131); Bright to Wilson, June 15, 1859 (Wilson Papers); Bright, *Public Addresses*, 157–60; Morley, *Cobden*, 695–6, 813–14; Smalley, *London Letters*, I, 135–6; McCarthy, *Reminiscences*, I, 249; C. S. Parker, *Life and Letters of Sir James Graham* (1907), II, 92; *Letters of Queen Victoria*, III, 349–50; Trevelyan, *Bright*, 282–3, 395–7, 405–13; Bright, *Diaries*, 191, 239–43; Chamberlain, *Down the Years*, 308.

109   4   Cobden to Peel, June 23, 1846, and Peel to Cobden, June 24, 1846 (Add. MSS., 40, 594, ff. 123–40); Cobden to Ashworth, July 10, 1849 (ibid., 43, 653); Cobden to Parkes, June 10, 1857 (ibid., 43, 664); Cobden, *Speeches*, I, 239; Morley, *Cobden*, ch. XVII; A. Briggs, 'Peel', in *British Prime Ministers* (ed. Duff Cooper, 1953); Briggs, *Chartist Studies*, 297–8.

## 3 International Bearings

116   1   Cobden to Bright, Oct. 18, 1846 (Add. MSS., 43, 649), Sept. 17, 1855 (ibid., 43,650); Cobden to Wilson, March 31, June 21, 1847, Sept. 23, 1856 (Wilson Papers); Cobden to Ashworth, May 8, 1848, Oct. 16, 1852 (Add. MSS., 43, 653); Cobden to Sturge, Sept. 12, 16, 1848,

*page*

June 15, 1849 (ibid., 43, 656); Cobden to Combe, June 19, 1849 (ibid., 43, 660); Bright, *Speeches*, 470, and *passim*; Cobden, *Speeches*, I, 469–70, II, 6, 223, 228, 353, and *passim*; Gibbon, *Combe*, II, 217; Morley, *Cobden*, ch. XVIII, 408–9, 474, 622–3, 627; Bright, *Public Letters*, 238–9; Hobson, *Cobden*, *passim*; W. H. Dawson, *Richard Cobden and Foreign Policy* (1926), 144–5, 148–50, 302–3, and *passim*.

### 4 Peace and War

117  1  Cobden to Baines, March 1, 1848 (Baines Collection); Cobden to Tait, Jan. 29, 1853 (Add. MSS., 43, 665); Cobden to Bright, Nov. 9, 1855 (ibid., 43, 650); Gibbon, *Combe*, II, 11; Morley, *Cobden*, 633; Robertson, *Bright*, III, 190; Bright, *Public Letters*, 238–9; Mackie, *McLaren*, II, 10–11; *Stevenson's Book of Quotations* (9th ed., 1958), 1471, 1555.

120  2  Cobden to Wilson, Jan. 17, 1848, Sept. 23, Nov. 17, 1856 (Wilson Papers); Cobden, *Speeches*, esp. vol. II; Bright, *Speeches*, 224–76, 459–65; Morley, *Cobden*, 230, 508–13, 538–40, 544–7, 556, 597–609; Bright, *Public Letters*, 1–5; Miall, *Richard*, chs. III–VIII; Trevelyan, *Bright*, 187–92; Hobson, *Cobden*, 180; Dawson, *Cobden*, ch. VI; Bright, *Diaries*, 110–13; G. B. Henderson, *Crimean War Diplomacy* (1947), ch. VI.

121  3  Cobden, *Speeches*, II, 179–210; Morley, *Cobden*, 529–34, 563–71; Trevelyan, *Bright*, 195.

124  4  Cobden to Baines, Dec. 11, 1854 (Baines Collection); Cobden to Smith, Oct. 3, 1855, Jan. 4, 1856 (Smith Papers); *Leeds Mercury*, Jan. 20, 1855; Cobden, *Speeches*, II, 3–55, 314; Morley, *Cobden*, ch. XXIV; Hobson, *Cobden*, chs. VI, VII; Dawson, *Cobden*, ch. X. On the Crimean War see R. W. Seton-Watson, *Britain in Europe, 1789–1914* (1945), chs. VIII, IX; K. Martin, *The Triumph of Lord Palmerston* (2nd ed., 1963); A. J. P. Taylor, *The Trouble Makers* (1964), ch. II.

132  5  Bright to his wife, Feb. 28, April 19, June 8, July 21, 22, 1855 (Bright MSS.); *Punch*, XXVII (1854), 241; *Manchester Guardian*, April 5, 1854; Bright, *Speeches*, 224–76, 459–65; Robertson, *Bright*, III, 25–72; Bright, *Public Letters*, 22–42; Trevelyan, *Bright*, ch. X; Watkin, *Journal*, 286–91, 303–20; Bright, *Diaries*, 179, 189–91; A. J. P. Taylor, *Englishmen and Others* (1956), ch. 8; Taylor, *Trouble Makers*, ch. II.

132  6  Bright to Cobden, Jan. 31, 1855 (Add. MSS., 43, 384); Robertson, *Bright*, III, 68; Trevelyan, *Bright*, 216.

134  7  Bright to Sturge, Nov. 11, Dec. 28, 1854 (Add. MSS., 43,723); Bright to his wife, Feb. 28, April 19, 1855 (Bright MSS.); Bright to Wilson, June 13, 1855 (Wilson Papers); *The Times*, Nov. 28, 1854; Morley, *Cobden*, 626–7; Trevelyan, *Bright*, 215–16, 249; Mills, *Bright*, II, 349; Williams, Manchester and the Manchester School, ch. XII.

139  8  Bright to Cobden, April 16, 1857 (Add. MSS., 43, 384); Cobden to Wilson, May 30, 1857 (Wilson Papers); Bright to his wife, April 23, 1858 (Bright MSS.); *Manchester Guardian*, *Manchester Examiner*,

March 1857; Cobden, *Speeches*, II, 57–82, 121–56; Morley, *Cobden*, ch. XXVI, 689; Robertson, *Bright*, chs. XXXIV, XXXV, III, 181–3; Vince, *Bright*, 145–6; Mrs. Salis Schwabe, *Reminiscences of Richard Cobden* (1895), 291–2; Trevelyan, *Bright*, ch. XII; Hobson, *Cobden*, ch. VIII; *Later Correspondence of Lord John Russell* (1925), II, 221; Bright, *Diaries*, 223–6; Thompson, 'Whigs and Liberals in the West Riding', 238–9; Williams, 'Manchester and the Manchester School', ch. XIII.

146  9  Bright to Cobden, Oct. 6, 1859, July 25, 1860 (Add. MSS., 43, 384); Cobden to Bright, Oct. 11, 1859, Jan. 30, April 13, 1860, Feb. 6, 1861 (ibid., 43, 651); Cobden to Gladstone, Oct. 29, 1859, Nov. 12, 1860 (ibid., 44, 135); Cobden to Palmerston, July 12, 1860 (ibid., 43, 670, ff. 49–50); Cobden to Baines, July 13, 1860 (ibid., 43, 664); Bright, *Speeches*, II, 231–55; Ashworth, *Cobden*, 480–8; Cobden, *Speeches*, II, 231–55; Ashworth, *Cobden*, 244–56; Morley, *Cobden*, chs. XXIX–XXXII; Robertson, *Bright*, ch. XXXVII; W. E. Gladstone, 'The History of 1852–60, and Greville's Letters and Journals', *English Historical Review*, II (1887) 296–302; S. Buxton, *Finance and Politics* (1888), ch. XI; Morley, *Gladstone*, I, 652–87; Trevelyan, *Bright*, 284–95; Hobson, *Cobden*, ch. X, 348; A. L. Dunham, *The Anglo-French Treaty of Commerce of 1860* (1930); Bright, *Diaries*, 244–5; W. E. Williams, *The Rise of Gladstone to the Leadership of the Liberal Party* (1934), chs. III–V; Grampp, *Manchester School*, 119–20.

149  10  Cobden to Gladstone, Jan. 13, 1860 (Add. MSS., 44, 135); Cobden to Ashworth, July 1, 1864 (ibid., 43, 654); E. Ashley, *Life of Henry John Temple, Viscount Palmerston, 1846–1865* (1876), II, 221; Morley, *Cobden*, 628, 917; Bright, *Public Addresses*, 298; A. Trollope, *Lord Palmerston* (1882), 201; Robertson, *Bright*, V, 191–2; Bright, *Public Letters*, 189–96; Taylor, *Englishmen and Others*, 64; Taylor, *Trouble Makers*, 61–2; D. Beales, *England and Italy, 1859–60* (1961); R. T. Shannon, *Gladstone and the Bulgarian Agitation, 1876* (1963), 6, 79, 118, 124–5, 139–40, 168, 229–30, 268; Vincent, *Liberal Party*, 33–5.

## 5 Retrenchment and Reform

151  1  Cobden to Parkes, Dec. 7, 1885 (Add. MSS., 43, 664); Cobden to Gladstone, Feb. 25, June 11, 1860 (ibid., 44, 135); Jan. 15, 1862 (ibid., 44, 136); Cobden to Bright, June 30, July 12, 25, Aug. 25, 1860, Jan. 10, Oct. 14, 1861 (ibid., 43, 651), Oct. 7, 1862 (ibid., 43, 652); Cobden *Speeches*, II, 258–9, 367–72; Morley, *Cobden*, 683–4, 772; Morley, *Gladstone*, I, 680, II, 422, 815–16; Trevelyan, *Bright*, 265, 284; Hobson, *Cobden*, 201–2; P. Guedalla (ed.), *Gladstone and Palmerston* (1928), 212–13; Williams, *Gladstone*, ch. V; Vincent, *Liberal Party*, 202–5.

152  2  Cobden to Bright, Nov. 16, 23, Dec. 22, 23, 27, 1848, Jan. 3, 1849 (Add. MSS., 43, 649); Cobden to Ashworth, Dec. 23, 1848 (ibid., 43, 653); Cobden to ?, Dec. 10, 1862 (ibid., 43, 671, ff. 44–7); Cobden to Wilson, Sept. 23, 1856 (Wilson Papers); *Tracts of the Liverpool*

*Financial Reform Association* (1851); Cobden, *Speeches*, I, 455–606; Morley, *Cobden*, 494–507, 812; Hobson, *Cobden*, 105; Frances E. Gillespie, *Labor and Politics in England 1850–1867* (1927), ch. III; W. N. C. Calkins, 'A Victorian Free Trade Lobby', *Economic History Review*, second series, XIII (1960–1).

153   3   *Punch*, Feb. 4, 1865; Cobden, *Speeches*, II, 556–7; Morley, *Cobden*, 881.

157   4   Cobden to Sturge, July 16, 1846 (Add. MSS., 50, 131), March 23, 1852 (ibid., 43, 656), April 23, 1857 (ibid., 43, 722); Cobden to Baines, April 13, 1848 (Baines Collection); Cobden to Wilson, May 8, 1848 (Wilson Papers); Cobden to Bright, Nov. 7, 1851, Sept. 9, 1852 (Add. MSS., 43, 649), Jan. 8, 1853 (ibid., 43, 650); Cobden to Combe, Oct. 15, 1852 (ibid., 43, 661); Cobden to Hargreaves, June 1, 1860, Feb. 11, 1865 (ibid., 43, 655); Bright to Wilson, April 18, 1848, Feb. 22, Sept. 18, 1849, Sept. 26, 1851 (Wilson Papers); Bright to Cobden, Oct. 24, 1851, Jan. 14, 1853 (Add. MSS., 43, 383); *Parliamentary Debates*, third series, LXII (1842), 967–70; Cobden, *Speeches*, II, 467–563; Bright, *Public Addresses*, 29; Morley, *Cobden*, 127, 500–1, 557–63, 565–6, 811–12; Trevelyan, *Bright*, ch. VIII, 209–12; Gillespie, *Labor and Politics*, 144; Bright, *Diaries*, 133.

158   5   Cobden, *Speeches*, II, 485-501; Morley, *Cobden*, 501, 516–17, 520–2, 566; Trevelyan, *Bright*, 185–6; Gillespie, *Labor and Politics*, 95 n. 1; S. Maccoby, *English Radicalism, 1832–1852* (1935), 316–17; Sir H. Bellman, *Bricks and Mortals* (1949), ch. II, 206–18; S. J. Price, *Building Societies, Their Origin and History* (2nd ed., 1959), 50–3, 126–7, 131; W. L. Burn, *The Age of Equipoise* (1964), 77–8; E. J. Cleary, *The Building Society Movement* (1965), 49–54.

161   6   Cobden to Hargreaves, April 30, 1860, Feb. 21, 1864, Jan. 5, 1865 (Add. MSS., 43, 655); Cobden to Bright, March 30, 1863, Feb. 4, March 1, 1865 (ibid., 43, 652); Cobden to Kell, March 8, 1865 (ibid., 43, 671, ff. 212–14); Note on Cobden and Co-Operation (ibid., 43, 670, ff. 149–51); Morley, *Cobden*, 565–6, 829–30, 881–2, 911, 945–6; G. Howell, *Labour Legislation, Labour Movements, and Labour Leaders* (1905), I, 144–5; Hobson, *Cobden*, 166; G. J. Holyoake, *The History of the Rochdale Pioneers* (5th ed., 1922), 171; A. D. Bell, The Reform League from its Origins to the Reform Act of 1867 (D.Phil. thesis, Oxford Univ., 1961), 337 ff.; T. R. Tholfsen, 'The Transition to Democracy in Victorian England', *International Review of Social History*, VI (1961); Vincent, *Liberal Party*, 191.

162   7   Bright to Sturge, Nov. 26, 1851 (Add. MSS., 43, 723); Bright to Cobden, Nov. 14, 1858 (ibid., 43, 384); T. Frost, *Forty Years' Recollections* (1880), 272–4; Vincent, *Liberal Party*, 164, 186–7.

163   8   *Northern Tribune*, I (1854), 125–7.

166   9   Bright, *Speeches*, 277–328; Robertson, *Bright*, III, 135–80, IV, 234–5, 237–40; Bright, *Public Letters*, 49–56, 69–74; Trevelyan, *Bright*,

267–82; Gillespie, *Labor and Politics*, chs. VI, VII; Bright, *Diaries*, 234–8, 248; J. Saville (ed.), *Ernest Jones* (1952), 186–9; Vincent, *Liberal Party*, 60, 187–9.

176  10   Cobden to Bright, Feb. 4, March 1, 1865 (Add. MSS., 43, 652); Bright to Wilson, June 27, July 10, 1866 (Wilson Papers); Russell to Gladstone, April 20, 1867 (Add. MSS., 44, 293, f. 270); Bright to Gladstone, Jan. 17, 1875, July 13, 1882 (ibid., 44, 113); *The Times*, Feb. 21, 24, March 13, 17, 1865; *Parliamentary Debates*, third series, CLXXXVI (1867), 626–42, 1953–63; Bright, *Speeches*, 192–9, 329–414, 545; Bright, *Public Addresses*, 270–9; Robertson, *Bright*, chs. XLI, XLII; Bright, *Public Letters*, 72, 99–100, 106–14, 128–38, 163–5; Morley, *Gladstone*, bk. V, ch. XIV; Howell, *Labour Legislation*, I, 144–5; Trevelyan, *Bright*, chs. XVI, XVII; Gillespie, *Labor and Politics*, ch. IX; Bright, *Diaries*, ch. XII; A Briggs, *Victorian People* (1954), chs. VIII–X; Bell, Reform League, 337 ff.; F. B. Smith, ' "Democracy" in the Second Reform Debates', *Historical Studies, Australia and New Zealand*, no. 43 (1964); R. Harrison, *Before the Socialists* (1965), ch. III; Vincent, *Liberal Party*, esp. ch. 3; F. B. Smith, *The Making of the Second Reform Bill* (1966), esp. 13, 25–7, chs. 4, 5; Gertrude Himmelfarb, 'The Politics of Democracy: the English Reform Act of 1867', *Journal of British Studies*, VI (1966), esp. 123–7; *Karl Marx and Frederick Engels: Selected Correspondence* (n.d.), 172; M. Cowling, *1867: Disraeli, Gladstone and Revolution* (1967), esp. 35, ch. VII, 292–5.

177  11   Cobden, *Speeches*, II, 561; Bright, *Public Addresses*, 44–5, 256–60; Morley, *Cobden*, 925–6; Smith, *Bright*, 338; Bright, *Public Letters*, 179–81.

177  12   Trevelyan, *Bright*, 379–80; Millicent G. Fawcett, *What I Remember* (1925), 65; R. Fulford, *Votes for Women* (1957), 60, 63–6; Vincent, *Liberal Party*, 209–10.

## 6 Education

179  1   Cobden to Combe, Oct. 15, 1852 (Add. MSS., 43, 661); Cobden to Bright, Dec. 29, 1853 (ibid., 43, 650); Cobden to Robertson, Jan. 22, 1864 (ibid., 43, 665, ff. 338–40); *Manchester Times*, Dec. 17, 1836; *Postage Sel. Comm. Third Rep. Mins of Evid.*, P.P. 1837–8, xx, pt. II, 708, Q. 6, 712; Cobden, *Speeches*, II, 567–622; Morley, *Cobden*, 22–4, 128, 485–6; Watkin, *Cobden*, 114–39, 202; Schwabe, *Cobden*, 122–50, 162–76; Robbins, *Theory of Economic Policy*, 90–3; La Nauze, 'New Letters of Richard Cobden', 200–2.

181  2   Cobden to Baines, Dec. 28, 1848 (Add. MSS., 43, 664); Cobden to Combe, Sept. 4, 1852 (ibid., 43, 661); Cobden, *Speeches*, II, 590–1, 603, 605–6; Smiles, *Autobiography*, 170–1, 174; Hobson, *Cobden*, 164–5; S. E. Maltby, *Manchester and the Movement for National Elementary Education* (1918); Cobden, *Diaries*, esp. 26–8, 69, 71; Thistlethwaite, *America and the Atlantic Community*, 147–50; Williams,

Manchester and the Manchester School, ch. XI; Fielden, *Cobden and America*, 221–68.

181  3   Bright to Baines, Feb. 1, 1848 (Baines Collection); Bright, *Speeches*, 529–37; Bright, *Diaries*, 155–6; Cobden, *Diaries*, 28; Vincent, *Liberal Party*, 207–8.

182  4   Cobden to Coppock, April 13, 1845 (Cobden Papers, no. 41); *Parliamentary Debates*, third series, LXXIX (1845), 818–23, 963–8; Bright, *Speeches*, 149–52; Morley, *Cobden*, 326–7; Trevelyan, *Bright*, 160–2; McCord, *Anti-Corn Law League*, 191–2.

183  5   Bright, *Public Addresses*, 201–4, 276–7, 340, 344–6; T. Wemyss Reid, *Life of the Right Honourable William Edward Forster* (1889), 307–16; Trevelyan, *Bright*, 405–9; P. Fraser, *Joseph Chamberlain* (1966), 11–12, 18–19.

## 7 Newspapers

185  1   Cobden to Bright, Nov. 22, Dec. 19, 1853 (Add. MSS., 43, 650); *Newspaper Stamps Sel. Comm. Rep. Mins of Evid.*, P.P. 1851, xvii, 558; Cobden, *Political Writings*, I, 124–5; Cobden, *Speeches*, II, 77; Bright, *Public Addresses*, 26–7, 337–9; Morley, *Cobden*, 565, 884–5; H. R. Fox Bourne, *English Newspapers* (1887), ch. XX; Watkin, *Cobden*, 140–62; C. D. Collet, *History of the Taxes on Knowledge* (1899), Trevelyan, *Bright*, 212–14, 337–8; Bright, *Diaries*, 171–2, 196; *History of The Times*, II (1939), ch. X; A. P. Wadsworth, *Newspaper Circulations, 1800–1954* (Manchester Statistical Society, 1955), 3, 8–10; F. Williams, *Dangerous Estate* (1957), ch. VI; R. D. Altick, *The English Common Reader* (1963), 348–54; Fielden, *Cobden and America*, 253–9.

186  2   Cobden to Bright, Sept. 9, 1852 (Add. MSS., 43, 649), Jan. 12, 1855, Nov. 22, 1855, Oct. 20, 1856 (ibid., 43, 650); Cobden to Sturge, Oct. 29, 1856 (ibid., 43, 722); Bright to Cobden, Dec. 14, 1855, Nov. 24, 1857 (ibid., 43, 384); *Manchester Examiner*, Jan. 1, 1862; J. Grant, *The Newspaper Press* (1871), I, 376–9; Morley, *Cobden*, 637; Bourne, *English Newspapers*, chs. XXI, XXII; McCarthy, *Reminiscences*, chs. VI, IX; Hobson, *Cobden*, 129–31, 141–2, 230–2; *History of the Times*, II, ch. XIV; Williams, *Dangerous Estate*, ch. VII; Altick, *English Common Reader*, 354–7; Vincent, *Liberal Party*, 61–2, 178; Fielden, *Cobden and America*, 260–7.

188  3   Cobden to Bright, Dec. 10, 16, 25, 1863, Jan. 7, 1864 (Add. MSS., 43, 652); *Cobden-Delane Controversy, Opinions of the Liberal Press* (1864); *The Times*, April 4, 1865; Bright, *Speeches*, 445–8; Morley, *Cobden*, ch. XXXV; Bourne, *English Newspapers*, II, 264–9; A. I. Dasent, *John Thadeus Delane* (1908), II, 81–93; *History of The Times*, II, 335–6.

## 8 The Land

191  1   Cobden to Combe, Oct. 4, 1848 (Add. MSS., 43, 680); Cobden to Kell, March 8, 1865 (ibid., 43, 671, ff. 212–14); Bright to Cobden,

# References

page

Sept. 25, 1851 (ibid., 43, 383); Bright, *Speeches*, 3,3, 380–2, 445–58; Cobden, *Speeches*, I, 382, II, 116–17, 367; Bright, *Public Addresses*, 125–8, 186, 274–5, 426–7; Morley, *Cobden*, 518, 561–2, 679–80, 920–1; Robertson, *Bright*, VI, 333–6; Bright, *Public Letters*, 160–1, 239–41, 328–9; Miall, *Richard*, 132–3; Anne Cobden-Sanderson, *Richard Cobden and the Land of the People* (1909); Trevelyan, *Bright*, 337, 438; Bright, *Diaries*, 371; Kirby, 'Game Laws', 35–7; T. W. Fletcher, 'The Great Depression of English Agriculture, 1873–1896', *Economic History Review*, second series, XIII (1961); Lord Ernle, *English Farming Past and Present* (6th ed., 1961), cxxxiv–vii; Burn, *Age of Equipoise*, ch. 6; F. M. L. Thompson, 'Land and Politics in England in the Nineteenth Century', *Trans. Royal Historical Soc.*, 5th series, 15 (1965); Chambers and Mingay, *Agricultural Revolution*, 160–8; Vincent, *Liberal Party*, 35, 175–7.

## 9 Ireland

200  1  Bright to his wife, Aug. 23, 1849 (Bright MSS.); Bright to Smith, Nov. 7, 1866 (Smith Papers); Bright to Gladstone, Oct. 4, 1881; Gladstone to Bright, Dec. 7, 22, 1880, Sept. 29, 1881 (Add. MSS., 44, 113); Bright to Northy, July 27, Dec. 27, 1886, June 22, 1887, (ibid., 44, 877); *Manchester Times*, Dec. 17, 1836; Cobden, *Political Writings*, I, 48–96; Bright, *Speeches*, 149–213; Bright, *Public Addresses*, 70–88, 171–7, 222–3, 508–26; Morley, *Cobden*, 11–12, 489–94, 513–15; Robertson, *Bright*, chs. XXIX, XLIII; Bright, *Public Letters*, 5–22, 94–6, 138–44, 144–50, 181–3; ibid. (2nd ed., 1895), 125–64; *The Times*, July 2, 1886, Oct. 24, 1887; *Mr. John Bright on Home Rule* (Home Rule Union Leaflet, no. 2, n.d.); R. B. O'Brien, *Life of Charles Stewart Parnell* (1898), II, 145–52; Morley, *Gladstone*, bk. VI, ch. II, vol. II, 566–9, 576, 582; Trevelyan, *Bright*, 159–69, 337, 347–50, 388–93, 402, 410, ch. XXI; Bright, *Diaries*, chs. VI, XIII, 415–70, 533–47; J. L. Garvin, *Life of Joseph Chamberlain*, II (1933), chs. XXIX–XXXIV; Mills, *Bright*, II, 136–8; E. L. Woodward, *Age of Reform* (1949), 347; J. L. Hammond, *Gladstone and the Irish Nation* (1964), esp. 24, 99, 105–6, 185–6, 213, 230, ch. XXV; Vincent, *Liberal Party*, 181, 187; Fraser, *Chamberlain*, ch. 4.

## 10 Empire

209  1  Cobden to Tait, July 3, 1838 (Add. MSS., 43, 665); Cobden to Combe, July 9, 1848 (ibid., 43, 660); Cobden to Bright, Oct. 18, 1850 (ibid., 43, 649), Aug. 24, Sept. 22, 1857 (ibid., 43, 650), Aug. 28, 31, 1862 (ibid., 43, 652); Cobden to Sturge, April 19, 1852 (ibid., 43, 656), July 1, 5, Aug. 31, 1857 (ibid., 43, 722); Cobden to Smith, May 19, Aug. 8, 1857 (Smith Papers); Cobden to Gladstone, Feb. 24, 25, 1862 (Add. MSS., 44, 136); Cobden to Ashworth, Dec. 4, 1862 (ibid., 43, 654); Bright to Baines, March 27, June 7, 1853 (Baines Collection); Bright to Cobden, Oct. 24, 1861, Aug. 6, Sept. 6, 1862 (Add. MSS., 43, 384); *Growth of Cotton in India Sel. Comm. Rep.*

*Mins. of Evid., P.P.* 1847–8, ix, 511; Cobden, *Political Writings*, I, 25–31, II, 23–106; Cobden, *Speeches*, I, 486, II, 357–8, 377–99; Bright, *Speeches*, 1–84, 101–6; Bright, *Public Addresses*, 158–9, 445–8, 497–504; Morley, *Cobden*, 230–1, 520, 670–8, 824–5, 866–7, 934–5; Robertson, *Bright*, I, 63, II, 390–3; Bright, *Public Letters*, 47–9, 75–6, 117–27, 205–7, 281–2, 309–10; J. H. Bell, *British Folks and British India Fifty Years Ago* (1891), esp. 99–100, 137; Trevelyan, *Bright*, 169–71, 261–7, 317–18, 368–9, 432–7; Hobson, *Cobden*, 58–62, 86–7, 88–9, 91–2, 223–4, 238–9, 271–2, 315–16, 339–40; Dawson, *Cobden*, ch. IX; Mills, *Bright*, II, 191–8; Hirst, *Golden Days*, 50; J. Gallagher and R. Robinson, 'The Imperialism of Free Trade', *Economic History Review*, second series, VI (1953); C. A. Bodelson, *Studies in Mid-Victorian Imperialism* (1960), 53–4; J. Gallagher and R. Robinson, *Africa and the Victorians* (1961), esp. chs. I, XV; O. MacDonagh, 'The Anti-Imperialism of Free Trade', *Economic History Review*, second series, XIV (1962); Thistlethwaite, *America and the Atlantic Community*, ch. I; R. J. Moore, 'Imperialism and "Free Trade" Policy in India, 1853–4', *Economic History Review*, second series, XVII (1964); B. Winch, *Classical Political Economy and Colonies* (1965); A. W. Silver, *Manchester Men and Indian Cotton, 1847–1872* (1966); Fraser, *Chamberlain*, 43; R. J. Moore, *Sir Charles Wood's Indian Policy* (1966), 125–32, 141, 147.

11 Economics

218 1 Cobden to Combe, Nov. 8, 1847 (Add. MSS., 43, 660); Cobden to E. Potter, Dec. 29, 1853 (Cobden Papers, no. 55); Cobden to Bright, Nov. 5, 1855 (Add. MSS., 43, 650); Cobden to Ashworth, April 8, 21, 1863 (ibid., 43, 654); Cobden to Cassell, Sept. 8, 22, 1849 (ibid., 43, 668, ff. 19–23); Cobden to Livesey, Oct. 11, 1849 (ibid., ff. 27–40); Chadwick to Cobden, May 14, 1848, Cobden to Chadwick in reply, n.d. (Chadwick Papers, University College, London); Bright to Cobden, Nov. 5, 1853 (Add. MSS., 43, 383), Nov. 14, 1857 (ibid., 43, 384); Bright to Gladstone, Jan. 17, 1875 (ibid., 44, 113); *Parliamentary Debates*, third series, LXXIV (1844), 330–3, 1063–71, LXXVII (1845), 832, LXXVIII (1845), 728, LXXXIII (1846), 408–11, LXXXVI (1846), 1050–60, 1075–9, XCI (1847), 122–6, C (1848), 1174, CXVIII (1851), 1366–7; *Ten Hours Advocate*, Dec. 19, 1846, May 1, 1847; *Manchester Guardian*, Dec. 27, 1875, Dec. 24, 1895; Bright, *Speeches*, 440; Cobden, *Speeches*, I, 383, 577–600, II, 71–2, 101, 180, 194, 253–4, 305–13, 336–7; Bright, *Public Addresses*, 136–8, 343–4; Morley, *Cobden*, 226–7, 298–302, 951–5; Robertson, *Bright*, II, 357–60, III, 165–6; Bright, *Public Letters*, 76–82, 171–4, 223–4, 292, 298; Hodder, *Shaftesbury*, I, 423–5, II, 23, 89, 203–6, 210; Vince, *Bright*, 42–3; Smiles, *Autobiography*, 174; Trevelyan, *Bright*, 16–17, 154–9, 182; Hobson, *Cobden*, 166–7; Bright, *Diaries*, 75–6, 144; Mills, *Bright*, II, 75–6, 171–99; J. H. Clapham, *Economic History of Modern Britain*, III (1938), ch. VII; M. Arnold, *Culture and Anarchy* (ed. J. Dover Wilson,

1948), xxvii, 18–19; MacGregor, *Economic Thought and Policy*, ch. III; Robbins, *Theory of Economic Policy*, esp. chs. III, IV; Wallas, *Place*, 217–18; S. E. Finer, *Life and Times of Sir Edwin Chadwick* (1952), 417–18, 437; R. A. Lewis, *Edwin Chadwick and the Public Health Movement* (1952), 120, 172, 275; La Nauze, 'Letters of Richard Cobden,', 200–2; A. Briggs, *The Age of Improvement* (1959) 438; Grampp, *Manchester School*, 85–91, 103–4; J. B. Brebner, 'Laissez-Faire and State Intervention in Nineteenth-Century Britain', in *Essays in Economic History*, III (ed. Eleanora Carus-Wilson, 1962), 252–62; J. T. Ward, *The Factory Movement* (1962), esp. 287, 325, 342, 403, 425–6; Vincent, *Liberal Party*, 168–75; B. L. Hutchins and A. Harrison, *History of Factory Legislation* (3rd ed., 1966), 122; Silver, *Manchester Men and Indian Cotton*, vii, 67, 216–17.

## 12 The American Civil War

229  1  Cobden to Bright, April 29, 1859, May 19, Dec. 3, 7, 1861 (Add. MSS., 43, 651), Jan. 7, 10, 23, Oct. 6, 7, Dec. 29, 1862, Oct. 4, Nov. 10, 1864 (ibid., 43, 652); Cobden to Hargreaves, Feb. 25, 1861, Jan. 10, Dec. 18, 1862, Jan. 19, 1863 (ibid., 43, 655); Cobden to Parkes, Nov. 3, 1861 (ibid., 43, 664); Cobden to Gladstone, Dec. 11, 1861 (ibid., 44, 136); Cobden to Paulton, Dec. 27, 1861, Oct. 11, 1862 (ibid., 43, 662); Cobden to Cassell, March 19, 1862, Jan 11, 1863 (ibid., 43, 671, ff. 22–5, 48–51); Cobden to Wilson, July 16, 1863 (Wilson Papers); Bright to Cobden, Aug. 31, Oct. 3, Dec. 9, 1861, Jan. 9, 13, 20, Aug. 6, Oct. 8, 1862 (Add. MSS., 43, 384); Bright to Smith, Jan. 13, 1862 (Smith Papers); Bright to his wife, July 27, 1862, June 22, 1863, July 24, 1864, April 23, 1865; *The Times*, Dec. 6, 1861, March 27, Sept. 24, 1863; *Manchester Guardian*, Dec. 31, 1862; Cobden, *Political Writings*, II, 5–22; Bright, *Speeches*, 85–148; Cobden, *Speeches*, II, 83–119, 253, 279–303, 313–21, 360–66; Bright, *Public Addresses*, 1–14, 363–4; Morley, *Cobden*, ch. XXXIV, 914–16; Robertson, *Bright*, ch. XXXVIII; Reid, *Forster*, ch. IX; *Correspondence of John Lothrop Motley* (1889), II, 48, 51–3, 119–22, 204–7; Watkin, *Cobden*, 195; E. L. Pierce, *Memoir and Letters of Charles Sumner* (1893), IV, 59–60; H. Solly, *These Eighty Years* (1893), II, 247; Morley, *Gladstone*, I, 713–17; *Massachusetts Historical Society, Proceedings*, XLV (1911–12), 35–159, 243–333, 508–30; Trevelyan, *Bright*, ch. XIV; Hobson, *Cobden*, chs. XI, XII; E. D. Adams, *Great Britain and the American Civil War* (1925), esp. II, 102–12, 222–5, ch. XVIII; Dawson, *Cobden*, chs. VIII, IX; Bright, *Diaries*, ch. XI; J. G. Randall, *Lincoln, the Liberal Statesman* (n.d.), ch. VI; Cobden, *Diaries*, 38–81, 143–220; H. C. Allen, *Great Britain and the United States* (1954), ch. 13; H. Pelling, *America and the British Left* (1956), ch. II; O. Maurer, '*Punch* on Slavery and Civil War in America', *Victorian Studies*, I (1957); Harrison, *Before the Socialists*, ch. II; Fielden, Cobden and America, ch. VII.

# References

CHAPTER IV: CONCLUSION

## 1 Deathbeds

232 1 Cobden to W. Cobden, Aug. 21, 1825 (Cobden Papers, no. 19); Cobden to his wife, Jan. 14, 1844 (Add. MSS., 50, 748), Nov. 26, 1864 (ibid., 50, 749); Cobden to Parkes, Feb. 1, 1865 (ibid., 43, 664); Bright to Cobden, Nov. 17, Dec. 14, 1864, Jan. 22, 1865 (ibid., 43, 384); Morley, *Cobden*, 834, ch. XXXVIII; Robertson, *Bright*, IV; 343, 356-7; Bright, *Diaries*, 285-9.

233 2 Vince, *Bright*, 110; Trevelyan, *Bright*, 437, ch. XXII; Beatrice Webb, *My Apprenticeship* (2nd ed., n.d.), 108-9; Bright, *Diaries*, 461, 486; Mills, *Bright*, ch. XX.

## 2 Cobden and Bright in History

235 1 Cobden to Sturge, Nov. 28, 1841 (Add. MSS., 50, 131); Cobden to Fitzmayer, March 22, 1856 (ibid., 43, 665, ff. 30-1); *Punch*, April 8, 1865; *Rt. Hon. John Bright M.P., Cartoons from the Collection of Mr. Punch* (1878); Bright, *Public Letters*, 152-3; M. H. Spielmann, *The History of Punch* (1895), 101, 205; Duke of Argyll, *Autobiography and Memoirs* (1906), II, 188; Mrs. Russell Barrington, *Life of Walter Bagehot* (1914), 424-5; *Works and Life of Walter Bagehot* (ed. Barrington, 1915), IX, 76-8, 188-92; Cavendish, *Diary*, II, 67; Bright, *Diaries*, 439-41; *The Queen and Mr. Gladstone* (ed. P. Guedalla, 1933), I, 263; Vincent, *Liberal Party*, 197-8.

237 2 J. McCarthy, *A History of Our Own Times* (1880 ed.), III, 122; Holyoake, *Sixty Years*, II, 270-89; McCarthy, *Reminiscences*, I, chs. IV-VI; T. P. O'Connor, *Memoirs of an Old Parliamentarian* (1929), I, 257.

249 3 Cobden to Paulton, Nov. 8, 1863 (Add. MSS., 43, 662); *Leeds Mercury*, April 3, 1865, March 28, 29, 1889; *Manchester Guardian*, April 4, 1865, June 27, 1871, July 20, Oct. 17, 1892, Jan. 23, 1901; *The Times*, Aug. 13, 1866; Cobden, *Speeches*, II, 358, 421; J. E. T. Rogers, *Cobden and Modern Political Opinion* (1873), 131; Buxton, *Political Questions*, 125-8; Bright, *Public Letters*, 311-14; R. Gowing et al., *Richard Cobden and the Jubilee of Free Trade* (1896); J. Chamberlain, *Imperial Union and Tariff Reform* (1903); G. Armitage-Smith, *The Free-Trade Movement and its Results* (2nd ed., 1903), esp. 152-3, 202-3; W. J. Ashley, *The Tariff Problem* (1903); W. Smart, *The Return to Protection* (1904); F. List, *The National System of Political Economy* (1904 ed.), esp. 102-3; Smiles, *Autobiography*, 259-60; C. J. Fuchs, *The Trade Policy of Great Britain and her Colonies since 1860* (1905); W. Cunningham, *The Rise and Decline of the Free Trade Movement* (2nd ed., 1912); Helen Bosanquet, *Free Trade and Peace in the Nineteenth Century* (1924); A. Marshall, *Official Papers* (1926), ch. VI; Dunham, *Anglo-French Treaty of Commerce*, chs. XVI, XVII; *The Great Victorians*, 143-8; J. H. Clapham, *Economic History of*

# References

*Modern Britain*, II (1932), ch. VI; Sir C. Petrie, *The Chamberlain Tradition* (1938), 121; S. H. Zebel, 'Fair Trade: and English Reaction to the Breakdown of the Cobden Treaty System', *Journal of Modern History*, XII (1940); W. K. Hancock, *Survey of British Commonwealth Affairs*, II, part I (1942), esp. sect. IV; B. H. Brown, *The Tariff Reform Movement in Great Britain* (1943); Sir J. H. Clapham, *Corn Laws Repeal, Free Trade and History* (Manchester Statistical Society, 1946); W. Ashworth, *A Short History of the International Economy* (1952), ch. VI; W. H. Chaloner, *The Hungry Forties* (1957), 3–6 (but see *Notes and Queries*, tenth series, III (1905), 87, 111); Thornton, *The Imperial Idea*, chs. II–IV; Sir S. Unwin, *The Truth about a Publisher* (1960), 89–91; S. B. Saul, *Studies in British Overseas Trade* (1960), esp. chs. II, III, VI; *Edwardian England* (ed. S. Nowell-Smith, 1964), 57–63; Read, *English Provinces*, 184–90; F. Crouzet, 'Commerce et Empire: L'Expérience Britannique du Libre-Echange à la Première Guerre Mondiale', *Annales, Economies, Sociétés, Civilisations*, 19 (1964); S. H. Beer, *Modern British Politics* (1965), 279–92.

# Index

# Index

Collet, C. D., 184
Colonies. *See* Empire
Complete suffrage, 29–30
Constantinople, 12, 123
Co-operative movement, 159
Corn Laws, 20; repeal of, viii, 10, 17, 18, 20, 22–68, 74–5, 78–82, 92–7, 137–8, 233
Cotton industry, 7–9, 202–4, 226, 246; depression in, 22, 49, 57
Coventry, 69
Crimean War, viii, 83–4, 86, 90, 102–3, 104, 109, 112, 116, 119, 120, 121–34, 163

*Daily Mail*, 186
*Daily Mirror*, 186
*Daily News*, 186
*Daily Telegraph*, 185, 186
Delane, J. T., 187–8
Derby, Lord, 73, 164, 170, 173
Dickens, C., 2, 5
Disestablishment, 16, 192–4
Disraeli, B., 8, 27–8, 103, 118, 148, 166, 174, 175, 192, 208, 240
Dunford, 1, 39, 41, 230, 231
Durham city, 93–4

Eastern Question. *See* Crimean War *and* Free trade
Education, 16, 19, 70, 75–7, 177–83
Empire, 16, 200–9
Engels, F., 10, 239
*England, Ireland and America*, 6, 13, 21, 22, 109, 112, 122–3
Erasmus, 111
European Economic Community, 247–8

Factory legislation, 36, 67, 179, 210–14
Fair Trade League, 242–3
Fenton, J., 74
Foreign policy. *See* Free trade
Forster, W. E., 212, 223–4
Free trade, 10, 12, 13–14, 16, 32–5, 65–8, 107–8, 109–53, 197, 216–17, 233, 237–49. *See also* Corn Laws
Free Trade Hall, 45, 54
Freehold purchase, 56, 157–8
French Revolution of 1789, 52, 58, 67

Game Laws. *See* The Land
Gammage, R. G., 37
Garibaldi, 169
Gaskell, Mrs., 40
Gaulle, Gen. de, 247
George III, 51
George, H., 189
Gibson, T. Milner, 46, 102, 104, 105, 134–6, 184, 231
Giffen, R., 106
Gladstone, W. E., viii, 31, 33–4, 71, 88, 90, 99, 106, 118, 132, 134, 139–47, 148–9, 149–51, 166, 167–75, 182, 185, 193, 195–9, 202, 208, 213, 226, 231, 232, 235
Glasgow, 42, 204
Glasgow Trades Council, 167
Graham, Sir J., 126, 213
Great Exhibition, 119, 177–8
Grote, Mrs., 40
Grotius, 111

Hammond, J. L., viii, 248
Herbert, S., 60
Hickin, J., 53
Hill, R., 19
Hobson, J. A., vii, 245
Holman, 72
Holyoake, G. J., 236
Home Office, 50–1
Home Rule, 195–200, 225, 236
*Hornby* v. *Close*, 174
Horsman, E., 170
*How Wars are got up in India*, 201
Howell, G., 160, 172
Huddersfield, 42, 134
Hume, J., 155
Hume, J. Deacon, 141
Hunt, Henry, 52, 73

272

# Index

## Index